Investigations in Number, Data,

Schools and Families
Creating a Math Partnership

Megan Murray

Editorial Offices Glenview, Illinois • Parsippany, New Jersey • New York, New York

Sales Offices Parsippany, New Jersey • Duluth, Georgia • Glenview, Illinois
Coppell, Texas • Ontario, California

T E R C

This project was supported, in part,
by the
National Science Foundation
Opinions expressed are those of the authors
and not necessarily those of the Foundation

The *Investigations* curriculum was developed at TERC (formerly Technical Education
Research Centers) in collaboration with Kent State University and the State University of
New York at Buffalo. The work was supported in part by National Science Foundation
Grant No. ESI-9050210. TERC is a nonprofit company working to improve mathematics and
science education. TERC is located at 2067 Massachusetts Avenue, Cambridge, MA 02140.

ISBN 0-328-01881-3

3 4 5 6 7 8 9 10 xxxx 10 09 08 07 06 05 04 03

Contents

Section One: **Inviting Families into a Math Partnership**

Tackles the often-asked question, "But how do we get parents and families to come to school?" and outlines issues and barriers facing both educators and families, as well as some strategies for overcoming various impediments

Outlines important issues in hosting an event for parents, with a general overview of what such a night might look like

Describes one teacher's part in grade-level math night for parents and offers activity suggestions for each grade

Provides additional models and suggestions for other ways to set up parent math events

Sample responses to the most frequently heard questions and concerns of parents, gathered from teachers, administrators, and mathematics education researchers

The role of homework in *Investigations* and suggestions for developing a homework policy, communicating that policy to parents, and involving them in the process

Formal and informal ways to make the math program visible and generate interest in it, while sharing with families the mathematical thinking of their children

Five models for working with parents on school mathematics in longer, more in-depth programs, plus a summary of what facilitators are learning about making such courses work

Contents

Preface

At a conference I recently attended, one presenter described a program for developing parent leaders in mathematics, science, and technology. What struck me were the statistics she shared on the participants in this program, most of whom said they were taking the course in order to be able to help their children with mathematics. More than 50 percent of those attending one class were grandparents (Silverman, 2001). While writing this book, I have heard teachers mention being in contact with their students' siblings, aunts, and grandparents; with neighbors and family friends; and with mentors and volunteers. I was constantly reminded of the variety of people with whom schools must communicate about the children in their classrooms. Thus, the terms *parents* and *family* used throughout this publication are meant to include the wide variety of primary caretakers, relatives and nonrelatives alike, responsible for the welfare of children in our communities.

This book grew out of the work of the *Investigations in Number, Data, and Space* Implementation Center. As we at the Implementation Center work with teachers and administrators to support the effective implementation of the *Investigations in Number, Data, and Space* curriculum in schools and districts around the country, we consistently hear questions and comments about informing and involving parents and the community:

- How (and when) do we best begin and continue conversations with parents about changes in mathematics teaching and learning?
- How do we earn and capitalize on the support of parents?
- We have a small but vocal group of parents who are concerned about *Investigations;* how do we best work with these parents and address their concerns?
- Parents in a neighboring district are criticizing the use of the program there. How can we prevent that from happening here?

This book began as a brochure, to be distributed in response to such questions. The centerpiece was to have been a chapter written by veteran *Investigations* teacher and workshop leader Margie Riddle, who captured in writing a talk—"Engaging Parents as Partners"—that she had given at a math conference. As we discussed other issues that needed attention, the brochure quickly became a pamphlet, and then a monograph, and finally this book. Margie's thoughtful and practical contribution is still here as chapter 9.

Another *Investigations* Implementation Center project is developing "stories" that describe the implementation process of several districts that have been using the

Investigations curriculum for a number of years. To collect information for these stories, Implementation Center staff visited each district, collected artifacts and data pertaining to the implementation, observed in classrooms in several schools, and interviewed a range of district staff, including assistant superintendents; math coordinators; directors of math; math and science specialists; principals; staff developers; teacher leaders; teachers on special assignment; and classroom teachers at every grade level. The focus of these interviews was what it takes to successfully implement a curriculum like *Investigations*. One set of questions was particularly relevant to the work of this book:

- How has your school or district garnered community support for change?
- How has your school or district communicated with parents and other stakeholders about changes in the mathematics curriculum? What concerns have parents had? How have these concerns been addressed? How have those concerns evolved since the first year of implementation? What parent concerns remain? How are these concerns being addressed? Have parents played a role in supporting implementation efforts? How has parent support been developed and utilized?
- When you think about the parents in your community, what's working well, in their minds, and what do they see as needing improvement?
- Were you involved in parent outreach initiatives? How did you communicate with parents about the *Investigations* curriculum? What concerns or questions did parents have? How have you responded to parents' concerns? How did your interactions with parents change over time?
- In hindsight, are there things you would have done differently in gathering support for the program from the community? in addressing parent concerns or utilizing parent support?

The majority of the quotes appearing in this book comes directly from these interviews with teachers and administrators across the country. I hope that I have accurately captured the practices and expertise that these educators bring to their work with parents. I gratefully thank all the people interviewed, particularly those quoted, from Brookline Public Schools (Massachusetts), Clark County School District (Nevada), Community School District 2 (New York), and Madison School District 38 (Arizona).

Once an initial draft of the book was complete, I used an *Investigations* Implementation Institute to recruit readers to provide feedback. These institutes offer teams of educators the chance to come together to develop and revise implementation plans, experience professional development sessions, and network with other educators from districts from around the country that are using *Investigations*. In this way I found another author: Susan Pfohman, a panelist at one Institute, who shared her perspective as a parent in a district adopting *Investigations*. Her thoughtful presentation and feedback on that initial draft inspired me to include the voice and perspective of a parent within the pages of this book. Sandy Rummel and Patty Lofgren were members of the same panel who also made several contributions, as did Annette Raphel, a presenter on homework at another Institute. Paula O'Brien-Broome's comments on the draft provided another quote, and a team from SciMathMN (Minnesota) suggested an approach for parent nights over time. Both Susan and Margie put me in contact with parents and school staff for the quotes included in their particular chapters.

Implementation Institute participants shared ideas as well as sample newsletters, brochures, and other materials. These ideas and examples informed my work, and some grace the pages of this book, thanks to folks from Newtown Friends School (PA); the Florence E. Smith School of Science, Math and Technology (CT); Fayerweather Street School (MA); Milwaukee Public Schools (WI); Brookline Public Schools (MA); P.S. 116 of Community School District 2 (NY); Fitchburg Public Schools (MA); and Wellesley Public Schools (MA).

Two of the teachers quoted are colleagues via the Internet. Holli Hall often shares vignettes from her classroom with the members of the Exxon Listserve. She kindly allowed me to use one of those vignettes in chapter 3, "Math Night for One Classroom or Grade Level." Similarly, Missy Taft let me reprint part of a conversation from the CESAME Support Site for *Investigations* Users. I thank them both.

Patty Lofgren and Ruth Parker, both of the Mathematics Education Collaborative, offered much valuable feedback, including the suggestion for the chapter "Answering Those Frequently Asked Questions." The creation of this chapter led me to tap the expertise of a veteran group of *Investigations* teachers and consultants: the leaders of TERC's summer workshops (*Investigations* Workshops for Transforming Mathematics). Their thoughtful responses to the questions and concerns of parents make chapter 5 a particularly useful resource.

Chapter 8, "Seminars, Workshops, and Classes for Parents," describes some new and exciting ways of working with parents. Thanks to Sandy James, Lucy Wittenberg, Marta Civil, Nancy Buell, Rose Christiansen, Amy Morse, Polly Wagner, and Liz Sweeney—first for undertaking such thoughtful and groundbreaking work, and second for sharing it with me, and thereby with a much wider audience.

Many other people offered additional suggestions that changed the book in productive ways, including Diane Schaefer of the Department of Education in Rhode Island and my colleagues at TERC, EDC, and SummerMath for Teachers who make up the Professional Development Study Group. Particular thanks are due to my colleagues at TERC: Karen Economopoulos, Lucy Wittenberg, Jan Mokros, Myriam Steinback, Cornelia Tierney, Marlene Kliman, Andee Rubin, and Lorraine Brooks, to name a few. They shared their ideas and experiences about working with parents, both as classroom teachers and as educational researchers and consultants. They read and commented on drafts; shared and translated useful information and resources; worked wonders in laying out and formatting the text, art, and many quotes; and supported me in undertaking what at times felt like a Herculean task. Finally, special thanks are due to two more people. I can't quite imagine working with an editor other than Beverly Cory—her wisdom and patience are greatly appreciated. Above all, I could not have written this book without the support and leadership of Susan Jo Russell. Her knowledge about how children learn mathematics and how teachers and curricula can support this learning consistently resulted in thoughtful and insightful feedback. Her ideas about content, audience, mathematics, teaching, and learning have helped shape and grow this book into what it is today.

This book was written specifically to support teachers and administrators in schools and districts that are using the *Investigations* curriculum. The artwork and student work comes from *Investigations* units and classrooms. The activity and game examples are from the *Investigations* curriculum, and the people quoted are using *Investigations* in their classrooms, schools, and districts. However, much of this book will be useful to anyone looking for ways to communicate with all stakeholders about how and why mathematics teaching and learning is changing.

Megan Murray
November 2001

Resources and Readings

While this book was being written, many people shared ideas about resources that have worked well to support the design and implementation of a program of family involvement. Some of their suggestions are included in the "Resources and Readings" sections at the end of most chapters. Many more are listed on the *Investigations* website (described below).

Some of these resources may represent some differences in philosophy, approach, pedagogy, and content; readers will need to assess how to use and adapt the information to best suit the needs of their particular communities.

Schools and districts that are committed to ongoing communication with families should become familiar with the following websites and publications and, if possible, make them available for reference by both teachers and parents.

Websites

The *Investigations* website (www.terc.edu/investigations) lists and maintains much information that is helpful to teachers, administrators, and parents. Visit this site for the following:

- information about the curriculum, including sample activities and components such as family letters and foreign language materials. This is a good place to send parents who are looking for more information about *Investigations*.
- descriptive lists of professional development packages and resources that include video components, often of children in *Investigations* classrooms. Many schools or districts implementing *Investigations* find videos of students working on math to be particularly powerful for communicating with parents.
- many relevant articles on a variety of topics, by *Investigations* authors and others, available to download and print. Many schools and teachers compile a set of resources and articles that parents find useful in learning more about *Investigations* and about mathematics teaching and learning. They use these to stock a library or offer them as handouts.
- books, articles, and links to other websites useful to both educators and parents on topics such as math education, mathematical activities for families, resources for communicating with families, and organizations working with parents and families.
- sample websites from schools or districts that use their sites to communicate information about math and *Investigations*.

The CESAME Support Site for *Investigations* Users contains information about *Investigations* games, units, and helpful resources and about schools and districts around the country that are using *Investigations*. It offers a "Spotlight" feature where implementation issues are addressed and an "Ask an Author" feature where *Investigations* authors answer questions submitted by teachers and administrators. This site also has a variety of interactive features, such as topic-specific, grade-level discussion groups and places to find a peer partner or share success stories. These discussion groups are a place for teachers to discuss the issues and ideas of this book with other teachers and a place to send parents to talk with other parents and to hear from practicing teachers. The CESAME Support Site is at www.lab.brown.edu/investigations.

The U.S. Department of Education publishes a wealth of information. Many of their most popular pamphlets and brochures are available online through its website (www.ed.gov/pubs/index.html), and others can be ordered by calling 877-433-7827 or by writing to ED Pubs, P.O. Box 1398, Jessup, MD 20794-1398. Some are available in Spanish, and most are available at no charge.

One valuable title available online at the Department of Education site is *Family Involvement in Children's Education: Successful Local Approaches* (Funkhouser, Gonzales & Moles, 1997). This "Idea Book" supports those who are working to develop and maintain school-family partnerships. It describes how twenty Title I programs have overcome common barriers to parent involvement and suggests ways that schools can work to build strong partnerships with families and com- munities. Sections include: Overcoming Time and Resource Constraints, Providing Information and Training to Parents and School Staff, Restructuring Schools to Support Family Involvement, Bridging School-Family Differences, and Tapping External Supports for Partnerships.

Another Department of Education brochure, available free or online, is *Reaching All Families and Creating Family-Friendly Schools* (Moles, 1996). This booklet offers outreach strategies to involve parents in their children's education. Some strategies, such as open houses and parent-teacher conferences, will be familiar; others, such as parent resource centers and positive phone calls, are less com- monly used. There is help for communicating with families about school policies and programs, individual student progress, and activities for the home to support children's learning. One section of this booklet focuses on reaching special groups, such as LEP parents, single parents, working parents, and fathers. Also addressed are: planning and publicizing events, creating a welcoming atmosphere in school, finding potential roles for parent liaisons, and devising parent workshops.

The Eisenhower National Clearinghouse (ENC) for Mathematics and Science publishes a magazine called *ENC Focus*. One issue from 1998 focused particularly on *Family Involvement in Education*. Available online at ENC's website (http://enc.org), this issue offers a variety of articles, including an interview with Margie Riddle that offers another perspective on her strategies for working with parents (which she describes in this book in chapter 9, "A Teacher's Perspective: Engaging Parents as Partners"). An article on helping with math homework and information about a variety of projects and people who are currently working with parents are also available. The ENC website also describes many selected resources on the topic.

Books

Susan Swap's (1993) *Developing Home-School Partnerships* reviews the research on parent involvement and explores the barriers to home-and-school partnerships, as well as strategies for overcoming them. She describes three commonly used models of family involvement—a protective model, a model based on transmission, a curriculum enrichment model—as well as a new model she calls the partnership model. Much of the book describes this new model and strategies for implementing it.

Classroom teacher Nancy Litton (1998), in *Getting Your Math Message Out to Parents,* shares her strategies for engaging parents with her math program. She includes information on the use of newsletters and the benefits of rewriting letters provided by the curriculum, choosing student work to share with parents, hosting parent volunteers in the classroom during math, and using a homework diary to communicate with parents. She describes how she prepares for and organizes events for parents and provides images of the newsletters, student work, portfolios, and agendas she uses for parent visits and for math nights.

Beyond Arithmetic: Changing Mathematics in the Elementary Classroom, written by three of the *Investigations* authors (Mokros, Russell, & Economopoulos, 1995), is a useful resource for teachers, administrators, and curriculum specialists who are transforming the teaching and learning of mathematics while implementing curricula such as *Investigations.* This book was written to answer many of the questions elementary educators (and parents) have about how and why mathematics instruction is changing. It includes a section on promoting math to parents, with a list of books for parents who are interested in learning more about math for children.

A valuable addition to a school's lending library for families is another book by an *Investigations* author, *Beyond Facts and Flashcards: Exploring Math with Your Kids* (Mokros, 1996). In addition to providing math games and activities that can easily be woven into a family's everyday life, the book helps parents understand what makes a good school math program and how they can support their child's teacher.

Introduction

Many parents and teachers of school-aged children have similar memories of their own elementary school experiences in mathematics. Desks were in rows, with the teacher at the front of the room. In a typical math lesson, the teacher presented a new procedure—such as long division or subtraction with regrouping—and then children practiced that procedure by doing a page of similar problems from a textbook. One perennial task was to memorize the multiplication tables. For this, some recall taking timed tests; others recall flashcards.

But in the late 1980s, mathematics education started to change, prompted in part by a call from the National Council of Teachers of Mathematics (NCTM), a nonprofit association of math educators dedicated to improving the teaching and learning of mathematics for all students. In response to research about U.S. mathematics education and how children best learn mathematics, NCTM published the *Curriculum and Evaluation Standards for School Mathematics* (1989), proposing a plan to improve and update the mathematics curriculum and overhaul the country's approach to assessment. These *Standards* were updated just over a decade later in *Principles and Standards for School Mathematics* (NCTM, 2000).

In the intervening years, schools have begun using a number of new mathematics curricula based on the NCTM *Standards,* including *Investigations in Number, Data, and Space* (TERC, 1998). These curricula offer students a much different experience in mathematics. Classrooms often look and sound busy. Children sit at tables or desks grouped together. They may walk across the room to get manipulatives from a shelf, play a mathematical game on the floor in a corner of the room, or build a structure with blocks according to given constraints. They participate in energetic class discussions that require them to explain, justify, listen, evaluate, and reevaluate. Consider the following example from a classroom using the *Investigations* curriculum, with a teacher orchestrating a discussion of what makes numbers odd or even.

The children in this fifth grade class are solving Number Puzzles. Each puzzle gives four clues that, when taken in combination, result in a single number or set of numbers. The children at Table 2 have come up with three answers—11,000, 11,002, and 11,004—for a number puzzle that the whole class has solved. One of the four clues says, "The number is even."

Following is the dialogue that ensued.

> *Teacher:* Do Table 2's answers fit the bill?
>
> *Evan:* No! They're not even numbers.
>
> *Teacher:* Which?
>
> *Caitlyn:* 11,000.
>
> *Other Voices:* Yes, it is. That's even.
>
> *Caitlyn:* 11,000 is *not* even.
>
> *Evan:* Because of the 11.
>
> *Diego:* It ends in zero so it's even.
>
> *Teacher:* How could you prove to me it's odd or even?
>
> *Diego:* Clear the calculator and then do + 2 = = = = ...
>
> *Teacher:* All the way? [Diego nods.] Well, that would take a lot of time ...
>
> *Giselle:* Divide it by 2. If it goes in evenly, then it's even.

Shakita: If 1 is an odd number, then the numbers that come before and after it [0 and 2] are even.

Giselle: Zero makes odd numbers even. Like 30.

Caitlyn: Well, that's true for 200, 400, 600, 800, 10, 12, …

Evan: 1, 3, 5, 7, 9, 11. 11 is an odd number.

Teacher: So you think 11,000 is odd?

Diego: It's not odd because then the whole number'd be odd, but there are zeros.

Brendan: Because it's like going by tens.

Shakita: It's the last number that counts.

Giselle: That's like 10. Without the zero, it's odd.

The teacher writes two numbers on the board: 11,000 and 11,001. As she writes the second number …

Shakita: That's odd.

Evan: Are you trying to say that thousands are even numbers?

Teacher: I'm not trying to say anything. You tell me …

—J. Pepicelli, grade 5 teacher (Massachusetts)

This teacher doesn't simply tell the class the answer or explain how to tell whether a number is even or odd. Instead, she asks questions that push students' thinking further, encourages them to clarify their ideas, and challenges them to find efficient ways to prove their theories. As the children work to explain their ideas, the teacher is learning about what they think and understand about numbers.

This helps her plan appropriate next experiences for individual children and for the class as a whole.

She is also pleased that the class is discussing big mathematical ideas in, for example, place value and number theory. (Is it the 11 in 11,000 that's important in this discussion? Or the fact that it's 11 *thousand,* as represented by the 000? Why are all numbers with 0, 2, 4, 6, or 8 in the ones place even?) The students are developing a variety of ways to prove a number is even:

- if you can count to it by twos, starting from zero
- if it is divisible by 2 with no remainder
- if it is a multiple of an even number

They are simultaneously thinking about *why* those ways work. Students clarify their ideas as they articulate their thoughts and try to prove their theories—and as they hear others do the same. For the teacher, this discussion has supported one key goal: moving students from a strategy that works for one particular problem to a theory that is generalizable to *any* problem. The process represents a major mathematical leap for fifth grade students.

This kind of classroom looks and feels quite different from those that live in the memories of today's adults. As a result, parents have many questions about this way of teaching and learning mathematics. Is this math? Why isn't my child getting flashcards and sheets of practice problems? Isn't this just a lot of fun and games? Why is math being taught so differently? What was wrong with how I was taught? How do I help with homework? How can I tell if (and what) my child is (or isn't) learning? How can the teacher? How does working in groups help my child learn math? How will my child succeed if she doesn't learn the standard algorithm for subtraction (or multiplication)? Why not teach standard algorithms as well as use students' invented strategies? Why doesn't my child have his own textbook? How will my child do in the next grade? in a different school? on standardized tests?

Because this kind of math class is quite different and is unfamiliar to many families, schools must be prepared for these questions and concerns. They need to find many ways to communicate with families and to involve them in thinking about several important aspects of this new mathematics classroom:

- the math program itself, how and why it is different, and how it will benefit their child
- the value, for all children, of participating in the kind of learning community that develops in an *Investigations* classroom
- the mathematics that students are investigating, why it is important, and what children are grappling with as they learn it
- how children learn mathematics and how and why mathematics can be about making sense of problems and situations
- how their child is doing mathematically, as an individual and as a student in a particular class
- how families can help their children with math at home

A Partnership That Benefits Everyone

Research has clearly shown that successful efforts at family involvement in mathematics benefit everyone: teachers, parents, and children (Ford, Follmer, & Litz, 1998). Teachers who actively involve parents in their math program find many families get excited about mathematics. Parents become interested in how their children learn math. They enjoy doing math activities with their child, and they lend support to the school's efforts to teach math in a new and rigorous way. Children share their explorations of math at school with their families, and they share their experiences at home with teachers and classmates. The result is a learning community that bridges the home and the classroom in meaningful and respectful ways.

How, then, do teachers benefit?

- Families help expand and deepen the mathematics that happens in class. They become the teachers' allies in the search for mathematical experiences that challenge, empower, and engage children.
- Children's thinking steadily progresses as families explore mathematics together.
- Teachers gain a pool of potential volunteers and mathematical tutors who can work with children to support the classroom goals.
- Parents who understand the power of the mathematics become advocates for these programs in the schools.

Talking to Parents: One Teacher's Story

Most of the parents I deal with were educated in Mexico, where you borrow and you carry and that's it—which is really how most of our parents were educated. This is the way you do it, and you learn how to do it that way, period. So sometimes I see the kids go home with homework, and their parent will say, "You didn't do it the right way." That's a big issue for the children, because we spend so much time discussing the fact that *there is more than one way to do it.* Sometimes the kids are confused about something, and the parents will show them a way to do it that the kids don't understand. They can *do* it that way, but they don't understand the math behind what they're doing.

So we've really worked hard on talking to the parents. We send home the letter at the beginning of the unit so they know what we're talking about and get some understanding of the math. Also, I have nine parents who volunteer in my classroom for an hour during math time, three days a week. It's really interesting because when we do word problems, they see that the kids are using all these different strategies, and they start saying, "Oh, yeah, that makes sense; yeah, you can do that." They weren't saying that earlier.

I remember this happening with one parent in particular, Emilio. His son Felipe was having a really hard time with subtraction, with anything that would require regrouping. His dad went over it and over it with him. Every time I'd send home subtraction homework, I'd get it back, and I could tell from the work that the dad had done all the regrouping and all the steps of the traditional algorithm. Clearly, Felipe couldn't find the answer on his own.

Then one day, Emilio was in my classroom while we were sharing subtraction strategies, and he said, "Oh!" and I said, "What, Emilio? What did you see?" and he said, "You don't have to do it this way!" It was one of those big "Aha!" moments. He said, "This way that I was positive was the only way my son could do it and get it right—that's not the only way. And all along I've probably been confusing him more by trying to show him something that was different from what you're doing in class."

And then, just as sure as can be, the next day on his homework, Felipe had it done a different way. He still is struggling, but he has a much better understanding, and they're really helping him at home. Plus, now Emilio was the expert, and he was able to show the other parents that there was another way of doing it.

—*K. Lively, ESL teacher, grades 3–4 (Arizona)*

And what are the benefits to parents?

- They are welcomed into the ongoing process of educating their children, in a mutually respectful relationship with the school.
- They experience the pride of knowing they play a crucial role in their children's math education.
- They gain a deeper understanding of their children and how they think mathematically.
- They can overcome any residual fear of mathematics and recognize that this—like reading—is an area where they *can* help their child.
- They have the chance to discover, share, and reconnect to their own mathematical strengths.

And the children? They benefit as well. Research shows that programs of family involvement, when implemented systematically and thoughtfully, exert a powerful influence on student achievement, as well as improve "self-esteem, attendance, and behavior" (Swap, 1993, p. 11). As one group reports,

> When families are involved in their children's education, children earn higher grades and receive higher scores on tests, attend school more regularly, complete more homework, demonstrate more positive attitudes and behaviors, graduate from high school at higher rates, and are more likely to enroll in higher education than students with less involved families. (Funkhouser, Gonzales, & Moles, 1997, "Executive Summary")

Furthermore, studies show long-range effects: "The evidence is now beyond dispute. When schools work together with families to support learning, children tend to succeed not just in school, but throughout life" (Henderson & Berla, 1994, p. 1).

The benefits are clear and justify a concerted effort by schools and teachers.

Schools must take leadership in developing and implementing practices that enable more parents to become and remain involved in their children's education. … When schools develop their programs of partnership, families appreciate the assistance, more families become involved, and more students improve their achievements, attitudes, and behaviors. (Hidalgo, Siu, Bright, Swap, & Epstein, 1995, p. 409)

As to the evidence that families will respond in kind, "studies suggest that parents are very willing to become involved in school or home-based learning activities when the activities are meaningful, congruent with family priorities, and likely to be useful" (Swap, 1993, p. 11).

Building a Family Partnership Program

What does it take to create and implement a successful program of family involvement? The goal of this book is to help schools and districts answer this question, particularly as they work to implement a new math curriculum. However, there are several overarching assumptions to consider before diving into the details of "what next" and "how to."

It's About Genuine Partnerships

Districts that develop successful school-home partnerships view parents as partners who have much to offer. As families share information about their children and their culture, as well as what they want for their children both in school and in life, the schools get a more complete and accurate picture of a particular child, group, or neighborhood. With this knowledge, they can better support and reflect the community they serve.

A true partnership is a transforming vision of school culture based on collegiality, experimentation for school improvement, mutual support, and joint problem solving. It is based on the assumption that parents and educators are members of a partnership who have a common goal: generally, improving the school or supporting the success of all children in school. Although parents and educators may have different contributions to make to the partnership and educators may be primarily responsible for initiating it, the assumption is that the common mission cannot be accomplished without collaboration. (Swap, 1993, p. 56)

Once schools discover the particular strengths and expertise that reside in the community, they can build on and use those strengths. Acknowledging a variety of cultures and perspectives both widens and deepens the mathematical conversations. When schools genuinely make use of the contributions of families, they pay tribute to children and parents alike, further strengthening the collaboration between school and home.

It's About All Families

Schools with successful programs of family involvement view *all* parents as potential partners. These educators

- assume that parents want their children to succeed in school and want to help their children succeed.
- understand that many parents have been excluded from the dialogue surrounding education and are unclear about school terminology and how they can support classroom instruction.
- do not necessarily assume that parents don't care simply because they are not present at school. There are many ways for parents to become involved in their children's education,

and it is what parents do to encourage learning in the home that is most crucial. (Vopat, 1998, pp. 66–67)

What's more, research shows that family involvement is determined more by teachers' efforts than by variables such as race, class, ethnicity, and work or marital status. Similarly, family involvement is more important to student success in school than any of those same characteristics of family background. In fact, across the K–12 spectrum, "surveys of parents, teachers, principals, and students reveal that if schools invest in practices to involve families, then parents respond by conducting those practices, including many parents who might not have otherwise become involved on their own" (Epstein, 1996, p. 217).

It's a Whole-School Project

According to a study conducted in cooperation with the Partnership for Family Involvement in Education, "Developing a successful school-family partnership must be a whole school endeavor, not the work of a single person or program" (Funkhouser, Gonzales, & Moles, 1997).

Many people assume it is the teacher's job to inform and involve the families of students in their classes. This is a dangerous assumption. Classroom teachers already have a full-time job that often spills over into non-work hours. To send teachers the message that forging the school-home link is their job alone is both overwhelming and unfair.

Although a principal or a teacher may be a leader in working with some families or with groups in the community, one person cannot create a lasting, comprehensive program that involves all families as their children progress through the grades. (Epstein, 1995, p. 707)

> [While reading a book about getting the math message out to parents,] my thoughts turned to how I might feel if someone suggested I try all the ideas. ... My reaction would probably be, *how am I supposed to find time to put so much effort into communicating with parents plus teach my class and fulfill all my other teaching responsibilities? My professional life is taking over my personal life and I don't like it!* (Litton, 1998, p. 134)

Successful programs are comprehensive; they make a difference for more than just one or two classes of students. They provide a variety of offerings tailored to all parents, and they support families year after year as their children progress through the school system. These efforts require the participation of many people across a school or district, working at different levels, with different responsibilities. Districtwide administrators, school-based staff, building administrators, and classroom teachers each have different roles to play. Within the teaching ranks, different individuals will have different strengths to share. It is each person's responsibility to find ways to contribute to the common goal of true partnership with all families.

It's About Patience and Flexibility

Implementing a successful program of family involvement takes time: time to develop trust and respect among parents and educators, time to create and implement a variety of programs and activities, and time to see the effects in families' attendance or children's school performance. It also takes persistence. Successful schools provide a range of activities, but sometimes only a few people show up. Other times, the planned event doesn't work very well or doesn't seem to fit the wants and needs of the participants. These schools don't give up. They use the feedback to adapt and adjust, and to design new offerings.

It's About Mathematics

Schools who are implementing *Investigations* need to help families learn about and come to appreciate a new math curriculum. They also need to support parents in helping their child with math at home and in seeing their child's math abilities and potential. These goals require detailed, curriculum-specific kinds of information and opportunities—something workshop leaders say parents are open to and even seeking.

> There need to be more opportunities for parents to connect in meaningful and intentional ways with the classroom curriculum and teachers ... Given the questions [parents in workshops] ask and their enthusiasm to experience learning along with their children, it seems that parents' interest in how they can interact and support classroom instruction is often underestimated and therefore underutilized ... The fact that parents [surveyed] were most often interested in information about the school's program, primarily its curriculum and method of instruction ... validates workshop experiences and perhaps helps explain why parents are not drawn to school activities that they perceive as peripheral to what really matters: the education of their children. (Vopat, 1998, pp. 4–5)

About This Book

This book is organized in two sections. The first section describes, in some detail, concrete ideas for communicating and collaborating with parents on the subject of school mathematics. The second section offers three perspectives on establishing effective school-home relationships, looking specifically at the role of classroom teachers, parent leaders, and school administrators.

Districts, schools, and teachers who hope to engage parents as partners in math teaching and learning must find a variety of meaningful and diverse ways to reach out to all the families in their community. The purpose of this book is to offer a range of suggestions and ideas from which schools can gather ideas that might work best with their particular students, families, and community. Many possibilities, drawn from the experiences of many different students and teachers, are described in this resource. The hope is that readers will be inspired to find respectful and effective ways to involve parents and families in their child's math education—and keep them involved.

Resources and Readings

The following resources describe research detailing the benefits of involving families in their children's education, to students, teachers, and parents.

Anne T. Henderson and Nancy Berla (1994) have summarized the results of many studies about how parent involvement affects children's success in school in *A New Generation of Evidence: The Family Is Critical to Student Achievement.*

The entire February 1998 issue of *Teaching Children Mathematics* focuses on family involvement. Especially useful is the article by Dominic D. Peressini, "What's All the Fuss About Involving Parents in Mathematics Education?"

Inviting Families into a Math Partnership

Chapter 1
How to Reach and Involve Parents

Finding ways to interest a wide range of families in math nights, math-share breakfasts, and conferences can be challenging. Getting families excited about a series of classes or meetings, such as a Family Math series or a mathematics seminar, can seem even more daunting. This chapter explores the barriers that hinder educators from reaching families, the barriers that keep families from getting involved, and some strategies schools have used to involve and engage families.

Barriers to Family Involvement

One educational researcher argues that the norms of schools do not support true partnerships: collaboration among adults is a rarity in school environments, many school norms focus on avoiding conflict, and there is little information available about how to establish successful partnerships. Also, neither time nor money is generally invested in building relationships with parents (Swap, 1993). Others agree, citing the lack of preservice or inservice training on how to develop successful family-school partnerships and describing the risks of such oversight:

> Uninformed teachers are more likely to view parents' absence in school as an indication that parents don't care about the education of their children [and] are more likely than knowledgeable teachers to believe that parents who do come to school are trying to subvert their professional judgment and classroom authority (U.S. Department of Education, 1997, pp. 19–20).

However, even informed teachers and schools that actively try to recruit families for a partnership run into inevitable barriers.

Time and Economics

Changes in the demographics of families and in the situations facing those in the workforce raise serious barriers to partnerships. There are more single-parent families, more working mothers in all families, more children in poverty, and more families with both parents working, many of them longer hours than ever before. For example, "the number of single-parent households headed by women has almost doubled since 1970," leading to predictions that "half of all children will spend at least part of their lives in single-parent homes" (Fuller & Olsen, 1998, pp. 8, 21).

Parents in all families are feeling the stresses of work. Approximately 79 percent of parents work in the paid labor force, 86 percent of men and 73 percent of women. Only 1 in 6 mothers is a stay-at-home parent (Hewlett & West, 1998). In fact, mothers are estimated to spend more than 80 hours per week on a combination of paid work and household work (Crittenden, 2001).

Evidence also suggests that families are working harder: "It takes more hours of work—or an additional job—to provide the level of financial security that one forty-hour-a-week job delivered a generation ago. In 1996, 7.5 million adult Americans held two or more jobs, a figure that has grown 64.6 percent since 1980" (Hewlett & West, 1998, p. 71). Poverty, which affected 1 in 5 U.S. children in 1998, and disproportionately affects non-white children and those in families headed by single women, also compounds the difficulties. As research shows, "lower-income parents and parents with less education participate less often in school-based parent involvement activities than do higher-income parents with higher education levels" (Funkhouser, Gonzales, & Moles, 1997, p. 5).

These same factors also affect educators who are themselves parents, adding up to less time and more stress all around. The same pressures make it difficult for parents to attend school events during work hours or during their family time and for teachers to schedule events at a time convenient for everyone.

> Eighty-seven percent of principals in K–8 Title I schools report that lack of time on the part of parents is a barrier to parent involvement in their schools, and 56 percent report that lack of time on the part of school staff is a significant barrier. In fact, principals identified these two barriers— lack of time for both parents and staff—as significant more often than any other items. (U.S. Department of Education, 1997, p. 8)

Diversity

The increasing diversity of children in classrooms, which has not been matched by increasing diversity of the teaching force, is another complicating factor.

> It is projected that, by the year 2020, children of color will comprise upwards of one-half of the children in classrooms … [Yet] most of our nation's teachers come from a rather homogeneous group; approximately 88 to 90 percent are European American and middle class. (Cushner, McClelland, & Safford, 2000, pp. 10–11)

In many cases, teachers may not be well informed about the cultural values and expectations of the students and their families. Other factors, such as a different first language, add to the challenges facing children who are trying to bridge the worlds of school and home. From the family perspective, "a sense of being different from school personnel may lessen parents' comfort in seeking contact with teachers or administrators. … Parents often do not know what is expected of them or how they might contribute to their child's schooling. Some parents respond to this confusion by withdrawing; others become angry and frustrated" (Swap, 1993, p. 25).

Logistics and Attitudes

There are also logistical and attitudinal barriers to overcome. Often, teachers have little access in their work environments to telephones or meeting spaces that offer any privacy. Families with younger siblings may not have suitable childcare arrangements. It may be difficult for some families to arrange transportation to the school; perhaps the family car is in use by a parent working the night shift or it takes several buses plus a substantial walk for them to reach the school. For some families, safety issues override their desire to attend. Some parents do not feel comfortable in a school setting, are unable to take time off from work, worry about their own educational background, or have given up because no one at school speaks their first language. Other parents have little time or energy to spare. Some may view schooling as the school's job alone. When invited to learn more about their children's mathematical learning, some parents feel no need to explore a subject in which they feel confident and competent; others have math anxiety and remember days of mathematical struggle they do not wish to revisit.

> We have found that childcare, transportation, language barriers, and a host of other complex issues can prevent some families from attending or participating in school events. The problem is compounded by the fact that parents have varying degrees of comfort or discomfort with mathematics, so coming out to evening mathematics sessions may not be a draw for them. We have worked to ensure that our sessions for parents are accessible. To date, both the written materials and the presentations have been translated into Russian, Vietnamese, and Spanish. For some families, these sessions were their first opportunity to attend school events conducted in their own language. —*P. Lofgren, Mathematics Education Collaborative (Oregon)*

Overcoming the Barriers

There is no question that changing demographics have made it more difficult for many families to participate in activities at school during the day. Parents will come to school activities, but with time so precious, they want to make sure that they are not wasting their time on activities where their involvement is not really wanted or valued, where their "second-class" status is underlined, or where they are not making a contribution to their child. (Swap, 1993, p. 25)

Sending a Clear Message

There is an urgent need to be clear in the message to families about school-based offerings. What is the purpose of these events? What will they involve? Why is this a useful and important way for them to spend their precious little spare time? What will parents get out of this? How will it help their child? Further, how do organizers communicate respect for parents and for all they would bring to such an event? How do they convey that all parents and caregivers are welcome and desired members of the school community, whatever their first language, mathematics background, or educational history? Organizers need to send the message that a more diverse group will mean a more valuable meeting. They also need to communicate the belief that this group will be a learning community—of peers, colleagues, and equals—working in partnership to improve mathematics education for their children.

Making the School a Welcoming Place

For a variety of reasons, some adults may not feel welcome or comfortable in a school setting. For this reason, it is especially important to make the school feel open, welcoming, and respectful of parents. One way to build trust between school and home is to plan informal social gatherings, both at school and in the community, where people meet and get to know each other, perhaps over food. For families who seem uncomfortable coming to school, meetings offered at a church, community center, public library, or com-munity leader's home can help build relationships and trust. One school set up a booth at a local flea market, while another used a neighborhood carnival to get the word out. One community organization drove a van through the neighborhood, announcing a workshop at the local library. Another approach is to reach parents in the workplace, offering lunchtime seminars on how to help their children with math.

School staff also need to consider the appearance of the building, how easy it is to find your way around, how parents are greeted in the office, and what strategies there are for communicating with visitors whose first language is not English. For example, are there signs to welcome visitors and help them find their way? Are they posted in the languages of all families? Some schools consciously create lively displays of student work in the entrance or office hallway; others have parent volunteers or aides who greet children and parents in the morning and send them on their way in the afternoon. Some schools create a parent center, an introductory video, or a parent newsletter; host special school-visiting periods; organize parent-outreach workers, who may do home visits; and set aside scheduled time for meetings and phone calls (Moles, 1996).

Being open to parents as classroom visitors, special guests, contributors in the classroom, and volunteers is another way to welcome parents and spread the word about what's happening in classrooms. One developer of workshops for parents says:

> Welcoming parents also means viewing them as allies in their children's education, not as obstacles to that education. The lack of a parent's physical presence at school does not necessarily mean a lack of motivation or interest. Blaming parents for a perceived lack of involvement will not miraculously produce the desired involvement; urging parent involvement only to treat them with disdain discourages the kind of partnerships necessary for children's educational success. (Vopat, 1998, pp. 66–67)

The school atmosphere is also important in its effect on teachers' attitudes toward parents. Teachers who feel that colleagues and parents are supportive of family involvement have more positive attitudes themselves. Moreover, those "positive attitudes also are positively correlated with more success in involving 'hard-to-reach' parents" (Epstein & Dauber, 1991, p. 293).

Knowing the Community and Planning Accordingly

Knowing the community well requires thinking about all the people and families in it. What groups are present? Which groups are typically represented at school functions, on committees, and in the school? Which voices and opinions are most commonly heard? How representative are those opinions of the parent population as a whole? Which groups are not typically present or heard? Why not? How might involvement from underrepresented groups be encouraged?

> The problem with the label "hard to reach" is that the difficulty in establishing communication is placed on the parents rather than on the methods educators have developed to reach out. My research … suggests that even "hard to reach" parents are not so hard to reach when they are offered programs that are respectful of their strengths and backgrounds, responsive to their needs, and scheduled at times and places that they can manage. (Swap, 1993, pp. 97–98)

Communities vary, as do the schools and families within them. Trying to use a one-size-fits-all model for developing family-school partnerships denies this diversity. A successful plan requires assessing the needs and wants, as well as the strengths and weaknesses, of the particular community— whether it be an entire district or school or a group within a school or district—and then customizing the approach to best serve that community. (Funkhouser et al., 1997; Hidalgo et al., 1995) More than one approach may be needed because

what works for one group may not work for others. For example, parents who are uncomfortable coming to school or who are uneasy about mathematics may require different forms of outreach and offerings than those who frequent the school or who have already been involved with the math program.

Scheduling is always an issue. Some schools find evening events are well attended, while others have only several participants for a parent night but draw many to breakfast or morning events. Afternoons might work well for parents who pick up children from the after-school program, while other parents prefer an evening since that gives them a bit of time at home after their work day before heading back out.

> Families that hesitate to become involved in schools often complain that administrators and teachers develop parent involvement strategies based on what they think parents want and need, and not on what parents say they want and need. (Funkhouser et al., 1997, p. 723)

In one low-income school, a new principal assessed the situation in the community and realized that hard work would be needed to establish relationships with neighborhood families. After several years of community outreach, the school reported impressive results.

> [The math nights were] very, very successful. This year we had to split them because last year we had K–5 in a small multi-purpose room, and we couldn't move, literally. So this year we did K–2, and that night we had about 150 families, which was phenomenal for a school of 570 children. And then we did a 3–5 night, and there were probably between 80 and 100 families.
>
> —W. Roselinsky, principal (Nevada)

How can schools and districts determine what it is that parents want and need? Some take surveys and collect data. One strategy is to sponsor community walks, where teachers and parents walk through the neighborhood to visit and talk with families, as well as introduce teachers to the community (Funkhouser et al., 1997). Teachers often use conferences or Parent Nights to ask what day of the week, what time of day, and what length of time works best. Once dates and times are established, giving as much advance notice as possible shows respect for parents' busy schedules. Schools also research transportation and childcare needs in order to design supports for the families of their students.

Careful planning can help eliminate roadblocks. Where transportation is an issue, some districts use a buddy system, connecting parents who have transportation with those who do not. Others offer PTA-funded cabs or school buses. Still others offer events within walking distance of most families or at convenient public locations. Where childcare is an issue, some schools hold events during the after-school program's hours. Others offer on-site babysitting courtesy of volunteers. Another option—if enough teachers are available—is hosting a parent-and-child event; some teachers run activities with the children while others meet with the parents. For parents who won't have had time to get themselves dinner before attending or who know they won't have time to prepare dinner afterwards, good food that is ethnically appropriate is an added benefit. Food, childcare, convenience, transportation, and other such considerations cannot be afterthoughts; they can be critical factors in developing connections with families.

Getting the Word Out
Schools find a variety of ways to advertise and reach out to a wide range of parents. The following are some examples.

Flyers These are sent home and posted at the school and in places like the town library, the grocery store, the community center, and the church. Flyers—and any written communications—should

be in parents' first language. ESL/bilingual teachers or volunteers might help with translation.

Letters School or district administration, classroom teachers, or the facilitators of a planned event may send an announcement describing the event, its importance, and what both the parent and the child are likely to gain from it. Periodic classroom, school, or district newsletters are another way to keep parents aware of what's happening at school and to announce upcoming events.

Invitations Some parents are more inclined to participate when the invitation comes from their child, so teachers often have their students design an invitation. In one invitation to a math workshop, children told their families which math game was their favorite and asked their parents to try that game at some point.

Children Children, and their excitement about school and learning, are often what gets parents involved. Some schools hold friendly competitions to see which class can generate the highest attendance. Others host events that include children, knowing that families are more likely to attend if they can come together.

Phone calls Workshop facilitators, parent leaders, volunteers, and ESL/bilingual teachers can call to inform families of a particular event, encourage attendance, and describe the event and what it offers to them as parents. Some schools institute a phone chain to get the message out. Other schools have a voicemail system that parents can call to check homework assignments and leave messages; this is another good place to make announcements.

School events A special math event can be advertised at other gatherings that draw families to the school, such as a PTA meeting, science fair, school play, or Back-to-School Night. Teachers can also talk with parents during conferences or informally as they see them at school.

Word of mouth People who are interested, or who are already signed up for an event, can be encouraged to bring a friend, talk to another parent about coming, or share a flyer with someone in their neighborhood.

Organizers need to have realistic expectations and definitions of success, particularly early on. Even schools that make concerted and well-intentioned efforts are sometimes left feeling unsuccessful when few parents or families attend.

> In the beginning stages of attracting parents to school, educators tend to be very disappointed if fewer people come than were expected. Instead, educators should focus on warmly welcoming and valuing the parents who *do* come and comforting event planners with the idea that it is great that *this* group of parents gave up time in their busy schedule to attend. Word of mouth is one of the best strategies for recruiting additional people, and if those who do come share their good experiences, then more family members are likely to come in the future. (Swap, 1993, p. 69)

Some schools find that piggybacking on another event that already brings parents in—such as a student performance or picture day—is a way to increase attendance. But overall, simply continuing with efforts that are respectful and well publicized tends to produce results. Individual teachers who work with parents, whether as classroom volunteers or in math seminars and workshops, also cite the power of getting even a few parents excited about and interested in what's happening in math.

> When our district curriculum department began to sponsor math nights for families, we offered five monthly sessions in each of five geographic areas of the district. When less than ten families would attend, I thought we were not reaching enough people. Gradually, however, the word spread as these few parents told their neighbors about the sessions, and attendance increased. Hands-on, minds-on experiences in these sessions often make mathematics accessible to parents who were not successful in math when they were young, and they become supporters. Students also enjoy showing their parents what and how they are learning in school.

—*L. Gregg, K–5 science and math specialist (Nevada)*

Conclusion

Teachers, schools, and districts that have been successful in working with parents list the following essentials:

- Ask parents about their interests, schedules, expertise, and hopes for what they might gain from school programs. Use this information to plan events and design programs that are based on (and tap) parent interests, strengths, and desires.
- Offer a variety of kinds of activities (from short, single-visit, presentation-style events to multi-session seminars for parents), at a variety of times (morning, after school, evening, weekends) and locations (at school and in the community).
- Try to minimize barriers by making parents feel welcome, valued, important, and appreciated, and by eliminating logistical barriers to participation, such as childcare, transportation, and language issues.
- Find a variety of ways to advertise events well in advance, to describe the purpose and benefits, and to encourage participation.
- Ask parents about the events they attend: What was useful? What wasn't? What was missing that would have been useful? How did you find out about this event? What made you decide to come? Then use their feedback to revise and improve upon what is offered in the future and how it is advertised.

- Don't give up! Partnerships are not easy to form and nurture. Educators and families need to get to know and trust one another, learn how to work together, and see that everyone is working toward the same goal—what's best for children. This development of trust and the ability to collaborate take time and effort.

These suggestions help increase the likelihood of reaching as many parents and families as possible; communicate respect for parents' time, ideas, and wishes; and generate more involvement and collaboration over time. Sometimes a single successful interaction can lead to a much deeper involvement. The most important message from people in the field is the last—don't give up! If turnout is lower than expected or if certain groups are underrepresented, the message is to keep trying—but try new things. Collect more data, work from and build on existing strengths, involve more people, build more relationships, and continue to focus on communicating respect for and trust in parents, along with the desire to work *with* them in doing the very best for their child.

Resources and Readings

Developing Home-School Partnerships (Swap, 1993) has more information about the barriers to school and family partnerships; see chapter 2. This book also shares ideas for creating a welcoming atmosphere at school and a description of parent centers.

An interesting and honest discussion of the challenges and complexities that may face teachers and parents—particularly if they are from different cultures—when a new math curriculum is introduced appears in the case study *Kathy: A Case of Innovative Mathematics Teaching in a Multicultural Classroom* (McDiarmid, 1992). In this case, a third grade teacher has introduced a new mathematics program in which students work towards mathematical understanding rather than learn mathematical rules.

Another good resource to help schools understand the difficulties of engaging some parent populations is a publication from the U.S. Department of Education (1997), *Overcoming Barriers to Family Involvement in Title I Schools: A Report to Congress*. Pages 29–40 examine family-school differences such as culture, language, socioeconomic status, and educational background, as well as age- and gender-related barriers to family participation.

Several publications offer ideas for dealing specifically with math anxiety as a barrier to parent involvement: Sheila Tobias's *Overcoming Math Anxiety* (1993), Marilyn Burns's *Math: Facing an American Phobia* (1998), and Patricia Clark Kenschaft's *Math Power: How to Help Your Child Love Math, Even If You Don't* (1997).

Chapter 2
Math Night for Parents

When considered across schools and districts, there are what can feel like a bewildering number of occasions aimed at informing parents about what's happening in the classroom and at school, such as adults-only Back-to-School Night, also known as Curriculum Night or Parent Night, and Open House, which often includes children and may be held either early or late in the year. These events present an overall picture of a particular classroom and its curriculum, from math to language arts, social studies, and science.

There are also a wide variety of options for events focused exclusively on math: a one-time event or a series of sessions over time; with children in attendance or without; with the parents of children in one classroom, at one grade level, or across grade levels. All are wonderful opportunities for teachers to meet the parents of their students, to open (or continue to build) lines of communication, and to present themselves and their program —all of which are particularly important when teachers are taking on a new math curriculum like *Investigations*. This chapter provides basic guidelines for setting up and running a successful math night for parents.

Logistics of the Event

Invitations
It is useful to think of math night not as a one-time event, but as the beginning of a conversation with parents that will continue throughout the year. It is important to encourage *all* parents to attend, but particularly parents who have expressed concerns about the math program, since this will be an opportunity to present, describe, and discuss the program in some detail. It can be equally important to make an effort to attract parents who are comfortable with and supportive of the math

program—and who might be less likely to attend, for those very reasons. These parents can be a real support to a teacher facing anxiety and concern from other parents and can add their own responses to some of the questions other parents pose.

> The good thing about holding math nights for parents is that if there are parents who are gnawing away at some issue, you can say, "Come to math night." And it's definitely a positive experience, for most people who go.
>
> —*K. Sillman, kindergarten teacher (New York)*

Teachers who host successful math nights plan around the typical barriers described in chapter 1—some parents may be hesitant to come to school, others have childcare or transportation issues, and still others have little time or energy to spare. Teachers make sure families know they are welcome and that their attendance is valued, perhaps by including an announcement in a newsletter, sending home a special notice, or having students design and make invitations. (See samples in figures 1–3 and on page 136.) They accommodate parents whose first language differs from that of the school—both in their announcements and at the math night itself—either using a translator or an "Open House" type of event at which the children can help with communication. Finally, they are understanding of parents who are unable to come, and they keep the lines of communication open by mailing any information that was handed out at the math night.

A Penny for Your Thoughts

Congratulations to Mrs. Lloyd's Readers!

They did enough reading and talking about the books they read last week to collect 373 pennies! These fourth grade readers are very motivated to help the students at Betances School in Hartford who  do not have the resources to enable them to have a library collection that is even close to what we are fortunate to enjoy here in West Hartford.

Our total amount for the first week was 675 pennies. We are encouraging all parents and guardians to assist children with this home-school project. Children should be reading from 10-20 minutes every night. Kindergartners should be read to. A brief discussion about one thing in the book should follow the reading. In order to support the concept of "A Penny for your Thoughts," we are asking that you give children a penny for thinking and talking a bit about a book, chapter, poem, magazine article, etc. This daily activity will help all participants with their reading skills, and the pennies will go toward a good cause - kids helping kids read good books!

Please contact your child's teacher or Ms. Leone in the library media center for more information or to answer any questions you might have about the program.

Thank You

To everyone who helped make this year's **World of Food** a great success including the WHEE students and staff who decorated the beautiful table covering. Thanks also to everyone who helped with set up and clean up. A special thank you to **Laura Renfro, Sara Dalton and Theresa Lerner.**

to **Lori Kessing** and the PTO for supplying the wonderful snacks for teachers during conference week.

Family Math Night

Investigating Numbers, Data & Space
5th Annual Family Math Night
Thursday, April 6, 2000
6:30 - 8:15 p.m.

Take this opportunity to sample some of our favorite activities from the *Investigations in Number, Data and Space* Curriculum and learn about the philosophy of this powerful math program. Get a close look at the wide array of games that compliment your child's daily math instruction. You'll experience, first-hand, activities from each grade level and math strand. Bring your number sense and get ready to have fun.

If anyone is willing to donate a jar filled with "goodies" for our "estimation station" or an item for our math raffle, please call **Natalie Simpson, Curriculum Specialist, at 236-3315.**

Surf's Up

Travel back in time to ancient Egypt. Learn about life at the time of the Pharaohs, find out about the gods and goddesses that influenced the lives of these ancient people, explore

Figure 1 A math night may be announced to parents in a school-wide newsletter. This is one page from a newsletter sent out by the Florence E. Smith School of Science, Math and Technology in West Hartford, Connecticut. From N. Simpson and K. List. Reprinted with permission.

NOCHE DE MATEMÁTICAS PARA LOS PADRES DE P.S. 116

Venga a pasar una noche aprendiendo cómo su hijo/a aprende matemáticas y hable con los maestros de la P.S. 116 acerca del programa de matemáticas.

Lucy West, Coordinadora de Matemáticas del Distrito Dos, estará con nosotros para hablar sobre la Iniciativa Global de Matemáticas del Distrito.

Nos dividiremos en dos grupos pequeños para explorar juegos y actividades y aprender más acerca de nuestro currículo.

Cuando: jueves, 12 de noviembre
6:00 – 8:00 p.m.

Donde: Cafetería de P.S. 116

¡Por favor vengan!

Padres solamente por favor

+ +

Por favor devuelva esta porción a la escuela antes del viernes, 6 de noviembre.

___ Asistiré a la noche de Matemáticas para los Padres de P.S. 116

Nombres de los padres que piensan asistir:

_____

_____

Figure 2 Math night can also be announced through a special flyer like this one, sent home with children to invite parents to a school-wide, two-hour event at P.S. 116, Community School District 2, New York. From J. DiBrienza. Reprinted with permission.

To the parents of the students of
      Ginny,
      Michelle,
      Ms. Jaffe,
      Ms. Wing and
      Ms. DiBrienza,

you are invited to a very important second grade math meeting!

When: Tuesday, February 2nd
         6:30 - 8:00 pm
Where: P.S. 116 Music Room
Who: All second grade parents, second grade teachers and
         Lucy West, Director of Mathematics, District 2

Come learn about how we teach your children math, and how to help your child at home. Come talk to us about algorithms and alternative adding and subtracting strategies!
This could be the most important math meeting of your child's early math career! Please make every effort to be there!!!
We promise it will be interesting and informative!

                     Hope to see you all there!
+++
___ I will be attending PS 116's Second grade parent math night. Please save a spot for me!
      Parent name(s) _____
      Child's name _____ Class _____

Figure 3 This note, sent home with all of the second grade students, invited parents to a grade-level-specific discussion about mathematics at P.S. 116, Community School District 2, New York. From J. DiBrienza. Reprinted with permission.

Staffing

An important consideration in designing a math night, particularly in the early stages of implementing a new curriculum, is staffing. Teachers who are new to *Investigations* are often in the process of profoundly changing their teaching, which can leave them feeling overwhelmed and vulnerable. They are learning the nuts and bolts of the curriculum (what content is covered when, how the books and lessons are organized, how to teach the material), while also learning to manage the logistics for the new program (how to organize and manage students and materials, how to keep track of student work and their progress, and so forth).

For this reason, some schools invite outside experts or consultants to lead the first math night. Others have pairs or triads of teachers, all the teachers at a grade level, or even all the teachers in the school work together on their initial offering. This way teachers can support one another, field questions as a group, and provide an organized and coherent evening.

Brainstorming anticipated questions and possible responses as a staff can result in a consistent school-wide message, which is a positive in and of itself. But this arrangement also provides an arena for important conversations, giving teachers the chance to hear a variety of opinions and potential responses on "hot-button" issues and to find answers that resonate with them personally. The more that teachers hear others articulate their thoughts about key topics, the more ideas and language they will have to call upon, and the more comfortable and fluent they will feel talking about the curriculum themselves.

Structure

Math nights vary in content and structure, but successful events seem to share these features:

- a whole-group introduction that paints the big picture, places the school or district in that context, and introduces ideas about mathematics and the new curriculum
- time spent exploring mathematics, using activities appropriate for both adults and children
- time to discuss parents' questions and concerns

For some alternative structures, see chapter 4, "Variations on Math Night" (p. 56). Once the content and structure of the event are set, preparing an agenda gives families an overview of the event, as well as guidance throughout the evening (see figure 4).

The Role of Games in the *Investigations* Program

Games are a central part of the mathematics taught at all grade levels with the *Investigations* program. By playing games, students develop familiarity with the number system and with "landmarks" in the number system, such as 10's, 100's and 1000's. Games also provide students with engaging opportunities to practice computation.

Playing games encourages strategic mathematical thinking and demands that students find an optimal way (rather than just any way) to solve a problem. Games are included often enough throughout each unit and throughout the year for students to develop fluency with numbers. It is expected that students will play a game many times.

Games also provide a home link. As a parent, you can learn about the mathematical thinking your children are doing by playing mathematical games with them at home.

(from: "The Role of Games in *Investigations in Number Data and Space*, TERC, 1998)

Reminders

Children should remain with their adult family members throughout the evening.

Areas not in use are closed for the evening.

The Florence E. Smith School of Science, Math, and Technology

Family Math Night

"Investigating Number, Data and Space"

Thursday, April 6, 2000
6:30 - 8:00 p.m.

Welcome to
Family Math Night
"Investigating Number, Data and Space"

This evening highlights many of the games and activities presented in the *Investigations in Number, Data and Space* curriculum.

Each of these activities supports students in developing important concepts and skills in 3 key areas of mathematics:
- building number sense;
- interpreting data; and
- relating to objects in space.

As you play the various games tonight, try to answer the following questions:
- What mathematical ideas or understandings does this game promote?
- What mathematics is involved in effective strategies for <u>playing</u> this game?
- What numerical understanding is involved in <u>scoring</u> this game?
- How much of this game involves mathematical skill versus luck?

"Investigating Numbers"
Cafeteria

Station 1
Racing Bears
Close to 10, 20, 100, 1000

Station 2
Compare/Double Compare
Capture Fractions

Station 3
Capture Five

Station 4
101-200 Bingo

Station 5
Plus, Minus, Stay the Same

Station 6
Fraction Cookies
~~~~~~~~~~~~~~~~~~
"Investigating Data"
Primary hallway

Station 7
Would You Rather be an Eagle or a Whale?

Station 8
How Many Letters in Our Names?

Station 9
Sorting Shoes

Station 10
How Tall Are We?

Station 11
Meals and Chores
~~~~~~~~~~~~~~~~~~~~~~~
"Investigating Space"
Gym/specials hallway

Station 12
Learning About Length

Space - Station 13
Body Measurements

Station 14
How Far Can you Jump?

Station 15
Quilt Squares

Station 16
Cover and Count

Station 17
Building Geometric Solids
~~~~~~~~~~~~~~~~~~~~
More "Investigating"
Station 18   Front foyer
Estimating Numbers and Quantities

Station 19   Front hall
Representing Mathematical
Thinking Across the Grades

Figure 4 This fold-up brochure was created for the participants at a math night at the Florence E. Smith School of Science, Math and Technology in West Hartford, Connecticut. From N. Simpson and K. List. Reprinted with permission.

The Whole-Group Introduction

Perhaps the primary reason for starting the evening as a whole group—in addition to welcoming parents, thanking them for their attendance, and laying out the agenda for the evening—is that it gives a teacher, a group of teachers, a whole school, or an entire district the opportunity to send a strong, consistent message: "We are doing more for our students in mathematics, this is how, and this is why. We are all—teachers, principal, administrators—behind it, and we want to earn your support in working to provide your children with the best mathematics education possible." Following are four types of whole-group presentations that have proven successful.

Setting the Stage

This type of presentation establishes the national context in which curriculum reform is taking place. It describes the National Council of Teachers of Mathematics (NCTM), their *Principles and Standards for School Mathematics* (2000), and the effects these standards are having on school systems nationwide. It explains how the *Investigations* curriculum—funded by the National Science Foundation and based on research about how children learn—helps children meet those standards. More information that would be suitable for this introduction appears in the box, "How *Investigations* Came to Be" (p. 43).

The box "NCTM Principles and Standards for School Mathematics" (p. 36) offers a summary that would support this presentation. Also, NCTM offers an Outreach Kit for those who speak about the *Principles and Standards* to teachers, administrators, parents, and the community. This kit includes a video and PowerPoint presentations tailored to different audiences, along with speaker notes, handouts, and "frequently asked questions." Refer to the NCTM website for further information.

Asking "What Is Math?"

This type of introductory talk begins with the presenter gathering ideas from parents about what they think of as "mathematics." Most often, responses center on computation and maybe fractions. These ideas are represented on a board or flip chart in a diagram that will be expanded to illustrate the larger picture. The presenter acknowledges that computation is one crucial area of mathematics.

However, computation is only one set of ideas within the larger category of learning about numbers and our number system. Much of elementary school mathematics focuses on the construction of, and patterns in, our number system: ideas about place value, the importance of 10 and multiples of 10, and how to take numbers apart and put them back together. The presenter then embeds the original ideas about mathematics in a larger circle that includes the larger set of ideas about number.

Furthermore, our number system is itself only one part of the larger picture of mathematics. Geometry and measurement are also of great importance. (The presenter adds these to the diagram in an overlapping oval as shown below.) Students need to be able to name, describe, visualize, and manipulate 2-D and 3-D shapes. They need to develop spatial sense and explore relationships among shapes and between two- and three-dimensional shapes. Experiences in measurement often link to geometry and to number and computation, as when students learn to visualize and compute the area of 2-D shapes and the volume of 3-D shapes.

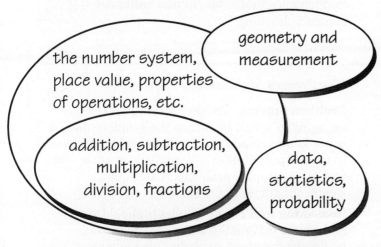

Similarly, in this information-laden world, the ability to interpret and analyze data is increasingly important. And again, many ideas in data and statistics involve number and computation—for example, finding the median or mean of a data set or comparing data within a set. The presenter then adds a third overlapping oval, demonstrating the place of data, statistics, and probability in the larger image.

This kind of discussion can help families think about the mathematics that children need to learn today and how that differs from the math they learned as children.

How Do We Use Math?

A similar introductory approach, more focused on computational proficiency and efficiency, asks parents to generate a list of ways they use math in their everyday lives. The group then sorts those items into two categories: times when an exact answer is needed and times when a good estimate is fine. Typically the two groups are about equal, although there are often spirited discussions about which way to categorize balancing the checkbook! This activity helps parents think about the purpose of teaching computation, what the expectations and goals for children should be, the role of estimation and traditional algorithms, and other important ideas in number.

A Video Introduction

Starting with a video like the one by Marilyn Burns, *Mathematics: What Are You Teaching My Child?* (Burns, 1994), helps families see how standards-based math curricula prepare students for the demands of the modern working world. This video also provides glimpses into real classrooms, offers images of students doing mathematics, and presents a math problem that intrigues and challenges adults. Some districts produce their own videos to introduce *Investigations* to parents, using footage from district classrooms. Other videos are also available; see "Resources and Readings"(p. 47) for some suggestions.

Six Principles for School Mathematics

Equity "Excellence in mathematics education requires equity—high expectations and strong support for all students."

Curriculum "A curriculum is more than a collection of activities: it must be coherent, focused on important mathematics, and well articulated across the grades."

Teaching "Effective mathematics teaching requires understanding what students know and need to learn and then challenging and supporting them to learn it well."

Learning "Students must learn mathematics with understanding, actively building new knowledge from experience and prior knowledge."

Assessment "Assessment should support the learning of important mathematics and furnish useful information to both teachers and students."

Technology "Technology is essential in teaching and learning mathematics; it influences the mathematics that is taught and enhances students' learning."

Ten Standards for School Mathematics

Five Content Standards

Number and Operations The focus is on making sense of our number system—understanding numbers and how to represent them, relationships among numbers and among operations, making reasonable estimates, and achieving computational fluency through "efficient and accurate methods that are supported by an understanding of numbers and operations."

Algebra The focus is on patterns and functions, using algebraic symbols and mathematical models to represent, understand, and analyze mathematical situations, and analyzing the way things change.

Geometry The focus is on the ability to visualize, reason spatially, and use geometric models and transformations to solve problems. Other important topics include coordinate geometry, symmetry, and the attributes and properties of 2-D and 3-D shapes.

Measurement The focus is on understanding and using appropriate attributes, units, tools, and processes to measure in a variety of contexts.

Data Analysis and Probability The focus is on collecting, organizing, displaying, and analyzing data to answer questions. Also important are making predictions based on data and considering the ways that data and probability are related.

Five Process Standards

Problem Solving "Problem solving means engaging in a task for which the solution method is not known in advance ... students should have frequent opportunities to formulate, grapple with, and solve complex problems that require a significant amount of effort."

Reasoning and Proof "Students should see and expect that mathematics makes sense ... by developing ideas, exploring phenomena, justifying results, and using mathematical conjectures in all areas."

Communication "Students who have opportunities, encouragement, and support for speaking, writing, reading, and listening in mathematics classes reap dual benefits, they communicate to learn mathematics, and they learn to communicate mathematically."

Connections "When students can connect mathematical ideas, their understanding is deeper and more lasting. They can see mathematical connections in the rich interplay among mathematical topics, in contexts that relate mathematics to other subjects, and in their own interest and experience."

Representation "When students gain access to mathematical representations and the ideas they represent, they have a set of tools that significantly expand their capacity to think mathematically."

Adapted from *Principles and Standards for School Mathematics* (NCTM, 2000): Principles, p. 11; Content Standards, pp. 29–71; Process Standards, pp. 52–67.

Exploring Mathematics

Successful math nights manage to engage parents with some mathematics at an adult level, while balancing the range of math competence in the room. Many teachers use a problem or game directly out of the classroom that requires adults to think specifically—even for a brief moment or two—about the mathematics. Sharing students' work on the same or a similar problem can be particularly powerful, as their work sometimes mirrors adults' thinking and often impresses parents with children's flexibility, efficiency, and understanding. Ideally, at least one game or activity should explicitly address computation since this is an ever-present concern of parents. It is also good to include an activity or game that explores content that may be new to many parents, such as geometry or data analysis.

> Right from the beginning, even in our open house, I have parents working on some problems and talking about the way that they're thinking about those problems, as a way of introducing them to the philosophy behind this math curriculum. I explain to them that this is often what you'll see in the classroom, a lot of discussion and talk about math problems. I think that the parents, in turn, are really surprised and amazed at how many different ways they come up with, as adults, to think about these problems.
>
> —M. Scott, grades 1–2 teacher
> (Massachusetts)

Activities

Suggested Activities from *Investigations*

Quick Images: an activity in many units across grades K–5

Number of the Day: a grade 2 classroom routine, adaptable to any level (For a detailed description of one teacher's work with parents using this routine, see chapter 3, "Math Night for One Classroom or Grade Level," p. 48.)

Counting Around the Class: a Ten-Minute Math activity in grades 3–5

Mental Math: a Ten-Minute Math activity in grades 3–5 (titled Estimation and Number Sense), focused on solving computation problems mentally

(For activities specific to each grade level, K–5, see the boxes at the end of chapter 3, "Math Night for One Classroom or Grade Level," pp. 54–55.)

One popular activity for math night is Quick Images, which appears throughout *Investigations*. In this activity, the teacher shows the class an image for just three seconds, then covers it and asks them to re-create the image themselves. A second brief showing gives them another look and a chance to revise their image. The time constraint forces students to work from the mental image they have formed.

One teacher reports that she presents several images to parents, including arrangements of dots (that focus on number) and arrangements of cubes (that focus on spatial and geometric ideas). She then discusses with parents the purpose of this activity and the reasoning behind the time limit. As parents explore the images, this teacher models how she does the activity in class, gathering a variety of strategies for seeing and remembering the image, methods for calculating how many, and notation for recording the strategies.

Most teachers say that it is important to explore some computation with parents, perhaps by asking them to solve a subtraction problem or a two-digit by one- or two-digit multiplication problem. Ideally, these teachers have examples of student work or a videotape of children solving the same problem to share and discuss. Depending on the audience, parents could be asked to find the answer by some method other than the standard U.S. algorithm. The teacher can then collect the parents' solutions and comment on the variety inherent in them, pointing out that not everyone understands number operations in the same way. However, it is also useful to help parents think about how the different methods are similar. That is, only a handful of basic approaches work well and make sense because they are based on how a particular operation works. Teachers stress that their goal is for children to think about what's reasonable when solving a problem, to use what they know about number and operations, and to consider the numbers in a problem when thinking about how to solve it. The main goal is that children develop fluency—efficient and accurate ways to solve problems and the flexibility to choose strategies that make sense to them and that best fit the problem at hand (Russell, 2000a, 2000b).

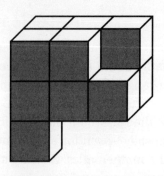

Figure 5 A Quick Image of a cube structure involves spatial ideas: How did you decide what to build with your cubes? What did you see? Would more than one cube structure match the image you saw? A Quick Image of dots, like the one shown in figure 6, works on number ideas: How many dots were there? How do you know? What patterns did you see?

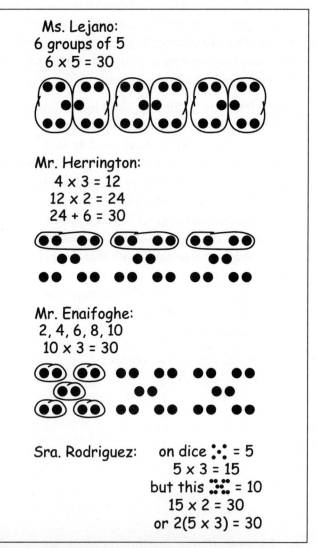

Figure 6 While demonstrating Quick Images to parents, a teacher models how she works with children by recording what the parents say about the way they "saw" a particular dot image.

One math night, I gave a problem that involved doubling. They were doubling 52—a relatively large number that was challenging for younger children, but they could grab some manipulatives and figure it out easily enough. One second-grade parent said that her child didn't have any strategies for doing this. When I spoke to the child about it, she actually did have some strategies. It wasn't 50 + 50 = 100, plus another 4 equals 104. It was more like, "I know that the 2 and 2 is 4," and beyond that, we needed to work together on the 50 + 50. But the girl was clearly making sense of the numbers. Still, the mother just wanted to see the columns, and since she didn't, she thought that her child didn't know math. Maybe the biggest thing with math night is that we can take a problem like 48 x 19 and actually show the parents seven or eight different ways the kids would solve that problem—and they're always impressed.

—S. Bridges, grade 5 teacher (New York)

Games

Suggested Games from *Investigations*

Capture 5: a grade 2 game

The Fraction Cookie Game: a grade 3 game

Close to 100: a grades 3–4 game that has variations appropriate for grade 2 (close to 20) and grades 4–5 (close to 1000)

(For games specific to each grade level, K–5, see pp. 54–55.)

Games are another popular route into the mathematics. Some worry that parents will think, "Is this math program nothing but fun and games?" Most teachers who use games for math night don't experience this reaction. These teachers circulate as parents play the games, asking questions and pointing out big ideas. They discuss the games afterward, asking "What did you learn about math while you were playing?" and "What do you think children will learn while playing?" Some teachers provide handouts for parents to jot down their ideas about the math in the various games and activities, while others post a list of the mathematical ideas in each game. One teacher had someone in each group tally the number of addition problems the group solved while playing Close to 100 to highlight the amount of computation practice children get while playing such a game.

Sometimes there is a push from some parents to go back to something a little more old-fashioned. But when they come to math night, they can't believe how much fun it is, and that's key. I know it's not all about fun; there is a goal and a purpose behind it. But having kids enjoy math—I mean, that's really powerful.

—S. Bridges, grade 5 teacher (New York)

The Math in "Close to 100"

- What are the mathematical ideas children might be working with as they play this game?

- What are some questions you might ask children as you watch them play this game?

- How would you change this game for a child who is having difficulty?

- How would you change this game for a child who needs more of a challenge?

Figure 7 This list of questions was written to help parents think about the math in Close to 100, a game introduced in *Investigations* grade 3. It could be used to make a handout for nearly any of the *Investigations* games. From R. Christiansen and N. Buell, Brookline, Massachusetts. Reprinted with permission.

Where's the Math in the Close To . . . Games?

By playing these games, children have opportunities to:

- recognize and learn about important "landmark" numbers - 10, 20, 100, 1000.
- explore what landmark numbers are like:
    - How many ways can you make 10?
    - What numbers can you count by to land exactly on 100?
    - How many 25's are in 1000?
- develop "number sense." (Number sense is like common sense - students use what they know to solve problems).
- round numbers.
- practice addition, subtraction, multiplication and division (depending on the level played).
- sharpen "mental math" skills.

Figure 8 Teachers might post a list like this on math night at stations for the Close to 20, Close to 100, and Close to 1000 games (*Investigations,* grades 2–5). From N. Simpson and K. List, the Florence E. Smith School of Science, Math and Technology in West Hartford, Connecticut. Reprinted with permission.

When games are used to introduce the mathematics to parents, teachers need to be clear that this curriculum is much more than "fun and games" and to talk explicitly with parents about the role of games in the classroom and at home, the mathematics in the games, the strategies and thinking skills children are developing as they play them, and the kinds of questions teachers (and parents) can ask children as they play. Such questions should be designed to find out what the children know and to push their thinking further. "The Purpose of Games in *Investigations*" (p. 41) can be used to make a handout for math nights.

One educator considers her parent night successful when parents are able to form a vision of what it would be like to do this activity or play this game with their child and become curious enough to actually try it. This means they are getting interested in and excited about how children think mathematically. Another educator says she feels successful when parents express the longing to have learned math this way themselves, or when someone struck by the alternative approaches to computation shares that, "This is what is always going on, secretly, in my head."

How teachers set up the activities and games for the Exploring Mathematics portion of math night varies, depending on the audience. The sample agenda on p. 33 shows how one school set up stations at different points around the school. Setting up this portion of math night for a single grade level, will be discussed in chapter 3, "Math Night for One Classroom or Grade Level," p. 48.

The Purpose of Games in *Investigations*

- Games are a central part of the mathematics in the units, not just enrichment.

- Games develop familiarity with the number system and with "landmarks" in the number system, such as 10's, 100's, and 1000's, and provide engaging opportunities for practicing computation.

- Playing games encourages strategic mathematical thinking as students find an optimal way (rather than just any way) of solving a problem.

- Games provide repeated practice without need for the teacher to provide the problems. The teacher is free to observe students or to work with a few students.

- Games are played often throughout a unit and throughout the year to develop fluency with numbers. It's expected that students will play a game many times.

- Games provide a school to home link. Parents learn about the mathematical thinking their children are doing by playing games with them at home.

From *Bridges to Classroom Mathematics* (COMAP, n.d.), a package of professional development materials for *Investigations*.

The Question-and-Answer Period

Structuring a Q&A

Most math nights include at least a short question-and-answer session. These tend to induce stress in teachers, especially those new to the curriculum. What questions will parents ask? How will I answer? Will I have an answer? What if they don't accept it? What if a question gets the group off track?

Many find that these sessions work best when several teachers join together to answer participants' questions. Thus, even if the math night is geared to individual classrooms, teachers will gather in larger grade-level or grade-band groups for this

part of the program to support each other in fielding questions. For examples of common questions and many sample responses from educators and researchers, see chapter 5, "Answering Those Frequently Asked Questions," p. 64.

One consideration is how to gather questions and comments. Handing out index cards early in the evening, so parents can jot immediate questions and turn them in, enables teachers to plan some answers ahead of time. Parents can use another card to keep track of further questions that arise during the evening. Using index cards can be helpful in several other ways. They provide a sense of the range of attitudes and indicate how many people are concerned about particular topics. They also give the presenters some control over how issues are presented and discussed. If there are combative or particularly critical-sounding questions, teachers can present them in a way that opens the conversation constructively: "Several people are wondering about basic facts and how this curriculum and I are going to handle getting the children to know their basic facts ..."

Another strategy is to have parents first talk in smaller groups. Each group discusses their questions and prioritizes them to bring to the whole-group discussion. This way parents hear a variety of different perspectives, and issues are sometimes resolved within the smaller group.

Anticipating Questions

Teachers say it's important to think beforehand about what the questions and comments might be. They think back to last year, think about the concerns in their community, and they ask more experienced teachers. Then, they plan concise, helpful responses that they feel comfortable communicating. Most teachers expect questions about the curriculum itself, why it's different, and how it benefits children, along with questions about facts and computation and about how families can help their children at home. Some teachers also prepare handouts about such common topics to distribute to parents who are interested.

My first year teaching second grade, I didn't have a sense of what parents' questions would be. I had a feeling that they would ask, "Why isn't there more drill? Why aren't there more just straight-out number problems?" But then they were seeing all those combining and comparing problems coming home, all the word problems. The parents really love those and saw that through them, the kids are working on math facts and building their sense of number. So I think with time, the parents become less anxious. But in the beginning, they definitely are. And so my first year, it was helpful for me to seek out the veteran teachers and say, "I know this is the first year with *Investigations*, but what do you foresee as some of the questions?" And they helped me reinforce the curriculum to parents.

—*S. Huard, grade 3 teacher (Massachusetts)*

Answering Questions About the Curriculum

Many parents will have questions about a curriculum like *Investigations* that looks and feels very different from what they remember. A well-planned "exploring mathematics" session, in which teachers and parents explore math together, helps parents understand how teachers work with children every day. Having lots of student work on display, along with the concrete materials they use, can help convey the nature of the curriculum. Video footage of children working can do the same. The following are some reassuring facts to communicate to parents:

- This curriculum is a complete, full-year mathematics curriculum. The children will use *Investigations in Number, Data, and Space* for math every day for at least one hour.
- This curriculum was funded by the National Science Foundation. It is based on research about how children learn mathematics, and it embodies the standards developed by NCTM.
- The curriculum was tested extensively in a wide variety of classrooms, with real teachers and

real students. It is currently used in school systems throughout the country and around the globe.

- The curriculum supports teachers by providing vital information about the mathematics, how children learn math, and what their students are likely to say and do with the activities.
- Research shows that *Investigations* students do *just as well as* other students on simple calculation problems, and *considerably better than* other students on word problems, multistep problems, and more complex problems (Mokros, 2000).

The background information in "How *Investigations* Came to Be" (p. 43) also answers some of the questions parents may have. Many related resources offer additional information that can help explain the curriculum: *Principles and Standards for School Mathematics* (NCTM, 2000), *Beyond Arithmetic* (Mokros, Russell, & Economopoulos, 1995), the *Investigations* units themselves, and articles referenced on the *Investigations* website. Ideally, these publications would be made available for parents to check out. The Implementation guide (Russell, Smith, Storeygard, & Murray, 1998) and the introductory text that appears in each unit of the curriculum are good sources for information that might be used to develop overheads or handouts to help explain the curriculum to parents.

How Investigations Came to Be

In the past few decades, data from a variety of sources have shown that mathematics education in the United States is not serving our students well. The data point out that U.S. students need to study more than arithmetic; they need mathematical experience and expertise in areas like geometry, data, and algebra. They also point to a curriculum that is "a mile wide and an inch deep." The conclusion: Our students need more significant mathematical experiences and the time and opportunity to think more deeply about mathematics.

In the face of developing knowledge about how children learn and about the weaknesses of U.S. students in mathematics, the National Council of Teachers of Mathematics (NCTM) took action, publishing three documents that laid the foundation for improving mathematics education in the United States:

The Curriculum and Evaluation Standards for School Mathematics (1989), *The Professional Standards for Teaching Mathematics* (1991), and *The Assessment Standards for School Mathematics* (1995).

These standards were designed to help teachers, curriculum developers, and assessment experts create a different vision of mathematics teaching and learning. NCTM updated the original *Standards* in *Principles and Standards for School Mathematics* (2000) to provide further guidance and focus for teachers and schools working to improve mathematics instruction for all children.

Following the publication of the 1989 NCTM *Standards,* the National Science Foundation funded a number of mathematics curriculum development projects at various grade levels (elementary, middle, and secondary). These projects aimed to provide new curriculum materials for school mathematics that would embody the vision of the NCTM *Standards.* One of those projects was *Investigations in Number, Data, and Space.*

Using the *Standards* and research about how children learn, a team of educators at TERC, a nonprofit organization working on issues in K–12 math, science, and technology, developed *Investigations* over nine years (1990–1998). During this extended period of development, the team spent literally thousands of hours in classrooms, observing teachers and students as they tried out activities, talking to teachers and students, and collecting student work. Such extensive classroom-based formative evaluation meant the developers were confident that *Investigations* worked well with a range of students and that the activities and the sequence of activities had been carefully evaluated to help students delve deeply into mathematical ideas.

For More Information

See the NCTM website (nctm.org) for additional information about the *Standards* and the changes they recommend. To read about each of the NSF-funded, standardsbased curricula, visit the website of the K–12 Mathematics Curriculum Center, hosted by the Education Development Center, Inc. (edc.org). For more details on *Investigations,* see the *Investigations* website (terc.edu).

The National Center for Education Statistics website (http://nces.ed.gov) has information about two assessments that yielded notably disappointing results in mathematics: the 1996 National Assessment of Educational Progress (NAEP) and the Third International Mathematics and Science Study (TIMSS). For more on TIMSS, see the Eisenhower National Clearinghouse (ENC) website (enc.org).

Answering Questions About Facts and Computation

Experienced teachers say that concern, anxiety, or criticism from some parents is likely in the areas of number, computation, algorithms, and basic facts. These are not unreasonable concerns from parents, and the school needs to show respect for these worries when responding. For example, teachers might say:

"This program does look and feel different from what most of us experienced as children, particularly in the way that it handles number and computation. You won't be seeing sheets of 30 computation problems for homework. But as you look more closely, you will see lots of practice with computation and basic facts as the children solve problems and play games. As they use facts to solve more complex problems, they quickly realize that it's very helpful to know them. We also work on finding ways to remember the facts that are hard for them. In working on facts this way, children are developing far more knowledge than just how to get the answer. For example, when the children know that 6 x 4 is 24 because they know first that "5 x 4 is 20, and 6 x 4 is just one more 4," they are understanding what it means to multiply, and they are making sense of the relationships among numbers, facts, and operations. They are learning that math, just like other subjects, is about making sense and figuring things out—not just about memorizing and repeating what they're told."

I tell the parents that math is not just crunching numbers, it's building number sense, building concepts between numbers. A lot of them will say, "It's not like when I was learning math." Well, ... I'm 29, and it's not like when I was learning math. I just memorized everything. So I'm very open with them about it, and, hopefully, ... give them an understanding about what the program is. And the parents have been very supportive.

—*S. Huard, grade 3 teacher (Massachusetts)*

Here's a similar way to convey the same message:

"It's important to me that the students are learning that mathematics is about making sense. When I was a student, math was about learning the one right way to add, subtract, multiply, and divide. I did well because I was good at memorizing, good at spitting it back out for the test. I never understood why carrying or borrowing worked or what long division was really about. What I want you to know is that learning math this way is asking far more of your children than we have in the past. They are learning so much more about numbers and how they work, about our number system, and about computation. They're not just learning how to add and subtract, multiply and divide. They are thinking about how to do it best for particular numbers, why a method works, whether the answer makes sense, and how a problem is (or isn't) related to an addition or multiplication problem we did earlier. You saw some evidence of that in the student work I showed earlier. For example, ..."

It's good to try for a balance between adequately answering specific questions about teaching facts and algorithms and addressing a broader range of issues. Parents who would like to talk more about very specific issues can be told to look forward to an upcoming newsletter or to set up a meeting with the teacher.

A back-to-school night is usually so tightly structured that I rarely have to face questions from highly critical parents. In any case, I much prefer to work with an unhappy parent one on one. So if a parent persists in asking questions that make me uncomfortable or that I am unable to answer, I suggest we discuss the issues at a separate meeting. So that the meeting will be as fruitful as possible, I ask the parent to jot down his or her most pressing concerns and send them to me, along with possible meeting dates and times. Knowing the specific concerns ahead of time enables me to prepare an honest and clear response. *(Litton, 1998, p. 40)*

Answering Questions About Homework

Families always have questions about helping their children with math at home. More detailed information is discussed in chapter 6, "Communicating Through Homework," page 88. For math night, one teacher shares the following with parents:

- Expect __ minutes of math homework each night. If your children have worked hard for __ minutes and have not finished, it's OK to consider the work done. If your children finish the assignment quickly, we have talked in school about ways to extend their work—they should be able to change the assignment on their own to make it appropriately challenging.
- Games will come home for homework. Particularly in the beginning, a lot of these games will take time for your children to master. Please give them time to think and talk about their ideas. Wait until they're ready to make their move or take their turn, and then ask questions about how they're thinking. You will see the sophistication of their strategies develop over time, particularly with repeated play.
- There's a lot to be learned from a wrong answer. Instead of just correcting your children, try to figure out what they were thinking and work together to see where things went wrong. This is the way we work in class.

- If your children have no idea how to do a homework assignment, that's important information for me. If this happens, please send your children back with a note and the unfinished assignment to work one-on-one with me.
- Besides homework, look for the ways math comes up everyday, while reading books, cooking, or doing chores. Take the time to build mathematics into the things you already do with your children daily.

I suggest that parents make up problems. I just tell parents, "When you're walking down the street, the city is the best place to do addition and subtraction. 'We're on 33rd Street. We have to go to 51st Street. How much farther do we have to go?'"

—*J. DiBrienza, teacher leader (New York)*

Two classroom teachers adapted information from the curriculum—material describing the teacher's role in an *Investigations* classroom (Russell et al., 1998)—to help parents think about *their* role in working with their children. According to these two teachers, the parents' role is as follows:

- to observe and listen carefully to their child
- to try to understand how their child is thinking
- to help their child articulate her/his thinking, both orally and in writing
- to place high value on their child's thinking hard about a problem
- to help their child keep track of her/his work and be able to explain or show her/his thinking
- to ask questions that push their child's mathematical thinking further
- to talk about important mathematical ideas
- to make decisions about how to modify the activity appropriately for their own child

This list makes a good overhead or handout for parents.

Encouraging Classroom Visitors and Volunteers

Some teachers use some of this whole-group, question-and-answer time to talk about parents visiting and volunteering in the classroom. She details upcoming classroom projects for which extra adults would be helpful and calls attention to sessions that might be particularly useful for parents curious about a particular topic. She describes past years when parents came in to share their mathematical expertise through activities such as sewing and quilting, origami, collecting, and cooking. She also describes trips the class has taken to visit a parent at work, to explore mathematics at the carpenter's shop or the grocery store.

Promising Ongoing Communication

Because one evening is such a short time, parents are reassured to learn that teachers will continue to be open to and available for questions, comments, meetings, and conversations. Many teachers close a math night by explaining the ways they will communicate with families about math and about this curriculum, including a school or classroom website, a school or grade-level newsletter, and classroom mailings. Teachers also clarify when and how they will be available—by phone, by e-mail, or for meetings. They encourage parents to attend scheduled conferences, when the teacher will have samples of each child's mathematical work to look at, discuss the child's strengths and weaknesses, and share what parents can be doing at home to further their child's progress.

Conclusion

Holding a math night can be a lot of work, but it is a wonderful opportunity for teachers to present themselves and their program to parents and to begin ongoing relationships that are respectful, collaborative, and mutually beneficial.

> We started math nights and we are still doing them. They are very successful. We have between 500 and 600 people who come out. We give everyone who attends a raffle ticket. We raffle off math books, games, and school supplies. The evenings are short and fun-filled. We think math nights are a great way to get parents and students working together on math activities.
>
> —*S. Goltz, principal (Arizona)*

A math night can be the perfect place to introduce families to a new math program and an ideal setting for involving family members in new ideas about mathematics. However, it is not a cure-all. Math night must be viewed as only one piece of a larger plan for reaching and interacting with families. In fact, these events sometimes raise a lot of questions that need to be answered in future forums, like those described elsewhere in this book. Building successful relationships with parents requires a meaningful exchange of thoughts and ideas, listening on both sides, acknowledging and responding to issues and concerns, and the development of trust and understanding. All of this requires sustained effort over time.

Resources and Readings

Litton's (1998) *Getting Your Math Message Out to Parents* offers a classroom teacher's thoughts on organizing the math portion of a Back-to-School Night, as well as support in choosing student work to share with parents (see especially pages 35–47).

Most videotapes that schools use for the introductory portion of a math night are not specifically designed for parents; rather, they appear as part of professional development packages for teachers. Nonetheless, these tapes are perfectly suitable for a parent audience and provide powerful images of children thinking and talking mathematics. They allow parents to glimpse what goes on in the classroom, to see the mathematical ideas children are struggling with and mastering, and to have the opportunity themselves to try to see the logic in children's mathematical ideas. In addition to the Marilyn Burns title suggested in the text (Burns, 1994), the following are some other possibilities:

- the *Math Time:* video series by Kathy Richardson, in particular *The Learning Environment, Thinking with Numbers,* and *A Look at Children's Thinking* (available from Didax Educational Resources).
- *Relearning to Teach Arithmetic* by Susan Jo Russell, David Smith, Judy Storeygard, and Megan Murray; two videotape packages (available from Pearson Learning).

- *Used Numbers,* two videotapes about students' work with real data (also available from Pearson Learning).
- *Talking Mathematics: Resource Package* by Rebecca B. Corwin, Sabra L. Price, Judith Storeygard, and David Smith; package includes seven videotapes (available from Heinemann).
- Videotapes are also included in two in-depth professional development series, *Bridges to Classroom Mathematics* (COMAP, n.d.) and *Developing Mathematical Ideas* (Schifter, Bastable, & Russell, 1999a, 1999b, 2001a, 2001b, in press).

More information about these and other videos can be found at the *Investigations* website.

The *Investigations* website also offers other support for those who are setting up a math night, including information for making handouts that will answer questions about the curriculum itself, why it's different, and how it benefits children; questions about facts and computation; and questions about how families can help their children at home.

Chapter 3
Math Night for One Classroom or Grade Level

This chapter describes how one teacher organizes her math night for parents. Although the specific suggestions relate to the grade 2 classroom, the structure can work for any grade level and can be broadened to apply to a grade band (such as K–1 or 3–5). A menu of *Investigations* activities that work well for each grade level appears at the end of this chapter (p. 54–55).

An Introduction to the Math

As suggested in the previous chapter, this evening begins with a whole-school group introduction. This teacher then gathers the parents of children in grade 2 and begins the mathematical portion of the evening with information about *Investigations*. She explains that the materials are based on research about how children learn, and that the curriculum was extensively tested in real classrooms and is used in school districts around the country. She displays the grade 2 units and hands out a packet of information taken from the units. She describes to parents how the materials in the handout support her work. Her handouts might include:

- the "About the Mathematics" section from one unit
- a Teacher Note that includes sample student work and an analysis of that work
- a Teacher Note about an important mathematical issue
- an "Observing the Students" section that guides teachers in what to look for as children work
- a Dialogue Box that offers a glimpse into the classroom and into children's strategies

Then, this teacher gives an overview of the mathematics in the *Investigations* units at her grade level, providing samples of student work wherever possible. The following are excerpts from her presentation:

"One of the major areas we will study in mathematics this year is data. We live in a data-rich society, confronted with more and more information on a daily basis. Graphs are everywhere—in newspapers, magazines, and on television. Interpreting the increasing amounts of data is an important skill for any citizen. Your children will be generating, asking, and refining questions. They will collect data and find ways to display the results and to explain what they think the data tell us. We will be exploring two kinds of data this year—*categorical* data, such as which animals live in our neighborhoods, what things sink and float, and what things scare us; and *numerical* data, such as how many teeth children have lost or how many pockets our class is wearing."

Figure 9 When discussing data, the teacher shows student work examples from previous classes. The graph below shows one representation of "Things That Scare Us." The line plot (bottom) displays data collected to answer the question "How Many Teeth Have the First Graders Lost?"

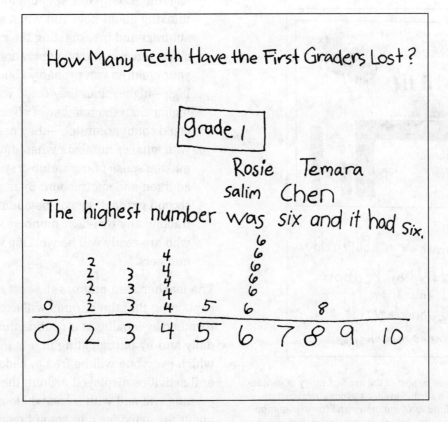

"Another major area we will be exploring is geometry—2-D and 3-D geometry and the connection between the two. For an example of what I mean, has anyone ever tried to put together a three-dimensional gas grill using instructions with two-dimensional pictures? When I went to school, geometry was mostly about memorizing definitions. We're going to be studying geometry differently. Children will be putting shapes together and taking them apart and really thinking hard about what makes a triangle a triangle or a rectangle a rectangle. For example, when pushed, many children think the *only* "real" triangle is an equilateral triangle. I want them to realize that any closed three-sided shape is a triangle, and to understand why. As we work on geometry, we will also explore ideas about the measurement of area (deciding how many tiles would cover a rectangle, for example), simple fractions (by looking at halves, fourths, and thirds of rectangles), and symmetry."

"Finally, we will be doing a lot of in-depth work with numbers. I'm interested in how children count, particularly how they count a set of objects. Do they organize them? count them one by one? use groups such as 2's, 5's, 10's, or even 25's? But the main emphasis of our work in second grade is understanding numbers—how you can take them apart and put them back together—and on place value. For example, I have 25 things. I can make 2 groups of 10 and a group of 5, but I can also make 5 groups of 5 or a group of 20 and a group of 5."

"We will also spend a lot of time studying addition and subtraction, including learning those important combinations lots of people call 'the facts.' We'll spend a lot of time thinking about how and when to add and subtract and investigating the relationships between the two operations. Although your children can probably count very high—higher than they could write and higher than the number of objects they could count accurately—they need to work with smaller numbers when they are making sense of our number system and addition and subtraction. By the end of second grade, they will be adding and subtracting any two-digit numbers, and those who are ready will be working with larger numbers."

The teacher then outlines the rest of the evening, explaining that the parents will explore some math together by looking at a routine that students do daily and by participating in a math workshop, in which everyone will be free to choose among several activities displayed around the room. The evening will end with some whole-group discussion about the activities and some time for questions.

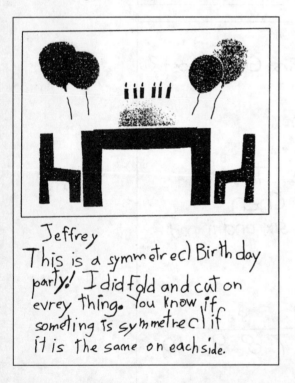

Figure 10 To explain one aspect of the grade 2 study of geometry, the teacher shows a second grader's symmetrical picture, which includes his definition of symmetry and his explanation of how he proved his picture has symmetry (by folding, cutting, and then comparing the sides).

How Far Is It From 38 To 65?

> I got it by counted on my figers.
> I started at 39 and I counted to 65.
> I got 27.

> 38 + 20 = 58   20 + 7 = 27
> 58 + 7 = 65   ☀27☀

> 38 | 48. 58. 68 - 2 = 66
> 66 - 1 = 65
> count by tens
> 27 answer

> the difference in between 40 and 65 is 25 but the number is 38
> 25 + 2 = 27
> 27 I counted on the 100 chart to check.

> the answer is 27 I counted on the 100s chart and went 1,2,3,4,5, 6,7,8,9,10,11,12,13,14,15,16,17,18, 19,20,21,22,23,24,25,26,27, but I didn't count the 38 cause you don't In the real game.

Figure 11 To further illustrate students' work with number, the teacher calls attention to a bulletin board display of second graders' work on the problem, "How far is it from 38 to 65?" She points out the variety of strategies used—some children counted by ones, others by tens, and some made larger jumps or used number relationships they knew.

Classroom Routines and Ten-Minute Math

In addition to the activities in each unit, *Investigations* teachers use certain standard Classroom Routines (at grades K–2) or Ten-Minute Math activities (at grades 3–5) throughout the year. Exploring one of these with parents gives teachers the chance to do the following:

- introduce the idea of Classroom Routines (or Ten-Minute Math), describe those that are current classroom activities, and explain the role they play in the mathematics curriculum
- connect parents to an activity children are doing regularly
- reveal some ways this curriculum addresses number, operations, and "basic facts"
- engage parents with some mathematics themselves and with the way math is being taught
- share student work

This second grade teacher often chooses to explore the Today's Number routine with parents. (How Many Pockets? is another mathematically rich second grade routine that explores many ideas in both data and number and would be an equally good choice.) As she describes the activity, she chooses a number for parents—ideally one that students have recently explored. For example:

> "Today's number is 19. The task is to find different ways to make Today's Number and record those ways in a number sentence. For example, 10 + 9 = 19. The children can use any ways that make sense to them, as long as they can explain their reasoning."

She collects some answers from parents on the overhead or board, modeling how she works with the children. That is, she might compare two different ways, record one way and ask if it reminds anyone of another way that's already been recorded or wonder aloud if that method would work for any number. For example: "It seems that you used doubles to get your answer (9 + 9 + 1). Could that strategy work for any number?" Or, "Does that remind anyone else of Mr. Wu's strategy (10 + 10 − 1)? In what way?"

The teacher then explains that when she wants children to explore particular content or embrace a challenge, she adds restrictions or limitations—for example, make 19 using only coin values or without using addition. Parents try another round using just such a limitation, making 19 using all 4 operations or in exactly 5 steps or using only subtraction. Again, they share methods and discuss the number sentences parents found, talking specifically about how the restrictions changed the activity for them. She then shares student work for the same problem.

Another second grade teacher shared the following vignette to illustrate for parents the benefits of a routine like Today's Number.

> Today was the 19th day of school and here are some ways to get 19 that the children came up with today.
>
> $10 \times 1 + 9$
>
> $100 − 81$
>
> $100 + 500 + 500 + 500 − 1600 + 19$
>
> $9 + 9 + 1$
>
> $17 + 2$

We do this every morning. The kids love it, and you can see that it challenges children who are at a variety of different levels. We have some pretty lively discussions as children explain and defend their ways. I have learned so much about how they think by doing this warm-up activity every day.

One of the things I want you to notice is the way children work on their "basic facts" as they do this activity. Knowing their combinations is an important goal, but we're coming at this from a different perspective. In the past, children learned the 2's, then the 3's, and so on. Now they're learning their facts as they use them to solve problems. For example, I'm pretty sure this way to make 19 [9 + 9 + 1] came from our recent work with doubles and with doubles plus and minus 1.

—*H. Hall, grade 2 teacher (Texas)*

Math Workshop or Choice Time

Choice Time or Math Workshop is a common way to offer parents a variety of activities to explore. Some teachers have their students host the stations; others illustrate each station with enlarged samples of student work (with no names). Some teachers post sample test questions related to the mathematics in each activity, while others give parents a short checklist or questionnaire to respond to as they rotate through the stations (for example, the handout with questions about Close to 100, p. 39). Posting the mathematical ideas children are exploring as they play (as shown for the "Close to …" games, p. 40) or having parents generate such a list while they play helps keep families focused on the mathematics.

One particular teacher sets up four stations:

- The first station has items on display, such as the mathematical children's literature being used in class and samples of student work, including any constructions or designs students would like to share using Geoblocks, pattern blocks, cubes, or tiles.

- The second station has several games and the materials needed to play them. Many games work for this setting. It is often better for parents to explore a few games in depth rather than race through many choices.
- The third and fourth stations contain a variety of number and other activities, the materials needed to do them, and possibly some student work for those activities. Displaying student work inspires interest and enlivens the activities for adults. (For a list of games and activities that work well at parent night, organized by grade level, see pp. 54–55.)

In addition, this teacher sets up an exhibit table of the *Investigations* units and materials, plus resources about math and math education that families can check out to take home.

Once the parents have begun working at the stations, this teacher circulates, much as she does in class. She asks questions, probes understanding, extends the problem, discusses the mathematical ideas, and describes what children struggle with and learn as they engage in these games and activities. She shares stories based on the day-to-day experiences of the class. For example,

> "One day Jillian shared this strategy for subtracting that you're looking at [in a piece of student work]. We were all puzzled about how and why it worked and wondered if it would work for any subtraction problem. A group of children spent the rest of that math class and most of the next exploring this strategy and convincing themselves it would always work. Now children who use this method often say, 'I solved it Jillian's way …'"

She also shares insights about individual children with their parents. For example:

> "The strategy you used to figure out how many paper clips are left in the box is just how Erin solves it in class. She starts at the number she has and counts up to 100. She

used to mostly count up by ones, but I've been excited because lately she's using bigger jumps, like 10 and multiples of 10. Her number sense and her ability to add 'friendly' numbers has really grown this year. She's comfortable adding 10 to any number now, not just to numbers that end in 0."

A Whole-Group Closing

After parents have had a chance to explore several activities in depth, it is useful to bring them back together to discuss their experiences with the activities and the mathematics, what they learned, and what they think children are learning. This is also a good time for teachers to explain the following:

- their mathematical goals for the grade level and how these activities help children reach those goals and prepare them for the mathematics in later grades
- their expectations of students—at school, at home, and regarding homework
- their method for keeping track of children's work

Many teachers build in a brief time during the parent night for parents to look through a portfolio of their child's work, with the understanding that parent-teacher conferences will allow for a more in-depth look and discussion of the work.

Finally, the teacher fields any questions and comments and offers ideas for helping the children at home. (How parents can help with math at home is further discussed in chapter 6, "Communicating Through Homework," p. 88.)

Games and Activities for Each Grade Level

The following lists provide, by grade level, a variety of *Investigations* games and activities appropriate for a parent math night. Whatever the structure, it is important to showcase a range of materials—displays, games, activities—and a range of content—number, geometry and measurement, and data. It's also important to keep the number of activities reasonable, enabling families to explore a few activities in some depth.

Note that when activities involve student-created riddles or story problems, parents can be encouraged to solve their child's problem and leave a note for the child that explains their strategy for solving it.

If teachers have completed the data unit(s) at their grade level, they will have student-collected data that parents can sort in different ways, such as Favorite Lunch Foods, Ways to Get to School, Sink and Float, Animals in Our Neighborhood, or What Scares Us. Another option is to collect similar data from parents early in the evening. For example, you might ask parents to respond to the question, "Would you rather be an eagle or a whale?" on a sticky note or index card as they arrive. The parents' responses are then made available for everyone to sort at one of the stations. Attribute blocks and shape cards are also good sorting activities for grades 1 and 2.

KINDERGARTEN

Display items: Student-made books ("The Counting Book" and "Book of Shapes") • The class Shape Mural

Games: Compare/Double Compare • Collect 10 or 15 Together • Racing Bears • What Comes Next? • Fill the Hexagons

Number activities: Grab and Count and its variations • Arranging Six Tiles • Towers of Six

Geometry, data, and other activities: Sorting Favorite Lunch Foods • Pattern Block Grab • Pattern Block Shapes (on- and off-computer) • Matching Faces • Geoblock Match-Up

GRADE 1

Display items: The student-made storybook "A Counting Adventure" • 3-D block town drawings • the class town of Geoblock buildings

Games: Compare/Double Compare • Collect 15 • Towers of Ten • Collect 25¢ • Tens Go Fish • Total of 20 • Five-in-a-Row

Number activities: How Many of Each? problems • Missing Numbers • How Many Squares?

Geometry, data, and other activities: Ways to Get to School or Would You Rather …? • Guess My Rule (Lids, Buttons, Shapes) • Who's the Mystery Person? (parents will need children's family portrait cards for this) • Which Holds More? • Pattern Block Pictures (on- and off-computer) • Blocks in a Sock • Drawing a Geoblock Building

GRADE 2

Display items: Student-made books such as "How to Make 10" and "Stories About 100"

Games: Double Compare • Tens Go Fish • Close to 20 • Roll-a-Square • Collect $1 • Get to 100 • Capture 5 • The Last Block Game

Number activities: Pinching Paper Clips • Cover Up • student-written story problems or Magic Pot Riddles for parents to solve

Geometry, data, and other activities: Fraction Flags • Which Rectangle Is Biggest? • Predict and Cover • Geoblock Count or Geoblock Footprints • sorting data or shape cards • student-written Rectangle Riddles for parents to solve

GRADE 3

Display items: Pictures of 100 • story problems or riddles students have written

Games: Plus, Minus, Stay the Same • Close to 100 • Array Games (Multiplication Pairs, Count and Compare) • The Game of Many Changes • The Fraction Cookie Game • Sorting Polyhedra • *Tumbling Tetrominoes* (on computer)

Number activities: Arranging Chairs puzzles • Riddles (including those written by children) • story problems • Related Problem Sets

Geometry, data, and other activities: The Perfect Cover-Up • *Get the Toys* (on computer) • patterns for two-cube boxes

GRADE 4

Display items: The 1000 book • skip counting books

Games: Array games (Multiplication Pairs, Count and Compare, Big Array/Small Array) • Close to 100 and Close to 1000 • Multiple and Division Bingo

Number activities: Multiplication plaids • story problems • multiplication and division clusters

Geometry, data, and other activities: Making cube buildings from pictures • matching silhouettes with geometric solids • Which Instructions Are Best? • instructions for making toys (parents can use their child's instructions to try to build the toy) • Crazy Cakes • dot paper/ Geoboards fourths • Mystery Data and Mystery Graphs

GRADE 5

Display items: The million dots display

Games: Close to 1000 • Close to 0 • the Digits Game • The Estimation Game • fraction, decimal, percent, and spinner games, possibly those designed by children

> (There are many appropriate fifth grade games. Some have more complex directions, so you might choose fewer and teach the rules to a group or choose only games with fairly easy-to-learn instructions.)

Number activities: Number Puzzles • multiplication and division clusters • How Do I Solve It? problems

Geometry, data, and other activities: Finding angle sizes in shape pieces • grid patterns for percents • packing problems • finding the amount of advertising on one newspaper page • *Trips* (on computer)

Chapter 4
Variations on Math Night

The basic math night described in the previous two chapters has countless variations. This chapter describes a number of models for events that have been used by schools and districts around the country to further family understanding and acceptance of standards-based mathematics curricula.

A Math Night for a Whole School

This evening event was held at one of the six elementary schools in a diverse New England urban district. The principal welcomed parents and presented the evening's agenda. The superintendent talked briefly about why math is changing and why the district chose *Investigations*. The math coordinator then spoke about the plan for implementing *Investigations,* how it would progress over time, and the support that was in place for teachers and parents. An outside consultant handled the rest of the evening. She started with a quick overview of the *Investigations* curriculum and its goals, discussed how math is changing, and asked parents to reflect on their own math experiences.

Next, the consultant did the grade 2 routine Today's Number with parents. Parents were fairly quiet as their children waved their hands wildly, so a variety of the children's ideas was shared and discussed. This raised the typical question, "Why is math changing?" The consultant talked about changes in today's workforce, describing both a Boeing job interview in which four candidates were asked to work together to solve a complicated problem and another situation in which job candidates were asked to build something using Legos and talk with the interviewer about its structure (Lewis, 2000).

The consultant then spoke about how state tests in Massachusetts are beginning to reflect this changing climate. She presented a typical math question from the state test, rephrased here:

> Karen's dog eats 28 pounds of dog food a month. What's the best estimate for how much the dog will eat in one year?

Parents shared their strategies for solving this:

- Round the 28 to 30, and 3 times 12 is 36, so 30 times 12 is 360; it's about 360.
- 28 times 10 is 280, and add 2 more 30s, and you get 340.

Once parent ideas were exhausted, one child shared her strategy, one that had not been suggested by any adult:

> "There's about 30 days in a month, and 28 [pounds of dog food] is really close to 30. I know there's 365 days in a year, so I knew it had to be less than 365—because it's about 1 pound a day, but a little less."

The presenter then talked about the reasoning inherent in this child's thinking, and how that's just the kind of fluent thinking *Investigations* is working toward: flexible, efficient, and accurate. She also showed particular units in *Investigations* that ask students to solve this type of problem and develop such powerful thinking.

The parents next watched video clips of students in the younger grades working on addition and subtraction and students in the older grades working on multiplication and division (Russell, 2000c, 2000d). Children then taught their parents math games from *Investigations,* and families ended the evening playing those games together.

Looking at Strands

This night, offered by a small private school in New England, began with the principal's whole-group overview, covering the national context of reform in mathematics education and the school's choice of curriculum. The rest of the evening focused on a particular strand of mathematics: in this case, multiplication and division. The strand of mathematics parents examined changed each year, but the multiplication and division topic was chosen the first year because it spanned grades K–8, was immediately recognized as "math," and involved complex issues in number and computation. In subsequent years the school helped parents examine number sense, 2-D and 3-D geometry, and algebraic thinking.

Stations were set up around the cafeteria by grade levels (one station each for K, 1–2, 3–4, 5–6, and 7–8), designed to guide parent exploration of this strand as presented through the curriculum. Teachers for each grade-level span had chosen several activities or games that highlighted the curriculum's work with multiplication and division. They had equipped the stations with materials and handouts, and they also staffed the tables to answer questions, talk with parents as they investigated the mathematics, and help clarify any directions.

The suggestion was that parents begin at their child's grade level and then rotate through the other stations, spending about 15 minutes at each. That way parents could begin with the kind of work their children were experiencing and then get a sense of where they're coming from (lower grades) and where they're heading (higher grades), all through the same strand of mathematics.

The evening ended with a whole-group discussion: What did you notice about the games and activities at your child's grade level? across the grade levels? What are the big mathematical ideas in this strand? There was a short time for general questions, and parents were encouraged to follow up any pressing concerns with their child's teacher.

A Sample Lesson

A school in an urban/suburban New England district used family night to present a sample math lesson to parents. That is, teachers actually taught a lesson to children while parents observed. This gave families the chance to see a "typical" math class. In one room, fourth grade students used geoboards and dot paper to find many different-shaped halves of the same-size square. In another room, a second grade teacher taught children to play Close to 20, a game in which they choose three numbers to make a total that is as close as possible to 20. Parents were impressed with the sophistication of the strategies children were developing, the flexibility children showed in solving problems in their heads, the ways children were composing and decomposing numbers to add them, and children's level of comfort in working with numbers. A district official spoke with parents afterwards and reported,

> The general message from everyone was, "This is wonderful. My kid is excited about math," and "They're not afraid of math."
>
> —D. Shein-Gerson, K–5 math coordinator (Massachusetts)

Take-the-Test Night

Another approach for educating parents about standards-based math curricula was reported in *The School Administrator*, a national journal.

> If we want parents and the public to accept and value standards-based assessments, we must inform them about the topic. Pittsburgh's director of public relations, Pat Crawford, created a successful way to provide such information. During "Take-the-Test Night," parents answered sample questions from our state and district tests, including the New Standards Reference Exam, had dinner, then scored their own tests and discussed the results. Parents were surprised at the level of questions on the NSRE and clearly recognized it as a good test of their children's knowledge. The news media gave good coverage to this event, so the public was also informed. (Briars, 1999)

A Math Panel

A small private school, several years into its work with *Investigations,* came up with a new approach after several years of math nights. The school offered a Math Panel made up of five people: the principal, a primary grade teacher, an intermediate grade teacher, and two parents. Both parents had previously been either concerned about or critical of the math program, but they had become convinced that it was in fact the best approach for children, including their own.

The principal opened the panel discussion with some history about the school's work on curriculum and on the changing mathematics curriculum in particular. The teachers followed, each explaining his or her mathematical goals for children.

Then one parent spoke, first from the perspective of his career in mathematics. He discussed what today's children need in order to become mathematicians and scientists and how that has changed in recent years. He also spoke as the father of a daughter in a society where children of different genders tend to experience unequal involvement and success in mathematics. He described how thrilled he was to watch his daughter developing mathematically powerful strategies.

The final speaker was the mother of several children in the school. Her initial reaction to *Investigations* had been very critical. She worried about what her children were *not* getting, worried that they were not learning their facts or the long-established algorithms for computation. She then described how she came to change her mind—through math nights, informational newsletters to which teachers occasionally attached both student work and Teacher Notes from the curriculum, and conversations with her children about their math homework.

This panel event ended with a brief period for comments and questions.

Parent-to-Parent

Tapping parent enthusiasm, as the previously described Math Panel did, can be a powerful strategy. Thus, teachers might work with parents (or encourage parents alone) to present a math event. In a typical "Choice Time" setup, parents could staff tables for a variety of activities from the curriculum and answer questions or explain the mathematics in the activities to their peers. Having parents who understand the math program talking with other parents breaks down barriers; it is no longer always just teachers telling parents. Chapter 10, "One Parent's View: Becoming a Parent Leader" (p. 141), explores how this idea has worked for a district in Portland, Oregon.

A Series of Math Nights

If interest is strong among families in a school, in a particular classroom, or at a given grade level or grade band, a series of math nights enables families to explore students' work in different strands of mathematics and with various mathematical materials and models. Teachers can all attend each meeting, or they can rotate the responsibility for facilitating the event.

The curriculum department in one large school district sponsored a series of math nights for families at the beginning of the implementation process. They offered one math night in each of the district's five geographic areas, five times during the school year.

> Some families actually traveled from their home school zone to attend all five sessions in their area. Some sessions were large (30 to 50 families) and some were small (8 to 12 families). It is hard for organizers when the turnout is small. However, a small group of key parents can become advocates, speaking positively to others about what they learned at the math night, calming concerns of other

parents. These sessions also provided professional development for teachers. Within four years, schools assumed responsibility for hosting the math nights for families.

—L. Gregg, K–5 science and math specialist (Nevada)

A school in a small Midwestern town on the fringe of an urban area was implementing *Investigations* when they decided to experiment with one math night per month. Announcing this schedule in advance made it far easier for parents to attend at least one math night; many families came several times. After the first month, parents helped set up subsequent meetings, and children in the class selected the activities they wanted to do with their families at the monthly get-togethers. As one of the teachers involved said,

Having the students and some parents involved in planning and helping out at the math nights resulted in greatly increased attendance. Wonderful things can happen if you just let them. Try it and see!

—K. Cayo, grade 4 teacher (Minnesota)

Further discussion of longer-term, in-depth ways to educate families in mathematical ideas can be found in chapter 8, "Seminars, Workshops, and Classes for Parents," p. 117.

Family Math

Educators interested in a series of math nights may want to consider the Family Math series of workshops from the EQUALS program at the Lawrence Hall of Science, University of California at Berkeley. Workshops are often led by teams of parents and teachers. In Family Math classes, adults and children come together once a week for several weeks. They work in small groups of two or three families and try the ideas introduced in class out at home. Several books (available in Spanish and English) provide information about

how to design and offer a Family Math series, along with interesting, easy-to-implement math activities for families to do together in class and at home, using common household items, such as beans, blocks, bottle caps, toothpicks, and coins. See "Resources and Readings," p. 7, for more details.

Family Math: *Investigations*

The math curriculum specialist at one school in an urban/suburban New England district of eight elementary schools organized a night specific to *Investigations,* using Family Math as a model. She started offering these nights when her school first started using the curriculum and developed them over the next several years. On this particular night, about a dozen volunteer-made *Investigations* games were set out with a "games menu" for people to take as they came into the cafeteria. Children wrote invitations to their parents, specifying a game that they especially wanted their parents to play.

In previous years, the organizer had set out a variety of games from Marilyn Burns's books, Mary Baratta-Lorton's *Mathematics Their Way* (1995), and other sources. As more teachers got involved with *Investigations,* the nights focused more on the curriculum and what can be found in it. The 200 or so people in attendance spent some time on games and some time in the auditorium, hearing an expert speak on two topics: finding and sharing math in your everyday life and helping your children with homework. She reported,

Parents were quite interested, engaged, and receptive. They asked some questions about algorithms, but seemed very open to thinking about new ways of computing, new ways of adding, subtracting, multiplying, and dividing.

—J. Mokros, TERC (Massachusetts)

A Mathematician's Chair

In many schools, an Author's Chair is an established way for children to share their writing with an audience. The Author's Chair can double as a Mathematician's Chair from which individuals, pairs, or small groups of children can share a significant piece of mathematical work.* For example, in a fifth grade *Investigations* unit, students plan and conduct a survey and then use what they've learned about fractions, decimals, and percents to present their findings. At a Mathematician's Chair event, a pair of children might explain how they determined their question, how they collected their data, and the strategies they used to analyze their results. The audience might include classmates, students from other classrooms, administrators, and parents. One teacher holds these events first thing in the morning several times a year and invites the parents of the participating children to a breakfast. Others set up the Mathematician's Chair for presentations during an Open House or Back-to-School Night.

Figure 12a These fifth graders compared the use of a local park by two age groups on a Saturday afternoon. From the Mathematician's Chair, they displayed and discussed the results of their research, expressed in fractions and as percents.

* For a description of a Mathematician's Chair that involves writing, sharing, and solving word problems, see "Integrating Mathematics with Problem Solving Using the Mathematician's Chair" (Hildebrand, Ludeman, & Mullin, 1999).

Figure 12b For a fourth grade project, students found a way to represent how many people were at home, hour by hour, over the course of 24 hours. They used their graphs to explain what they found out and what they learned from this project.

Math Shares

For this variation on math night, parents are invited to their child's classroom to learn what the children have been doing in mathematics. It's a good event to hold upon the completion of a fairly involved math project, so parents can hear about the project from their child. Alternatively, parents and children might work together on a math activity, explore a problem, or play math games at stations around the room. This type of event might be offered one morning before school (and before parents go to work). Two fourth grade teachers describe their experiences with Math Shares following a unit in 3-D geometry. Student work was hung in the classroom, and there were activities for parents to do with their children, but the highlight was a particular project the students had completed.

For our winter Math Share, the main project was the children's cube toy work from *Seeing Solids and Silhouettes* (a grade 4 *Investigations* unit). Students used interlocking cubes to create a cube toy. Then, they wrote instructions for how to build their toys. At our breakfast, parents tried to build their child's cube toy based on the written directions. It was really fun because the parents were getting hands-on experience in the math curriculum. Both as a new teacher and also as someone who's not as experienced with relating to parents, I was concerned that maybe parents would say, "This isn't math. What is this all about?" But parents loved it. The parents thought it was fantastic that their children were learning about two- and three-dimensional geometry. I was very pleased myself because I wasn't sure what to expect.

—R. Musser, grade 4 teacher (Massachusetts)

We had a long talk in class the day before, about how the children had had more work with 3-D geometry than many of their parents had. So we talked about, "How do you give hints to your parent," and "How are you gentle? How are you supportive?"

Once the parents created the toy, they had to go find the matching one that was over on the counter. The parents clearly appreciated the hard work the children did much more because they were involved in trying to understand the direction booklet. They read it with a much more focused eye than if they were just looking at the child's work, and they realized how difficult the work was.

—N. Buell, grade 4 teacher (Massachusetts)

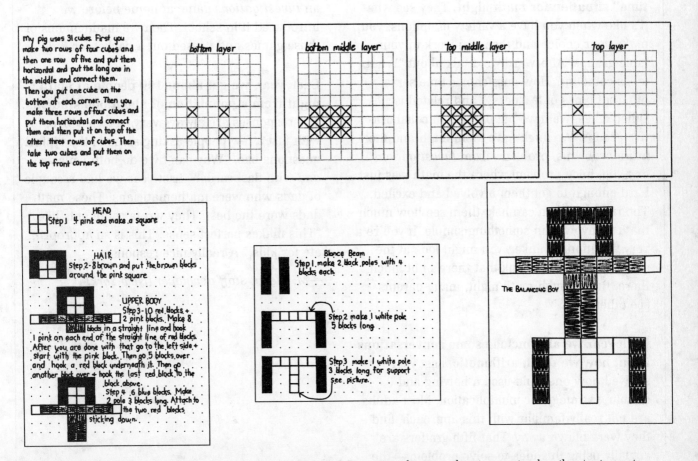

Figure 13 The mathematical thinking that students are doing in 3-D geometry becomes clear to parents when they try to create a 3-D toy from their child's written directions.

Our school, which is part of a large New York City district that adopted *Investigations,* has sponsored math nights for many years now. We've modeled them on a structure that has parents doing math. Only one year did we have children involved—a family math night, where the children came and families played games together. We haven't replicated that, even though it was very successful. It's like when I was teaching, I didn't have the children present at parent conferences. I liked to be able to sit down with the adult, use adult language, and get directly to the point. Given our limited time on math nights, that was our preference and the decision that we made.

Sometimes we have put parents in a "choice time" situation for math night. They see what it's like when you have a variety of options: you make your choice and then you work in your table groups. Afterward we'd talk about "What ideas came up? How does choice time serve different types of learners?" and related issues. Other times, we have put parents in collaborative groups. We might give them math-and-literature problems, problems from *Investigations,* or a big, juicy problem where the math was just hard enough to get them involved and excited. The right problem can help them see how much math is involved in something simple. If you're a very traditional thinker, you might look at the same problem and think that there's not much there. But through math night, many parents see otherwise.

Each year we also include some conversations about how we teach arithmetic. Last year we showed how one child used a halving and doubling strategy for multiplication. Most adults are not really familiar with this approach, and they were blown away. That fifth graders are actually using this idea to solve problems—the parents thought that was just incredible.

This year, we had them solve a few multiplication problems mentally and talk about their strategies, and the teachers shared their strategies as well. Then we showed a range of fifth graders' work for 47×19, so we could demonstrate how students are approaching this kind of computation in a number of different and really interesting ways.

The last couple of years, we have focused on how parents can help their child at home. We taught parents games that we think are worth playing at home—Close to 100 and Close to 1000. Experiencing and playing these with their children is great for everyone. We also pulled games from other resources, like Marilyn Burns, because we didn't want parents to use an *Investigations* game at home before we introduced it in school. Then we made menus of those games and passed out a packet for K–5.

Each year, we get about 100 people at math night from a population of about 600 students. The responses are always very, very positive, with just a few people asking some of the typical questions like, "Why can't we do both your way *and* with flashcards?" Last year we had a couple of dads who were mathematicians. These math dads were the best. They wrote comments like, "This makes perfect sense. This is so appropriate for kids." A really nice response.

—*M. Siena, staff developer (New York)*

Conclusion

With so many possible variations, math night can be a continually evolving feature of the school calendar. Teachers and administrators might change it a bit from one year to the next, experimenting with new approaches, responding to feedback from parents, keeping the event fresh and relevant so that parents continue to come and even look forward to this involvement in the math curriculum.

Resources and Readings

For additional images of what a math night might look like, Litton's *Getting Your Math Message Out to Parents* (1998) includes descriptions of several teachers' events (pages 121–132).

There are three *Family Math* books that provide support in developing a workshop series: *Family Math,* also available in Spanish as *Matemática para la familia* (Stenmark, Thompson, & Cossey, 1986), *Family Math for Young Children* (Coates & Stenmark, 1997), and *Family Math: The Middle School Years* (Thompson & Mayfield-Ingram, 1998).

Chapter 5
Answering Those Frequently Asked Questions

At math nights, during parent-teacher conferences, and even in casual conversations with parents, many of the same questions about changes in teaching math are heard. Administrators and teachers in *Investigations* classrooms were asked to list the most frequently asked questions voiced by parents about mathematics and the *Investigations* curriculum. These questions fell into five general categories, as follows:

1. Why change math, anyway?
- Why change? It worked for me.
- Why change? "If it ain't broke, don't fix it."

2. Will my child succeed?
- What's the evidence that these new methods work?
- Will my child succeed in a more traditional classroom, or in middle and high school?
- Will my child succeed on tests? in life?

3. Where are the rigor and the challenge?
- Is it hard enough? My child seems bored.
- Why give only two or three problems? Doesn't practice make perfect?
- Why so much group work? Won't it hold my child back?
- What's with all these games?
- How can there be more than one answer? In math, it's either right or wrong.
- I don't want my child using a calculator as a crutch.
- Why do the children have to show *how* they solved solved the problem? Why do you spend so much time *talking* and *writing* in mathematics?

4. What about computation and basic facts?
- I'm worried about the way you're teaching computation. Why are you doing it this way?
- What about algorithms? Why aren't you teaching the "one right way" that I learned?
- Shouldn't children know the basic math facts?

5. How do I help my child with math at home?

The same teachers and administrators who identified these common questions also supplied some strategies for responding, as well as answers that were helpful to the families in their communities. Their responses, combined with answers from research and the mathematics education community, are offered in this chapter. In providing a variety of possible responses, the aim is to help readers find the information, the voice, and the resources that best respond to the particular questions they are hearing in their own school districts.

Many parents' questions are based on a straightforward need for more information. Their children are doing math in a way that is unfamiliar to them, and they want to be able to understand and support their children's work. A few parents' questions arise from confusion, anxiety, misinformation, fear, or anger about change. Across the country, though, parents respond positively to their children's experiences in math. When asked about the "typical" response of parents in their district, people in the field shared many positive comments. For example, a teacher in Massachusetts reported:

> After five years or so of [using *Investigations*], we're starting to see wonderful continuity between grades, as students are building on these skills through the years. They're becoming very confident and solid math thinkers, and they're comfortable expressing their ideas and talking about their strategies. Even students who traditionally would not have thought of themselves as math thinkers or mathematicians now have this whole new confidence and really enjoy math. And the parents remark on all of this.

—M. Scott, grades 1–2 teacher (Massachusetts)

Other teachers speak of the support and even excitement they hear from parents. For example:

My parents are curious more than anything else. They ask, "Why couldn't I have learned math this way?" They want to become informed rather than debate. I haven't had a confrontational parent over math in years. I think that comes from my attitude—parents question teachers who aren't self-confident themselves.

—M. Riddle, grades 3–5 teacher (Massachusetts)

The parents are starting to say, "Wow, they brought home double-digit by double-digit multiplication. I guess you call it a cluster problem. And my kid did it pretty fast, and explained some exciting things to me." Or parents are saying, "I'm learning from my kid." These children are starting to really impress their parents.

—J. DiBrienza, teacher leader (New York)

Comments I hear all the time: "I am learning math from my child! We spend time together playing the math games ... and are enjoying it. I now understand why, but before I didn't know what I was doing and didn't like math. My child enjoys math class—I hated it. I wish you were my math teacher! This makes so much more sense."

And I hear things like this: "Your math homework drives me crazy ... but please let me know what the answer is and how you got it! My sister, mother, aunt, etc., etc., couldn't figure it out ... and we want to know what we were doing wrong."

—J. Pepicelli, grade 5 teacher (Massachusetts)

A parent of a child in my class came to me and said, "Rose, I don't know what you're doing, but my child knows math. I have not seen a lot of paperwork, however his mental math is good. He gives me hard problems in the car, and he can solve them before I can do them. I don't understand the way he thinks about numbers, but it is obvious that his methods work. Whatever you are doing is working."

—R. Christiansen, grades 1–2 teacher (Massachusetts)

One benefit of asking and listening to parents' thoughts about the new math program is the discovery of such excitement and support. However, in any parent population there will be the dubious, challenging, or worried voice. These parents are doing their job: they are looking out for their children's best interests. The job of teachers and administrators is to help these parents understand that the school, too, has their children's best interests at heart. It's not "us against them"—everyone is on the same side here. And so, the following pages model respectful responses to the five categories of most frequently asked questions and challenges from the parent community.

Why change math, anyway?

Parents may first realize that mathematics is changing when they see their elementary school child exploring ideas in 2-D and 3-D geometry; in data and statistics; in probability and chance; and in patterns, functions, and the mathematics of change. They wonder why their children are studying all these topics that were not a part of their own mathematics education. And, they wonder about the arithmetic that was the crux of their education—what happened to the rows and columns of practice problems for the long division algorithm? What happened to the one-and-only way to solve a multiplication problem?

Parents often want to know *why* mathematics teaching is changing. Speaking from the perspective of accomplished and successful adults, they may feel that the way they learned math worked for them, and if traditional methods worked for them, why aren't they good enough for their children? At the same time, those who aren't particularly confident in terms of mathematics, or weren't as students, often believe they failed simply because they didn't have the ability for math. They aren't aware that another approach might have better supported their own math learning.

Certain features of a standard-based math program or classroom may trigger this type of question. Parents will see children playing a lot of math games, hear a lot of talk and discussion in math class, see homework that is not the traditional sheet of computation problems. They might wonder why children are finding more than one way to solve a problem, why the teacher isn't showing or telling children how to solve problems, or why, in their homework, the children need to show or tell how they solved a problem. Answers to some of these more specific questions are elsewhere in this chapter, under "What's with all these games?" and "How do I help my child at home?"

To the more general questions about how and why math is changing, the following are some responses. The primary sources for these responses can be useful for schools and parents alike; see "References" (p. 164) for details.

We must judge schools not by remembrances of things past, but by necessary expectations for the future. Students must learn not only arithmetic, but also estimation, measurement, geometry, optimization, statistics, and probability—all of the ways in which mathematics occurs in everyday life. In the process, they must gain confidence in their ability to communicate and reason about mathematics; they should become mathematical problem-solvers. (National Research Council [NRC], 1989, p. 46)

During the past 20 years, the skills required to succeed in the economy have changed radically, but the skills taught in most schools have changed very little. As a result of the very-growing mismatch between the skills of most graduates and the skills required by high-wage employers, a U.S. high school diploma is no longer a ticket to the U.S. middle class … The issue is not that U.S. educational quality has declined—standardized test scores are modestly higher today than in the early 1980s. But the economy is changing much faster than the schools have improved. Many people—including half of recent graduates—have an education that is no longer in demand.

—*Robert W. Galvin and Edward W. Bales, Motorola* (Murnane & Levy, 1996, pp. 3–4)

Today's world is more mathematical than yesterday's and tomorrow's world will be more mathematical than today's. As computers increase in power, some parts of mathematics become less important while other parts become more important. While arithmetic proficiency may have been "good enough" for many in the middle of the century, anyone whose mathematical skills are limited to computation has little to offer today's society that is not done better by an inexpensive machine. (NRC, 1989, p. 45)

How would you react if your doctor treated you or your children with methods that were 10 to 15 years out-of-date, ignored current scientific findings about diseases and medical treatments, and contradicted all professional recommendations for practice? It is highly unlikely that you would passively ignore such practice. Yet that is exactly what happens with traditional mathematics teaching, which is still the norm in our nation's schools. For most students, school mathematics is an endless sequence of memorizing and forgetting facts and procedures that make little sense to them. Though the same topics are taught and retaught year after year, the students do not learn them. Numerous scientific studies have shown that traditional methods of teaching mathematics not only are ineffective but also seriously stunt the growth of students' mathematical reasoning and problem-solving skills ... Traditional methods ignore recommendations by professional organizations in mathematics education, and they ignore modern scientific research on how children learn mathematics. ... Just as medical treatment must be based on what current research tells us about disease and healing, mathematics teaching must be based on what current scientific research tells us about how students learn mathematics. (Battista, 1999, pp. 425–433)

The current debate about the future of mathematics education in this country often is treated as a comparison between the traditional "proven" approaches and the new "experimental" approaches ... Arguments against change sometimes claim that it is poor policy, and even unethical, to implement unproven new programs ... But, presuming that traditional approaches have proven to be successful is ignoring the largest database we have. The evidence indicates that the traditional curriculum and instructional methods in the United States are not serving our students well. The long-running experiment we have been conducting with traditional methods shows serious deficiencies, and we should attend carefully to the research findings that are accumulating regarding alternative programs. (Hiebert, 1999, pp. 12–13)

Why change? It worked for me.

For *some* people, traditional math did work. They could explain what they were doing and they knew how to apply their knowledge. Others learned the steps by rote, knew how to do the problem (i.e., get the right answer), but did not know how to use the information. Basically, the success they had in school getting the right answer/good grades was not applicable or useful beyond the school paper they wrote it on. Still others never could do the math because the steps were meaningless. How many adults still say, "I couldn't do math— it was my worst subject"? In the past it was thought that only some people were good at math. What we've begun to see is that, given the option to think about, make sense of, and understand a problem, many more kids (people) can solve complex problems.

—*B. Fox, grades 5–6 teacher (Massachusetts)*

There is a great deal of research that lets us know that the traditional way of teaching math did not prepare a high percentage of our current population. If it worked for you, consider yourself fortunate. In my classroom, I want *all* of my students to be well prepared for their future, in a world that is constantly changing. One of our jobs as parents and teachers is to help our young students navigate in an ever-changing society. We cannot possibly predict all of their future needs and experiences. We can, however, equip them with a variety of tools with which they are armed to tackle unknown challenges and opportunities.

—*B. Eston, grades K–1 teacher (Massachusetts)*

From the age of 9, African Americans and Hispanics do not perform as well as whites on national surveys of mathematics achievement. For example, NAEP mathematics assessments were conducted in 1973, 1978, and 1986. … The general picture of racial and/or ethnic disparities in mathematics achievement that come from the NAEP data is that Whites perform much better in mathematics than do Hispanics who, in turn, achieve slightly better than do African Americans. These cross-sectional data suggest that achievement disparities, which are great to begin with, increase over time as students grow older. (Secada, 1992, p. 628)

The vision of equity in mathematics education challenges a pervasive societal belief in North America that only some students are capable of learning mathematics. This belief, in contrast to the equally pervasive view that all students can and should learn to read and write in English, leads to low expectations for too many students. Low expectations are especially problematic because students who live in poverty, students who are not native speakers of English, students with disabilities, females, and many nonwhite students have traditionally been far more likely than their counterparts in other demographic groups to be the victims of low expectations. Expectations must be raised—mathematics can and must be learned by *all* students. (NCTM, 2000, pp. 11–12)

When someone says "the traditional way worked for me," I think of the two parts: "worked" and "for me." The traditional method stressed memorization of procedures presented by teachers. For many people, "worked" means that they memorized the procedures successfully. The way

we are trying to teach mathematics is based on children building understanding. Our goal is children who can do math efficiently and accurately, but who also understand the numbers, the operations, and the relationships. Then they can apply this deeper knowledge to novel situations and make original connections between ideas.

As for the "for me" part—the traditional methods worked for some people, but many other students were not successful. Our goal is for *all* students to gain deep and broad mathematical understandings and to develop efficient, accurate ways to approach and solve problems. Traditional methods shut many students out of math and gave them the message that they were not "good at math." If the one method presented did not make sense to them, they were unable to find a way into a problem because sense-making was not part of the process.

I have sometimes helped parents see that this way of teaching is beneficial to their children by telling them that what *they're* asking for is actually less than what I want children to get. I want the same accuracy and efficiency they want, but I also want children to have understanding, flexibility, and the feeling of being mathematically powerful.

—*L. Seyferth, kindergarten teacher (Massachusetts)*

Why change? "If it ain't broke, don't fix it."
Recent reports of the performance of our country's students from both the Third International Mathematics and Science Study (TIMSS) and the National Assessment of Educational Progress (NAEP) echo a dismal message of lackluster performance, now three decades old; it's time the nation heeded it—before it's too late. (The Glenn Commission, 2000)

Why change? The first thing to keep very clearly in mind as critics resist *Standards*-based proposals for change in school mathematics is the fact that reform initiatives have been prompted by overwhelming evidence that our traditional curricular and teaching practices are not yielding the kind of learning that is both desirable and possible. For almost 30 years, evidence from international comparative studies, our own National Assessment of Educational Progress, and the SAT/ACT college admission testing programs has suggested that, in relation to other countries that are our intellectual and economic competitors: our curricula do not challenge students to learn important topics in depth; our teaching traditions encourage students to acquire routine procedural skills through a passive classroom routine of listening and practicing; our assessment of student knowledge emphasizes multiple choice and short answer responses to low-level tasks. (Fey, 1999)

——————————

The effects of mathematical miseducation are like a long-term hidden illness that gradually incapacitates its victims. The results of testing by the National Assessment of Educational Progress indicate that only about 13% to 16% of 12th-graders are proficient in mathematics … And according to the National Research Council, 75% of Americans stop studying mathematics before they complete career or job prerequisites … Indeed, although virtually all students enter school mathematically healthy and enjoying mathematics as they solve problems in ways that make sense to them, most exit school apprehensive and unsure about doing all but the most trivial mathematical tasks.

Mathematics anxiety is widespread. So rampant is innumeracy that there is little stigma attached to it. Many adults readily confess, "I was never good at math," as if displaying a badge of courage for enduring what for them was a painful and useless experience. In contrast, people do not freely admit that they can't read. (Battista, 1999, p. 426)

——————————

On the 1982 National Assessment of Educational Progress (NAEP), 57% of 13 year old students and 72% of 17 year old students were able to accurately multiply two decimal numbers. When asked to *estimate* the answer to a similar problem, such as 3.04×5.3, the results were distressing. The answer choices provided were 1.6, 16, 160, 1600, and I don't know. If you multiply a little more than three by a little more than five, sixteen is the only mathematically reasonable answer. But less than 21% of 13 year olds and just under 37% of 17 year olds chose the correct answer. Although students were able to use a procedure to multiply decimals, they were unable to make sense of the quantities in a meaningful way (NAEP, 1983).

——————————

Average students in other countries often learn as much mathematics as the best students learn in the United States. Data from the Second International Mathematics Study (1982) show that the performance of the top 5 percent of U.S. students is matched by the top 50 percent of students in Japan. Our very best students—the top 1 percent—scored lowest of the top 1 percent in all participating countries. All U.S. students—whether below, at, or above average—can and must learn more mathematics. (NRC, 1989, p. 77)

——————————

Educators, parents, students, and the community are beginning to realize that all students must leave high school today with the knowledge and ability to apply what we once required of only the select few who continued their formal education in colleges and universities.

—*Thomas Payzant, Superintendent of Boston Public Schools* (Murnane & Levy, 1996, p. vii)

Will my child succeed?

Many parents express concern about their children's future and wonder if schools are experimenting on their children using untested methods. If children are learning math in this new way, how will they do? Will they succeed by school and district standards? on tests? Will they succeed with next year's teacher or school? Will they succeed in today's (and tomorrow's) competitive job market?

What's the evidence that these new methods work?

[There is a] myth … [that] no research is available to support reform efforts. On the contrary, for current instructional reforms in mathematics and for school children's mathematics achievement and performance, a sizable research base exists that supports the [NCTM] Standards. (Curcio, 1999, pp. 283–284)

The Standards proposed by NCTM are, in many ways, more ambitious than those of traditional programs. On the basis of beliefs about what students should know and be able to do, the Standards include conceptual understanding and the use of key mathematical processes as well as skill proficiency. The best evidence we have indicates that most traditional programs do not provide students with many opportunities to achieve these additional goals and, not surprisingly, most students do not achieve them. Alternative programs can be designed to provide these opportunities, and, when the programs have been implemented with fidelity for reasonable lengths of time, students have learned more and learned more deeply than in traditional programs. Although the primary evidence comes from elementary school, especially the primary grades, there is no inconsistent evidence. That is, there are no programs at any level that share the core instructional features, have been implemented as intended for reasonable lengths of time, and show that students perform more poorly than their traditionally taught peers. (Hiebert, 1999, pp. 15–16)

Research by Kamii and Dominick (1998) has shown that students who develop their own strategies for solving computation problems actually perform better than those who are taught the steps of a particular procedure or traditional algorithm, such as carrying and borrowing to add and subtract. For example, second and third graders who used their own strategies produced the highest percentage of correct answers when asked to find a mental solution to $7 + 52 + 186$ (or $6 + 53 + 185$), higher than fourth graders who were taught the algorithms, *on the same problem*. Further, the responses of children who were taught the algorithms were far more unreasonable than those in classes where students developed their own strategies. Moreover, these children did not notice the unreasonableness of answers like 144 and 783.

Additional studies done by the same researchers support that "children who use their own procedures are much more likely to produce correct answers than those who try to use algorithms" and that second graders compared "before and after they were taught algorithms … lose conceptual knowledge when they learn these rules." In fact, these educators argue that "algorithms not only are not helpful in learning arithmetic but also hinder children's development of numerical reasoning ... They encourage children to give up their own thinking ... and ... they 'unteach' place value, thereby preventing children from developing number sense." (Kamii & Dominick, 1998, pp. 130–136)

Currently, four studies—the goals of which were "to examine the effects of the curriculum on children's understanding of number and number operations"—have been conducted to study the achievement of students using the *Investigations* curriculum. To briefly summarize the findings, *Investigations* students do just as well as other students on simple calculation problems, and considerably better than other students on word problems, multi-step problems, and more complex problems. (Mokros, 2000)

A book entitled *Standards-Oriented School Mathematics Curricula: What Does the Research Say About Student Outcomes?* (Senk & Thompson, in press) offers more answers to the question "What's the evidence these new methods work?" The authors address the student achievement data available for each of the *Standards*-based, NSF-funded curricula at the elementary, middle, and secondary levels. The book includes a chapter about *Investigations* student achievement data, written by Jan Mokros: "Learning to Reason Numerically: The Impact of *Investigations*."

Will my child succeed in a more traditional classroom, or in middle and high school?

Our answers to parents are threefold. First, the children are really developing an understanding of math and a solid foundation that they will have no matter where they go. If asked to learn a new algorithm, it might take them a couple of days to learn the procedure, but they're going to

understand the ideas behind it. Because *Investigations* students have had the opportunity to explore the mathematics in depth, they have developed an understanding of mathematical concepts that will serve them well as they move into another school or on to the higher level math of the secondary curriculum. Secondly, another school isn't likely to care *how* children do math, just that they *can*. Your child can. Finally, we try to explain: "Our intent is to teach your child to the best of our abilities, based on research about how children best learn math. We can't not do that, just because your child might eventually go someplace that doesn't do math the same way. We're going to do the best we can for your child here, with the goal being real math thinking."

—*J. DiBrienza, teacher leader (New York) and N. Horowitz, grades 3–4 teacher (Massachusetts)*

Will my child succeed on tests?

On many of the new state tests, there are many items that necessitate making sense of nonroutine problems *and* explaining how you solve them. Fewer items on these tests are multiple choice. Fewer still are straight computation problems. How does "this math" help? First, children learn that they can make sense of math problems, even those problems that have unfamiliar content that has not been covered in class. Second, they have multiple ways of solving problems and checking on the accuracy of their solutions. Third, they develop the ability to show their thinking through words, equations, and diagrams. This ability to explain is critical to math and is also an important element of these new state tests, some of which have only three or four problems that are straightforward calculation items, such as 256×98. It is possible, even likely, that children from "traditional" classes, who have been drilled intensively on these skills, will do well on these items by using a memorized procedure. However, a child who has solid skills in thinking about numbers can do a problem like this using other methods.

For example:

$256 \times 98 =$

$256 \times 100 = 25,600$

$2 \times 256 = 512$

$25,600 - 512 = 25,088$

Instead of finding out how much 98×256 is, this child began with 100×256 since that was an easy problem. Then she knew to take away two of those 256's, or 512, to make it 98 rather than 100.

So a child using "this kind of math" can solve the calculation problem and also has the understanding to solve word problems and "thinking" problems.

—*J. Mokros, TERC (Massachusetts)*

One thing that we can tell parents is that the New York State math test is based on the same standards as *Investigations*. We can tell them that their children will be asked to explain their thinking on the test; they will be asked to show their thinking in numbers, words, and pictures. I think it's easier for parents to accept that, knowing that the test is going to be asking children to do the same sorts of things that we're asking of them.

—*R. Tsunoda, grade 4 teacher (New York)*

Will my child succeed in life?

Students who learn mathematics using *Investigations* and other *Standards*-based mathematics programs in higher grades will be well prepared for the jobs in today's world. Students in these *Standards*-based mathematics programs learn to be confident problem solvers. They have flexible ways of thinking and they can approach a task using more than one strategy. These students learn to work collaboratively and are able to listen and evaluate each others' ways of solving problems. They easily determine which strategy in their repertoire is best suited for a particular problem. These students also learn to use the appropriate tools and technology to aid them in solving a problem. They know how to ask the critical questions that lead them to successfully do the job. Students learning mathematics with understanding enjoy doing mathematics. Many of the students I've had in first and second grades come back and tell me that their favorite subject is mathematics. The positive attitude that they develop towards mathematics enables them to tackle a variety of challenging tasks.

—*R. Christiansen, grades 1–2 teacher (Massachusetts)*

Learning math in cooperative groups, sharing strategies, looking at problems from different perspectives and being able to vocalize their mathematical thinking empowers students immensely. Calculators and computers can answer computational questions in a very swift and effective way. What is needed from employees is an understanding of what the problem is asking and what procedures are needed to solve the problem. Employers are looking for people who can work in groups, think flexibly, and problem solve. Students need to be prepared to verbalize their thinking and explain their thought process. Teaching students to respond automatically, without a foundation of understanding, does nothing to prepare them for the job market.

—M. Perch-Little, grades 2–3 teacher
(Nevada)

Where are the rigor and the challenge?

Another set of questions arises from some parents' concern that their children are not encountering difficult and challenging mathematics.

What has been most distressing since we [NCTM] released the Standards documents is that our efforts to inform parents better have fallen short … Some parents are concerned that because other, previously disenfranchised students can now accomplish mathematics, this mathematics is not good enough for their children. This attitude has developed in spite of their mathematically promising students having said in interviews that they have never been more challenged by, or more interested in, mathematics. We have to help those parents bridge their fears and encourage them to join hands in providing a solid mathematics education for all children. (Price, 1996, p. 606)

Additionally, parents who remember math as a subject characterized by problems they did alone and problems with only one right method for solving them may have doubts about children working in groups on problems with many possible solution strategies. They worry when their child is solving problems

with relatively small numbers or when their child's computation strategies do not seem as efficient as the algorithm the parent knows. Some worry that playing games as part of math class, or using manipulatives like blocks or cubes, reduces mathematics to free play; they worry there is no rigor. A handout on "The Purpose of Games in *Investigations*" (see p. 41) is one answer to these questions.

Is it hard enough? My child seems bored.

Perhaps problems seem easy because your child *could* operate on larger numbers. However, when the numbers are more manageable, students can make better sense of what is happening in the problem. For example, your daughter can certainly solve harder problems, say 13 + 57. She might start with the 57 and count on 13 more. With smaller numbers, though, she is developing powerful, more efficient strategies based on the numbers in the problem and what she knows about them. For example, today she solved 12 + 13 in two ways. She said, "I know my doubles. 12 and 12 is 24, so 12 and 13 is one more or 25. Another way is 10 and 10 is 20, and 2 plus 3 is 5, so 25." My goal for her is to develop these strategies with smaller numbers and then apply them when tackling larger numbers.

—N. Liu, staff developer (New York)

There is enough math in these activities for children to delve as deeply as they want. Children don't always choose to challenge themselves, so often I suggest further questions for them to explore.

—K. Bloomfield, grades 3–4 teacher
(Massachusetts)

I've had parents say, "My second grader already knows the times tables. Why are you doing *this?*" I try to explain that the children are tackling really difficult investigations in the classroom, and sometimes that doesn't translate into a worksheet for homework. But if you've heard your child thinking, wondering, and questioning, you know that this is really rigorous.

—*T. Caccavale, grade 2 teacher (New York)*

The activities in the curriculum are designed to bring out and build mathematical thinking in every child, across the range of abilities found in any classroom. It is enough of a challenge for some children to find one solution to a problem; other children can be challenged to find multiple solutions, or *every* possibility, along with a proof that they have them all. Also, asking children to explain their thinking, make sense of others' thinking, and consider the efficiency of a variety of strategies to choose the best one for a given problem, provides challenge and depth of thinking for every student.

—*N. Liu, staff developer (New York)*

Why give only two or three problems? Doesn't practice make perfect?

I usually give students only two or three problems because that's their chance to show me how efficient and accurate they are or what weakness needs work. Imagine doing 25 examples … all wrong. That's a tough habit to break. Or, imagine doing 25 examples, all correctly, no variety. Your child loves to do the two or three problems, show them in different ways, and then create some for the rest of the class.

—*J. Pepicelli, grade 5 teacher (Massachusetts)*

Children can learn a lot about numbers and operations when they spend more time not just answering, but *examining* fewer problems. They also learn to think flexibly and develop a repertoire of strategies when they look closely at problems and think about what's unique and interesting about them, as well as when they consider how those problems relate to ones they've encountered before.

—*K. Bloomfield, grades 3–4 teacher (Massachusetts)*

Yes, we often give students just two or three problems to work on, *but* we ask them to solve those problems in more than one way. By doing problems in different ways, the students are demonstrating a better understanding of the concepts. When I was in school, I often had to do 20 problems, but I just did them by rote and never understood what the numbers meant. These students are asked to expand their thinking by solving the problem using different strategies.

—*J. Rook, grades 4–5 teacher (Massachusetts)*

Why so much group work? Won't it hold my child back?

Children often learn from each other in powerful ways—having children share their thinking multiplies their thought power!

—*K. Bloomfield, grades 3–4 teacher (Massachusetts)*

There are times when children need support from their peers—nothing I say matters very much. It's an opportunity to ground their understandings; they may even feel brave enough to admit *not* understanding because someone else doesn't either.

—J. Pepicelli, grade 5 teacher
  (Massachusetts)

Since the workplace is now driven by problem solving teams, children must learn to work together cooperatively in developing multiple solutions to real-world situations.

—Galvin & Bales (Murnane & Levy, 1996,
  p. xix)

What's with all these games?

Your son is very successful playing Close to 1000. He is doing mental math, estimating, and adding correctly. He's so proud. He supports the group in seeing how important (in a "fun" way) place value and accuracy are. When he brings this game home, ask him how he got the answer. In fact, these games are wonderful practice in computation, replacing those pages of practice examples (remember those?).

—J. Pepicelli, grade 5 teacher
  (Massachusetts)

If a parent questions the use of so many games, I agree that the *Investigations* curriculum uses a lot of games, but I explain that there are reasons for this. (Note that I often use the word *activity* rather than *game* with my students and would do the same with parents.) Games are an engaging way to have children practice skills in a way that is nonthreatening. Children think it's fun, but it's also getting at the

deeper mathematical issues. For example, there are lots of strategies involved in doing well in an activity like Close to 100 and Close to 1000. If you don't have a strategy, you won't be as successful, and the strategy is the math. If you don't understand how to put together groups of tens and groups of ones to equal 100, that is important information (for a parent and the teacher).

Also, there are usually variations of the games that challenge both the quick learner and the student who needs more practice with smaller numbers. I often suggest that the parents actually play the game with the child and ask themselves what issues came up for them, what skills were involved in playing. These math games are much like other games—the more you play, the more sophisticated your thinking. For example, chess is a game, but you can play it at all levels according to your understanding. The more you play, the better you get at figuring out those strategies. Similarly, while playing these games, kids often pick up ideas from other kids, so they are sharing ideas and teaching and learning from each other.

—J. Rook, grades 4–5 teacher
  (Massachusetts)

The games require mathematical thinking to play. As children become more and more familiar with this game, they not only practice computation skills but also discover more efficient ways to compute. Games, far more than traditional worksheets, provide motivation and context for children to build these skills. By asking children *how* they got their answers or *why* they chose their moves, teachers and parents can help children clarify and communicate their mathematical thinking. And by playing with each other, children are exposed to others' strategies and logical thinking.

—*N. Liu, staff developer (New York)*

These games are designed to help children learn important mathematics, such as the structure of the number system (as in the game Plus, Minus, Stay the Same), or relationships between numbers (as in Close to 100). Often students begin the game without strategies, but over time they start using strategies based on their developing knowledge of place value and number relationships. The games help children learn more sophisticated ways of operating on numbers. For example, Double Compare promotes strategies for learning basic facts. Close to 100 encourages mental strategies for adding two-digit numbers and for finding the difference between a two-digit number and the important landmark, 100. Games played on a hundred chart help children understand the structure of our number system.

—*J. Flowers, assistant professor,*
University of Michigan, and
K. Bloomfield, grades 3–4 teacher
(Massachusetts)

How can there be more than one answer? In math, it's either right or wrong.

Often there is only one right answer, but there are different ways to get to that answer. For example, Cary knows 6 times 7 by heart; Janice knows 6 times 6 is 36 and then adds on one more 6 in her head; Gail knows 7 times 5 is 35 and then adds on one more 7; and Gary thinks 3 times 7 is 21 and then doubles 21. Everyone figured out that 6 times 7 is 42 in an efficient way that made sense to them. It is also important for children to make sense of others' strategies and explore the connection between the methods—why do they all work?

There are also many math situations or problems that do have, potentially, more than one answer. For example: 36 divided by 8. If 36 people are going on a trip, how many vans do we need if each van holds 8 people? What if 8 people are going to share 36 crackers? 36 balloons? 36 dollars? How many rows of 8 seats would they fill up at the movies?

—*C. Mainhart, kindergarten teacher*
(Massachusetts), S. Smith, grade 3
teacher (Massachusetts), and G. Hanlon,
staff developer (New York)

[One] myth … [is that] answers that are close to correct are good enough. Nothing can be farther from the truth. If a problem requires an estimate rather than an exact result, a reasonable estimate is good enough. However, if a problem requires an exact answer, being *almost* correct is wrong. One controversial aspect of the new, state-of-the-art mathematics curricula that support the reform efforts is that they contain problems that can be solved in more than one way. This feature is a strength not a weakness because different learners bring different perspectives to solving problems. This situation is analogous to solving real-world, open-ended problems for which more than one right way is possible to get an answer. (Curcio, 1999, p. 283)

I don't want my child using a calculator as a crutch.

In [the *Investigations*] curriculum, calculators are considered tools for doing mathematics, similar to pattern blocks or interlocking cubes. Just as with other tools, students must learn both *how* to use calculators correctly and *when* they are appropriate to use. This knowledge is crucial for daily life, as calculators are now a standard way of handling numerical operations, both at work and at home. Using a calculator correctly is not a simple task; it depends on a good knowledge of the four operations and of the number system, so that students can select suitable calculations and also determine what a reasonable result would be. These skills are the basis of any work with numbers, whether or not a calculator is involved ...

[*Investigations* also recognizes] that, despite their importance, calculators are not always appropriate in mathematics instruction. Like any tools, calculators are useful for some tasks, but not for others ... [Teachers] will need to make decisions about when to allow students access to calculators and when to ask that they solve problems without them, so they can concentrate on other tools and skills ... [Teachers are also encouraged to help students] develop their own sense of which problems they can tackle with their own reasoning and which ones might be better solved with a combination of their own reasoning and the calculator. (Russell et al., 1998, *Investigations* unit introduction)

———————————

A comprehensive mathematics curriculum should help students learn to use calculators, computers, and other technological tools as a part of learning mathematics. These tools are helpful in doing and understanding mathematics and will be essential in the workplace and in the study of mathematics, science, or engineering in college. We would be remiss not to make their use an integral part of mathematics education. The *Standards* documents make it clear, however, that such tools do not replace the need to learn basic facts, to compute men

tally, or to do reasonable paper-and-pencil computation. The *Standards* suggest that when used appropriately, calculators and computers enable students to explore new areas of mathematics and to tackle many challenging mathematical problems that are impractical to attempt without the aid of such tools. Indeed, calculators and computers with appropriate software can transform the classroom into a laboratory where students can investigate and experiment with mathematical ideas. (NCTM, 1999, p. 7)

———————————

Do I like calculators? I love them. I think they're wonderful. I give parents examples of why, like the day I went into a first grade classroom and the kids were asking, "How many days are there in a whole year?" I could have simply said to them, "365; sometimes it's 366." Instead, I made it a problem to solve. Some kids took the calendar and started counting every day; some kids took the last number on each month's page and started adding. It was clearly a problem that most first graders could solve with a calculator. So I tell parents, "We don't use a calculator for 4×7 in third and fourth grade; you have to know 4×7. But this is an example of when we use a calculator."

—*D. Shein-Gerson, K–5 math coordinator (Massachusetts)*

———————————

Why do the children have to show *how* they solved the problem? Why do you spend so much time *talking* and *writing* in mathematics?
There are three reasons we ask students to explain their problem-solving strategies. First, we've found that students learn better and understand their own thinking better if they try to articulate their strategies. Second, when they explain their thinking, it helps us understand where they are in

their mathematical development so we can guide them more effectively. And third, as they explain their thinking, students help their classmates consider strategies they hadn't thought of themselves. Even so, we do not ask students to explain their thinking all the time, only when it serves one of these purposes.

—M. Riddle, grades 3–5 teacher (Massachusetts)

I explain that showing work isn't always required, but that it is a very important tool that lets the teacher assess what students understand. It enables teachers to examine student thinking. Mathematics as communication is also a very important aspect of helping children to fully understand how to solve problems. Those explanations help children clarify their thinking and learn from other students. Students offer their thinking to expand the voices in the classroom from one all-knowing expert to a community of experts. Math knowledge is meant to be shared rather than kept guarded.

—C. Mainhart, kindergarten teacher (Massachusetts) and S. Smith, grade 3 teacher (Massachusetts)

Sometimes this question makes me think about how and when I ask students to show their thinking. I've learned that in my eagerness to change my practice, I may have overused this part of the process. I've now come to a point where I pick and choose when to require this step, and from which students. Once students can easily articulate their understanding or show their thinking, I don't need to require this step from them. Just like in reading, I don't

require a book report for every book a child has read. I don't need second graders to tell me how 2 and 3 make 5, but I *do* want to see and hear how my kindergartners are making sense of this problem.

—B. Eston, grades K–1 teacher (Massachusetts)

What about computation and basic facts?

For many schools and districts, this topic represents the crux of parents' concerns. Many are looking for sheets of computation practice or flashcards for drilling children on their facts. They wonder when their children will master traditional algorithms for computing and when they will master the basic facts. These are reasonable concerns; fluency with the facts and the ability to solve computational problems are both important for success in mathematics. One important response to this type of question focuses on how the mathematics curriculum has been broadened, so that arithmetic is now connected to many other aspects of number and operations.

Understanding number and operations, developing number sense, and gaining fluency in arithmetic computation form the core of mathematics education for the elementary grades … Knowing basic number combinations—the single-digit addition and multiplication pairs and their counterparts for subtraction and division—is essential. Equally essential is computational fluency … Computational fluency refers to having efficient and accurate methods for computing. Students exhibit computational fluency when they demonstrate flexibility in the computational methods they choose, understand and can explain these methods, and produce accurate answers efficiently. The computational methods that a student uses should be based on mathematical ideas that the student understands well, including the structure of the base-ten number system, properties of [the operations], and number relationships. (NCTM, 2000, pp. 32, 152)

One of the concerns many people have about new mathematics programs is that students will not learn to add, subtract, multiply, and divide. A central objective of the *Investigations* program is to support students' learning about number, number relationships, the base ten number system, and number operations. The elementary grades are a critical period in the development of students' number and operation sense. The *Investigations* program spends a great percentage of time on this area, with a focus on the development of students' own strategies for solving problems. Fluency and accuracy *are* critical. Students *do* need to learn their addition and multiplication "facts," and many *Investigations* activities will help them do so. However, speed should not be confused with fluency, nor accuracy or memorization with a flexible knowledge of number relationships. (Russell et al., 1998, p. 9)

Students should model, explain, and develop proficiency with basic facts and algorithms. Computational proficiency has always been, and will continue to be, an integral part of mathematics education. Yet computational proficiency alone is not enough. To be successful in today's world, students need proficiency with basic facts, and they must be adept in reasoning, in problem solving, and in communicating mathematics. They must understand mathematical concepts and have the ability to make mathematical connections, and they must be able to use their computational

skills to apply mathematics problems to other disciplines. (NCTM, 1999, p. 7)

The teaching of mathematics is shifting from preoccupation with inculcating routine skills to developing broad-based mathematical power. Mathematical power requires that students be able to discern relations, reason logically, and use a broad spectrum of mathematical methods to solve a wide variety of non-routine problems. The repertoire of skills which now undergird mathematical power includes not only some traditional paper-and-pencil skills, but also many broader and more powerful capabilities. (NRC, 1989, pp. 82–83)

The very definition of teaching arithmetic needs to be revised. Arithmetic competence cannot be measured solely by evaluating students' mastery of computational algorithms. Mastery of arithmetic must include, as basic and integral, knowing which operations are appropriate to particular situations, which numbers are most reasonable to use, and what decisions can be made once the needed calculations have been done. It makes no sense to say that a child can do arithmetic but cannot apply it to situations. The basics of doing arithmetic must include being able to apply arithmetic operations to situations, as well as being able to calculate answers. (Burns, 1992, p. 142)

I'm worried about the way you're teaching computation. Why are you doing it this way?

I know you're concerned about your child being successful in school and learning how to add, subtract, multiply, and divide. I am, too. I want your child to be able to get right answers efficiently. I want your child to know "facts." There are lots of ways to get right answers, and sometimes the way you and I were taught is the fastest way. But there are many times when another way makes more sense. For example, 376 – 99 is much easier if I subtract 100 from 376 and then add 1 back. I can do that in my head much faster than crossing out and borrowing. If your child learns to understand how numbers relate to each other, how they can be broken up in different ways, he or she will have many ways to add (subtract, multiply, and divide) and be able to choose the best way for the particular numbers involved.

—C. Pardo, Title I math resource teacher (New Mexico)

Throughout the *Investigations* curriculum, we encourage students to find and use computation strategies that grow out of their developing number sense. Some students will have learned the standard algorithms; it is important that they learn other strategies as well. This is because the traditional algorithms have a serious drawback: They lead students away from thinking about the meaning of the problem and the relationships between the numbers in it. In their focus on the manipulation of individual digits, the students too often lose sight of the numbers as whole quantities.

There are many approaches to computation that keep more visible the connections between the numbers and the problem situation … When students develop their own procedures for addition or multiplication, for example, they tend to move from left to right in the problem, focusing on the largest part of the number first, rather than moving from right to left as in the historically taught procedure … Focusing on the largest part of the number(s) helps them maintain a sense of the size of the quantities involved. (Kliman, Russell, Tierney, & Murray, 1998, pp. 23–24)

I often give parents examples of, say, a subtraction situation where they probably wouldn't "take away" but instead would "add up." For example, the Knicks won last night 82–75. How much did they win by? I haven't found anyone who would use the traditional U.S. algorithm to solve this (borrowing 10 from the 80 to add to the 2, to subtract 5 from 12). Most people simply think 5 + 2 = 7. This gives us a place to start a conversation.

—J. DiBrienza, teacher leader (New York)

It's important to me to take the stance of not alienating or antagonizing parents. A debate about the algorithm might not be helpful—because they might feel threatened, vulnerable about their own understanding of math, or unsure of what else to do instead. So if I'm asked why I am not telling the children one way to solve a problem and having them practice it (or one of the many variations of that question), I say something like this:

My goal in teaching your child math is for her to develop deep understandings at these early grades that will help her continue to make sense as the math gets harder. It is true that we can teach students tricks that will help them do computation now, but what we know from looking at math in our country, and what I know from my experiences doing math, is that lots of us fail at math when it gets harder because our understandings of earlier math weren't sufficient. Or we can't use math in our everyday lives in a way that is comfortable and positive. [I find that parents will often confirm that math became hard for them at some point.] Children need to understand how our number system works and how numbers relate to each other—it's what we call number sense. A person who has a strong number sense can use math comfortably and successfully in everyday life. For example, if I were going on a trip and saw on a map that the two legs were 58 miles and 54 miles, I probably wouldn't take out a pencil and paper to figure out the total but would use my number sense: $50 + 50 = 100$, and $100 + 12 = 112$.

—*K. Schweitzer, grades K–2 teacher (Massachusetts)*

What about algorithms? Why aren't you teaching the "one right way" that I learned?

Everyone needs to know a couple of good ways to add, subtract, multiply, and divide. However, the ways that we were taught to do these operations aren't necessarily the best or most efficient ways. ... Borrowing, carrying, the procedure for long division—they're not universal. In other countries and at other times in our own country, students have been taught different and equally effective algorithms for the basic operations. Constructing effective algorithms, ones that can be used efficiently in a range of different situations, is in itself an important element of mathematical thinking. Students who invent algorithms that are easy to use are doing significant mathematical work. (Mokros, Russell, & Economopoulos, 1995, pp. 73–74)

"We've always done it this way!" is a common response to suggestions for change. But mathematics has not always been done in the same way. Although the calculations performed centuries ago are still valid today, the algorithms used most likely are not the same. (Mason, 1998, p. 91)

Although many people "believe that mathematical procedures are unique and timeless ... over the generations people have grappled with many methods in attempting to find those that were simpler, quicker, less wasteful of resources, or easier to communicate." (Rubenstein, 1998, p. 99)

The algorithms and notations usually taught in the United States are by no means universal. In many countries, division is presented in dramatically different ways ... Many other algorithms are found throughout the world. (Hirigoyen, 1997, p. 166)

Students' learning of symbolic manipulations must never become disconnected from their reasoning about quantities. For when it does, they become overwhelmed with trying to memorize countless rules for manipulating symbols. Even worse, when students lose sight of what symbol manipulations imply about real-world quantities, doing mathematics becomes an academic ritual that has no real-world usefulness. Indeed, to be able to use mathematics to make sense of the world, students must first make sense of mathematics. (Battista, 1999, p. 428)

It's important for children to understand that one particular algorithm may be no better or more efficient than another, and that many methods, including ones they invent themselves, are equally valid. There is no need for all students to do arithmetic calculations in the same way any more than it is essential for all children to develop identical handwritings or writing styles. A major risk of instruction that emphasizes the teaching of algorithms is the risk of interfering with children's learning to make sense of numbers. When learning algorithms, children focus on learning sequences of steps to carry out procedures, rather than on thinking and reasoning to make sense of numerical situations. Teachers know that it's common for children, when using standard algorithms, to make calculation errors and not even notice when they reach absurd solutions. (Burns, 1992, p. 153)

A common error when adding fractions is for students to add the numerators and denominators; for example: $\frac{1}{2} + \frac{1}{3} = \frac{2}{5}$. Students who do this are merely following a rule and, unfortunately, a rule that is totally inappropriate in this instance. Much of mathematics requires looking for the sense in the situation, not merely following a rule. It does not make sense to start with $\frac{1}{2}$, add to it, and wind up with an answer, $\frac{2}{5}$, that is less than the amount you started with. Yet many students do not notice this inconsistency or even think about looking for it. (Burns, 1992, p. 151)

I have some parents who come in and say, "Please just teach my child one way to do this because if they have to do it three different ways, they get so confused." I try to show them that it's really important for kids to have different strategies; that depending on the kind of problem, there will be a simpler strategy and a quicker strategy. And so when students have all this in their brains, they're able to pick and choose. I think parents are uncomfortable with the way kids are learning math because they're not familiar with it. So they almost want to push the kids, "Just do it one way; you'll get the right answer. You'll understand it later." I try to

tell parents, "Let me show you how we do it in the classroom. Then you can take this strategy and try to help your child at home." I give them a couple of problems in a parent conference so they can try it out on their own, and they're very receptive to that.

—*R. Musser, grade 4 teacher (Massachusetts)*

When children work with numbers written in vertical columns, they often focus on performing the operation on each column versus looking at the numbers as a whole. For example:

$$\begin{array}{r} 39 \\ -17 \\ \hline \end{array}$$

The children would say 9 – 7 is 2 and 3 – 1 is 2, often not giving thought to the fact that the 3 in 39 is 30 and that the 1 is a 10. This leads to other confusions when they encounter a problem like this:

$$\begin{array}{r} 37 \\ -19 \\ \hline \end{array}$$

When the children find that they can't subtract a larger number from a smaller number, they sometimes invert the two numbers being subtracted, doing 9 – 7 even though the problem says 7 – 9. Or they may "borrow" from the next column through a complicated set of steps:

$$\begin{array}{r} {\scriptstyle 2\ 17} \\ 3\!\!\!/7 \\ -19 \\ \hline 18 \end{array} \quad \text{or} \quad \begin{array}{r} {\scriptstyle 2\ 1} \\ 3\!\!\!/7 \\ -19 \\ \hline 18 \end{array}$$

They perform the borrowing algorithm but never realize that they are taking 1 ten from this 30 (which they see as 3), converting it into 10 ones, and adding it to the already existing 7 ones. The idea that "borrowing" is the right way to subtract ignores different strategies that may be more efficient. For example, a subtraction problem does not *have* to be solved through subtraction. Instead, a child might say, "How far is it from 19 to 37? If I start at 19 and add 1, that gets me to 20, plus another 10 is 30. Then 30 plus 7 is 37. The answer's 18."

—*C. Santiago, staff developer (New York)*

———————————

Sometimes, when a parent asks why I'm not teaching his child the "right way," the parent is screaming to learn more. This is an excellent opportunity to do a little math exploration with that parent. For example, I might explore with him a host of different ways to solve the same subtraction problem 72 − 37.

We could break the 37 into 30 and 7 and subtract one part at a time, starting with either the 30 or the 7, whichever seems easier for us:

72 − 30 = 42, and 42 − 7 = 35
72 − 7 = 65, and 65 − 30 = 35

We might see that 37 is close to 40 and subtract 40 from 72, then add the 3 to compensate for the difference between 37 and 40.

72 − 40 = 32, and 32 + 3 = 35

This whole problem could be done by adding. That is, we could add 3 to 37 to get to 40, then add another 32 to get to 72, and 3 + 32 = 35.

37 + 3 = 40, and 40 + 32 = 72
3 + 32 = 35

We might add an amount to both numbers to get numbers that are easier to work with:

72 + 3 = 75, and 37 + 3 = 40
75 − 40 = 35

Or we might subtract the tens, then the ones (in this case, resulting in a negative number), and add the two differences:

70 − 30 = 40
2 − 7 = −5
35

The goal is to have children "look to the numbers" to decide which strategy to use. Certain problems beg for different strategies.

—*G. Shevell, staff developer (New York)*

Shouldn't children know the basic math facts?

Children must still have a command of basic addition and multiplication facts. Learning basic facts is not a prerequisite for solving problems, but learning the facts becomes a necessity to solve problems that are meaningful, relevant, and interesting to learners. Basic facts are learned effortlessly by meaningful repetition in the context of games and activities rather than by meaningless rote memorization. By encountering a variety of contexts and tasks, learners have opportunities to develop and apply thinking strategies that support and complement learning the basic facts. (Curcio, 1999, p. 282)

———————————

To develop good computation strategies, students need to become fluent with the addition combinations from 0 + 0 to 10 + 10. These combinations are part of the repertoire of number knowledge that contributes to the rich interconnections among numbers that we call number sense. A great deal of emphasis has been put on learning these addition combinations in elementary school. While we agree that knowing these combinations is important, we want to stress two ideas:
(1) Students learn these combinations best

by using strategies, not simply by rote memorization. Relying on memory alone is not sufficient, as many of us know from our own schooling. If you forget—as we all do at times—you are left with nothing. If, on the other hand, your learning is based on understanding of numbers and their relationships, you have a way to rethink and restructure your knowledge when you don't remember something you thought you knew. (2) Knowing the number combinations should be judged by fluency in use, not necessarily by instantaneous recall. Through repeated use and familiarity, students will come to know most of the addition combinations quickly, and a few by using some quick and comfortable numerical reasoning strategy. (Economopoulos & Russell, 1998, p. 30)

Meaningful practice is necessary to develop fluency with basic number combinations … Practice needs to be motivating and systematic if students are to develop computational fluency, whether mentally, with manipulative materials, or with paper and pencil. Practice can be conducted in the context of other activities, including games that require computation as part of score keeping, questions that emerge from children's literature, situations in the classroom, or focused activities that are part of another mathematical investigation. Practice should be purposeful and should focus on developing thinking strategies and a knowledge of number relationships rather than drill isolated facts. (NCTM, 2000, p. 87)

When children typically study multiplication, they need to learn what multiplication is, how it relates to other things they've studied about mathematics, and how to apply it in a variety of problem-solving situations. Learning the times tables is important for every child, but memorization should build on, not precede, understanding. I want it all for children when they are learning mathematics— understanding and memorizing facts, in that order. I want children to learn to use numbers to solve problems, confidently analyze situations that call for the use of numerical calculations, and be able to arrive at reasonable numerical decisions they can explain and justify. Expecting any less is educationally foolish and shortsighted. (Burns, 1998, pp. 53–54)

I tell my parents, "If you're in the supermarket line and you don't have anything else to do, or if you're walking to school, you can ask him his facts. But, after you ask him what's 6×7, ask him how did he get there?" I think that's the most important question. It's what I say to them, I ask "How did you get there? How did you do that? How did you come up with that answer?" And then I see where their explanation takes them, see if they have a clear-cut understanding. It will only raise the level of the conversation and deepen their understanding.

—I. M. Marcial, grade 3 teacher (New York)

How do I help my child with math at home?

According to classroom teachers, this is one of the most common questions from parents and family members who are new to *Investigations*. It is voiced in many ways:

"I don't know what is OK to say and what's not OK."

"I don't understand this new program, so I don't know how to help. I'm afraid my child will fail."

"If I try to share the way I do it, she says that's not the way she does it in class." Teachers suggest the following responses. More ideas on helping at home can be found in chapter 6, "Communicating Through Homework" (p. 88).

—————————————

Early in the year, I encourage my parents to listen to how their children make sense of the math we're working on in school. We learn what not to say, even as teachers, by paying attention to how children respond to us. If the focus of our interaction is to show an interest in our students' ideas, rather than sharing our own ideas, we can learn pretty quickly whether our comments are helpful.

—A. O'Reilly, grade 2 teacher
    (Massachusetts)

—————————————

I let parents know it's OK to say, "I never learned math this way. I'm interested in learning about this new way." This makes it OK not to understand a child's homework. It's not related to smarts. Parents and students also need to know that parents' strategies are valid. I ask students to interview adults to see how they would solve a given problem that students also solve. We share the ways each group solves the problem, including the traditional algorithm, in class. Then, I include the information in a newsletter home, making sure to include the traditional algorithm.

—N. Buell, grade 4 teacher
    (Massachusetts)

—————————————

Talking to parents at Back-to-School Night, I share student-developed procedures from the previous year's class. I don't send home computation until we have estab-

lished strategies in the classroom. I let parents know that there is not one correct way and that I have not told the class any specific way to do it. I record and send home examples of the strategies developed by the class. I also show student-developed procedures during parent conferences and have children explain solutions to their parents.

—G. Lauinger, grades 4–5 teacher
    (California)

—————————————

It makes sense that you would worry that your child could "fail at math" without your help. Feeling as if you cannot help is frustrating! However, be aware that there are supports available in this curriculum. At the beginning of each unit, I send home the "Family Letter" that outlines the mathematics of the upcoming unit. I invite you to read the letter. Then, let me know if you have questions. Also, save the letter (perhaps on the refrigerator) so that you can refer to it when your child has a question. Knowing what your child is studying in class may help you say, "Oh, I know what this assignment is driving at!" Also, the *Student Activity Booklets* I use have a Family Note on the back of each assignment, specific to the activity, that explains what has been going on in the classroom, the math concepts in the assignment, and the materials needed.

When your child gets confused you can ask:

"What is this problem asking you to do?"
"How might you get started?"
"Can you think of anything you worked on at school that connects to the problem?"
"You said you don't get it. What part of the assignment is confusing you?"

Any one of (or a combination of) these questions may help you, as the parent, pinpoint where your child gets stuck. You might find that you *can* help your child get "unstuck." If you can't, just write a note on your child's unfinished homework with a few words about where you think your child got stuck. That way I know that your child needs help, and I'll provide that help.

Keep in mind that it takes time and practice to learn something. A few confusing nights of homework does not indicate failure!

You may find that you actually understand more of the math than you think at first. You also may find that you'll *learn* more math by working with your child on the games I send home and by reviewing your child's work on previous assignments.

Let your child teach you! When you see your child using a strategy you do not understand, say, "I want to learn from you. Can you explain your strategy to me?" Your child strengthens her or his understanding by verbalizing ideas while at the same time strengthening *your* understanding.

—K. Casey, grades 4–5 teacher (New York)

Suggest that the parents' role is to help their children reflect on what they know about the problem. They might ask, especially for a word problem, "What is the question you're trying to answer? What do you know so far?" Sometimes they can help by setting up a parallel problem with easier numbers. They should also know that it's OK if their child doesn't complete the problem. I'd rather get a note saying, "My child is confused" than a homework paper that is the parent's work rather than the child's.

—N. Buell, grade 4 teacher (Massachusetts)

When a parent comes in and says, "I need to know more, I want to learn about this math, I want to be able to help him, but I'm not quite sure where he's going," I find it helpful to provide Teacher Notes and Dialogue Boxes from the units, and most parents are comfortable taking those items home.

—N. Serafin, grades 3–4 teacher (Arizona)

Resources and Readings

In chapter 2 of *Teaching the New Basic Skills: Principles for Educating Children to Thrive in a Changing Economy,* Richard J. Murnane and Frank Levy (1996) consider the changing needs and practices of employers, including new interview techniques focused on such topics as problem solving and working with peers. Their book offers examples to bolster a presentation to parents.

Books with more answers to "Why change the teaching and learning of math? Change it how?" include *Math: Facing an American Phobia* (Burns, 1998), *Before It's Too Late* (The Glenn Commission, 2000; available online), *Beyond Arithmetic* (Mokros, Russell, & Economopoulos, 1995), *Principles and Standards for School Mathematics* (NCTM, 2000; available online), *Everybody Counts* (National Research Council, 1989; available online), and Susan Jo Russell's two articles on developing computational fluency with whole numbers (Russell, 2000a and 2000b; available online through the *Investigations* website). NCTM has also released a series of one-page documents called *Setting the Record Straight About Changes in Mathematics Education.* Each of these—"Commonsense Facts to Clear the Air," "Commonsense Facts About the NCTM Standards," and "Commonsense Facts About School Mathematics"—is available online and can be reproduced as a handout.

More information on "How do we know this way of teaching and learning math works?" can be found in an article in the February 1999 *Phi Delta Kappan,* "The Mathematical Miseducation of America's Youth: Ignoring Research and Scientific Study in Education" (Battista, 1999); this is also available online at the Phi Delta Kappa website. Another relevant article, "Relationships Between Research and the NCTM Standards" (Hiebert, 1999), can be found in the January 1999 *Journal for Research in Mathematics Education,* which is also available online.

For studies specific to the *Investigations* curriculum, see the IMPACT page of the *Investigations* website. One example is the article *The* Investigations *Curriculum and Children's Understanding of Whole Number Operations* (Mokros, 2000), which summarizes four studies examining the impact of the *Investigations* curriculum. (Individual summaries of three of the studies are also posted there.) These four studies are examined in more depth in a book from Lawrence Erlbaum edited by Sharon L. Senk and Denisse R. Thompson, *Standards-Oriented School Mathematics Curricula: What Does the Research Say About Student Outcomes?* (in press).

Chapter 6
Communicating Through Homework

Homework is an important means of communicating with families. It can be used to share ideas about what math content is important, give families the chance to see their children working mathematically, and offer a glimpse of how the children are learning and doing mathematics in class. In *Investigations* there aren't homework sheets filled with straight computation problems. There *are* sheets with one, two, or several problems, with plenty of room for children to show their solution process. Other homework consists of game directions and a score sheet or a request that children collect and record some data in a way that makes sense to them.

School policies vary widely on issues of homework. Some teachers are free to assign homework as they see fit, while others are required to assign work every night, every other night, or are held to some other schedule, depending on the age of their students. The *Investigations* curriculum supports teachers by providing enough homework to accommodate each of these situations.

Whatever the school policy, parents who expect nightly sheets of computational drill may worry that this curriculum is less rigorous. In fact, what *Investigations* is aiming for—in homework assignments and in classwork—is a much deeper understanding of mathematics. Children may be solving fewer problems, but those few problems require more thought. It is often not immediately obvious how to solve the problems, and there are usually several possible methods. Often these assignments require several solution attempts, the refining of strategies, and a picture or diagram showing the problem and solution. When children must find

ways to clearly explain a strategy, they must articulate—and therefore further clarify—key math ideas. One of the teacher's jobs is to help parents understand this purpose of homework, as well as parents' role in the process.

Homework Policy and Expectations

Students and their families need to have specific information about the nature of homework: how much to expect; how often to expect it; how to find out about, clarify, adapt, and expand assignments; what happens with finished work and how is it kept track of; what characterizes good work; and how parents can help at home. Developing clear homework expectations and routines encourages children to take responsibility for their own learning.

One good way to set expectations for homework is to share some papers from previous years (with no names), talking about what makes a good homework paper, asking what the students notice, and sharing what the teacher sees. The four examples of work on "Make Your Own Puzzle" (*Investigations* grade 5) illustrate what the teacher appreciates in these papers and where she feels more work is needed (figures 14–17). The teacher would explain to students and/or parents:

"Student 1 [figure 14] showed me how she solved the puzzle. She attached a 100 chart, and I can tell how she used it: She crossed out all the one- and three-digit numbers, circled multiples of 9, and crossed out any of those numbers that were even. And, if I couldn't tell from the 100 chart, the words are a clear explanation, too."

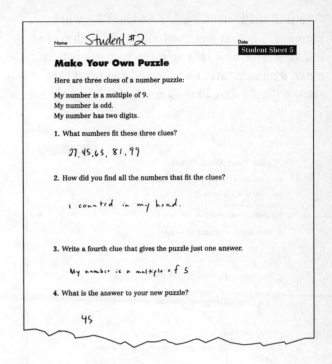

Figure 14 Student 1's work.

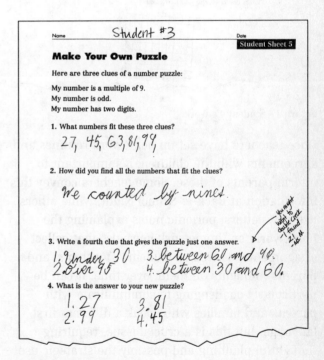

Figure 15 Student 2's work.

"Student 2 [figure 15] found all the numbers and found a way to make a puzzle with only one solution. But it's hard for me to tell how he thought about it. Writing 'I counted in my head' doesn't help me understand his method. It makes me wonder, How did you count in your head? What did you count by? How did you know when to stop counting?"

"Student 3 [figure 16] is an example of someone who did more than was expected. For part 3 of the problem, he found not just one but *four* ways to change the puzzle so it would have one answer. You can see I wrote him a note about one of his clues because I found two numbers that worked for that one."

Figure 16 Student 3's work.

"What is really useful about Student 4's work [figure 17] is that she used a picture to show her thinking. Her new clue said the number would make a square, and she showed me what that square would look like—9 rows of 9."

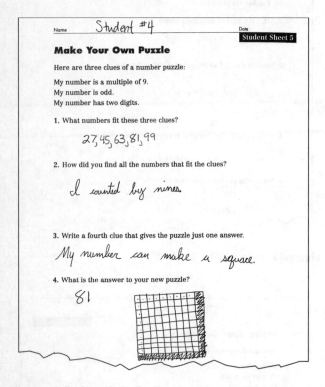

Figure 17 Student 4's work.

Once teachers have set up homework routines and agreements with the children, it's important to inform parents of these. Some teachers convey this information at Back-to-School Night, while others use newsletters, periodic notes explaining the homework, or "homework journals" that collect assignments, as well as students', teacher's, and parents' thoughts on them, over time. It can be particularly challenging to communicate with parents and families who speak a different first language, but this is a crucial issue, requiring thoughtful planning and possibly the strategic use of bilingual teachers or volunteer translators.

I try to use homework to solidify skills that the kids are learning in the classroom, but also I give certain math homework so that parents can see what we are doing. … I try to use some homework to assess the students' understanding. I really encourage parents to communicate with me if their child doesn't understand the homework. I want them to write a note to me right on the homework paper. A lot of parents do that, which is wonderful because then I know what kids are struggling with and what might be really easy for certain kids.

I will pass homework back to students and we go over it sometimes, but not all the time—just enough to let students know that they are being held accountable. I try to follow specifically what the *Investigations* curriculum recommends for homework. These homework sheets are great exercises for helping kids solidify their understanding.

—*R. Musser, grade 4 teacher (Massachusetts)*

In the beginning of the year, I encouraged parents to set up a game box with the children, to keep on their desk at home (or wherever they do homework). That way, they weren't losing all the materials. My first year (with *Investigations*), I didn't have that in place, and the kids would come in with half the cards, or they would forget pieces. Having a box labeled "Math Games" has helped keep them organized. Then if we revisit a game, if I say, "Tonight for homework, I want you to play Close to 50 again," now I don't hear Johnny saying, "I don't know where that is."

—*S. Huard, grade 3 teacher (Massachusetts)*

What Will Homework Look Like?

Because families often have preconceptions of what math homework should look like and how often to expect it, teachers need to let parents know—in newsletters, at Back-to-School Night, and on homework sheets—how homework is going to look and why. Families need to understand that math is about more than numbers and computation and that students will be exploring ideas in geometry, measurement, and data. At the same time, they need to be clear about the importance of number and computation in this curriculum— that these areas will be investigated in great depth, for long periods of time, and that fluency with the facts is an important goal.

For parents who express concern about "basic facts," teachers can highlight how the children will work on learning these number combinations. Across the grades, children are asked to think about which facts are hard for them and to develop strategies for remembering them. In second grade, that process might look like this: "8 + 9 is hard for me to remember. But 9 is almost 10, just 1 less, and I know 8 + 10 is 18. I added 1 too many, so take 1 away, and I have 17." In fourth grade, the process may sound like this: "I have a hard time remembering 8 times 7. But I know 7 times 7 is 49, and 8 times 7 is 1 more 7, and 49 + 7 is 56."

When first describing the homework in *Investigations*, teachers can give parents a sense of the range of assignments that are likely to come home during the year. Showing concrete examples of the materials involved, along with examples of typical homework assignments at their child's grade level, can help make activities come to life. With these examples, teachers can explain the math involved and the strategies children will be developing as they work. To illustrate activities for newsletters or handouts, teachers can copy student work from previous years or use pictures from the *Investigations* units (see figure 19 for an example that works for first grade; figure 20 for a similar example for third grade). Figure 21 shows a sheet of general information about math homework suitable for parents at all grade levels, and figure 22 is another handout that categorizes the types of homework somewhat differently.

Teachers who are just starting out with *Investigations,* or who are teaching only a few units, may not yet have a sense of the whole year's curriculum, the kinds of homework assignments that are likely, or the scope of the mathematics they will cover. They may want to preview each unit with an eye toward explaining the kind of homework in the unit to parents. They can also tap the expertise of others at their grade level, or collaborate with other teachers to present the information as a grade-level team.

8 + 6
6 + 8

Clue: 6 + 6

"I think of 6 + 6 is 12, and then it's 2 more, so it's 14."

8 + 6
6 + 8

Clue: 8 + 2 = 10

"I think of 8 and 2 is 10, so take 2 away from the 6 and there's 4 left, so it's 14."

8 + 6
6 + 8

Clue: 7 + 7 = 14

"I take 1 off the 8 and put it on the 6, so it's 7 +7, which I know is 14."

8 + 6
6 + 8

Clue: 10 + 6 = 16

"10 plus 6 is 16, so 8 plus 6 is 2 less."

Figure 18 Using "addition cards" from *Investigations,* these four children have each come up with a different strategy to help them remember the fact 8 + 6. All show good number sense.

First Grade Homework in *Investigations*

Dear Families,

Much of the math in first grade focuses on counting and comparing quantities and on developing strategies for solving addition and subtraction problems. To practice these skills, the children will go home to count, for example, all the windows or electrical outlets in their home and find a way to keep track of and record their findings. They will be playing counting games like "Compare" and "Collect 15¢." They will also solve number problems (12 + 13), story problems, and recurring problems like "How Many of Each?" For example:

> I have 7 items. Some are peas and some are carrots.
> How many of each could I have?

These examples (taken from one of the *Investigations* units) show some different ways students typically solve this problem. Some find just one solution; others find several. You might be interested to see how your child solves this problem!

—Ms. M.

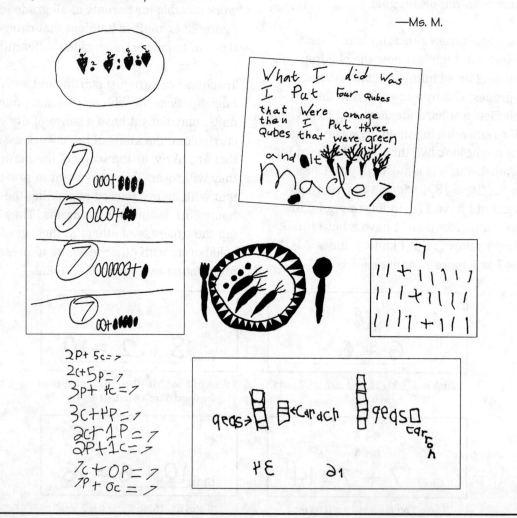

Figure 19 Parent handout giving examples of first grade math homework

Third Grade Homework in *Investigations*

Dear Families,

In third grade math, a major focus is on developing strategies for solving addition and subtraction problems. Your children will be working on this when they play addition and subtraction games like "Plus, Minus, Stay the Same" and "Close to 100," and as they solve number problems and story problems. You will also see your child beginning to think about multiplication and division. They'll be looking for things that come in groups, such as the two rows of 6 (or six rows of 2) in a carton of eggs. They will consider how they could share a group of things equally among everyone in their family, and they will play games with array cards. The girls in this picture (shown in one of the *Investigations* units) are using array cards to play the game "Multiplication Pairs," which offers children lots of practice with the multiplication "facts." You might want to ask your child a few facts and hear his/her strategy for remembering them!

—Mrs. C

Figure 20 Parent handout giving examples of third grade math homework

Things to Know Your About Your Child's
Math Homework

We give children a variety of math homework assignments through the grades. A few types of assignments are described here. Some come directly from the *Investigations Curriculum* that District 2 has adopted. Others come from other sources.

Games
Often games are assigned as homework. We play the games at school and would like you to play them with your children at home also. Not only are games motivating and challenging for children; they also contain important mathematical ideas and help children develop math skills. Playing them over and over helps children clarify their mathematical understandings and hone their skills. As you play the games with your children, ask them occasionally about what they notice and about their strategies for playing. And try to relax and have fun when you play with your child. Though games contain serious learning, they should not be taken seriously enough to cause unpleasantness between you and your child.

Problems to Solve
These problems may be short problems due the next day or, especially for grades 4 and 5, they may be "Problems of the Week," meant to be worked on over several days. These problems may call on your child to draw deeply on his or her math knowledge and skills. Sometimes your child may complain that "the teacher didn't show me how to do this;" and, in a way, this is true. Teachers cannot teach students to do every kind of problem; instead we try to help them develop strategies that will help them solve a wide variety of problems. Even if your child doesn't arrive at a final solution, the work they do toward a solution is important. Your help is welcome. Just be sure it isn't a matter of simply giving them an answer, as this robs your child of the chance to learn something from attempting the problem. Be assured that the problem will be discussed in class, and that strategies used by different students will be shared.

Tasks to Perform
Sometimes your child may be asked to do something such as collect data or take measurements at home. The information collected is information that will be discussed and used later in class. In fact, the next day's lesson may depend on everyone having performed this task. It may, for example, involve making a graph representing everyone's data.

Facts to Practice
So that they can become competent in estimating and computing, our goal is to help students learn their addition facts through 10 + 10 by the end of second grade and their multiplication facts through 10 x 10 by the end of fourth grade. We'll be working on this at school, but most children will also need extra help at home. Your children will be assigned games and given suggestions for learning these facts, and your encouragement and assistance are important. Remember, though, that this is a task that takes quite a while for many children; therefore, it will need to be worked on over time.

Sandra Nye, Math Staff Developer

Figure 21 Information about homework to give parents early in the year. From S. Nye, New York City. Reprinted with permission.

Types of Homework Assignments in *Investigations*

Here are a few examples of the kinds of homework assignments you might see coming home this year. The examples are from different grade levels, but they typify the work at any grade.

1. Children work on several problems that are similar to what they've been doing in class. For example, in school, fourth graders work with geoboards to show and compare fractions. For homework, they might bring home dot paper and design many ways to split a square into halves or fourths.

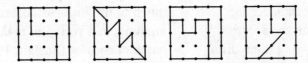

2. Children play a game with a family member or friend, like Close to 100 or Collect 15. These games, particularly when they are played repeatedly, give children needed practice with important concepts.

3. Children take a break from the math being explored in class by focusing on a different idea (such as geometry during a number unit) or they visit a past activity so they can keep practicing those ideas (such as a computation game during a geometry unit).

4. Children collect data at home and find ways to represent them. It might be the number or ages of siblings, the number of cars, people, or animals that pass by a window in ten minutes, the amount of ads in a half hour of television or radio programming, or a question decided upon by the child.

5. Children prepare a set of materials, such as array cards or Tetromino shapes (below), for an upcoming unit or lesson.

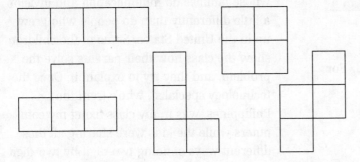

6. Children undertake a larger mathematical project, sometimes overlapping with science or other work. For example, they might investigate some aspect of conservation in their house, such as, "How much garbage do we generate in a week?"

Figure 22 A handout that includes some illustrations can help parents understand the variety of *Investigations* homework they might expect to see.

I always do the homework suggested in the units. Sometimes I'll make up a sheet on my computer to reinforce what we did in math that day. If we did word problems involving fractions—sharing brownies among a number of people—and I felt they needed more practice on it, then I would send that home for homework that night. Sometimes I give it to only a few students. Other times, I give it to the whole class. I save those all on my computer, and I also have different varieties in an extra work folder for some of the students who need or want extra math work, as opposed to just giving them ditto sheets from another book.

—*S. Huard, grade 3 teacher (Massachusetts)*

Homework that involves parents is another link between home and school. What I use comes mostly from the units, and a lot of it is the games. I think it's really important that the parents play the games with the kids, if possible. (It's not possible for every parent.) If the parents actually play the games, they see all the math that's in them, and the practice and strategizing, and that's important.

—*N. Buell, grade 4 teacher (Massachusetts)*

Sometimes *Investigations* teachers will assign homework that involves both parent and child. For example, a note to parents might say:

> "For homework tonight your child will solve this problem. Your job is to try to really understand and record your child's strategy for solving this problem. This can be hard work and will probably involve listening really carefully, several times, to the method your child uses. This is a great way to find out how your child is thinking mathematically, and to get a sense of what it feels like to be me, during math class!"

One teacher had children teach their parents a math activity at home, after investigating it on their own and teaching it to their friends (Hart, Smyth, Vetter, & Hart, 1996, pp. 180–186). Another teacher strove to make the connection between the math people do at home and "school math" by asking families to work together to describe a mathematical experience from their daily lives, such as estimating how much it costs to own and maintain the family pet, figuring out how much to tip for a restaurant meal, or altering the amounts in a recipe to make a larger (or smaller) batch of cookies (Ensign, 1998). Yet another teacher involved families by having parents and children work separately to solve the same problem; class discussion the next day focused on the strategies both children and parents used—which included several traditional algorithms.

A perfect way to bring the standard algorithm into the classroom is to have children go home and talk to their parents, ask an adult at home, "How would you solve this problem in two ways?" Then children come in to school and share the adult's way of solving the problem. Often you get the standard algorithms. It's so much fun because we have some children from South America, whose families do multiplication and division a little differently than do people who grew up in the United States. Some of the children show the class how their parents solve the problem, and they try to explain it. Once the technology specialist, who's from the Philippines, was in my class fixing my computers while the kids were sharing all these different ways of doing two-digit by two-digit multiplication. One child shared a way, and I just couldn't follow her reasoning. The technology specialist came up and said, "I know how to do this. This is the way we were taught." And he explained it so that we could understand what was happening.

—*N. Springer, grade 4 teacher (Massachusetts)*

Written Homework Notes

Notes to families on individual homework assignments can serve several purposes:

- explain the assignment and what to expect
- describe the mathematics in the activity
- offer ideas about how families can help

This is not necessary for *every* homework, but is useful for especially important assignments. Some teachers write their own notes, while others rely on those available in the *Investigations* curriculum. Blackline masters of sheets intended for homework have a short note to families on the front. In the *Student Activity Booklets,* homework assignments have a longer note to families on the back of those sheets. A grade 3 teacher's note might be:

> For homework tonight your child will work on a puzzle called Arranging Chairs. The challenge is to find different ways to place a particular number of chairs in rectangular arrangements. (For example, 10 chairs could be set up in 5 rows of 2, or 1 row of 10.) In this work, the children are finding factor pairs, practicing their facts, and building mental images of multiplication.
>
> We solved several of these puzzles in class, so your child should know what to do and how to begin. You can help by asking questions about the process. Good questions might be, "Will you try rows of 7? What about 2? Why or why not?" or "Do you think you have all the possibilities? How do you know? How could you find out for sure?" or "Is there any way you could change one rectangle to find another that works?"
>
> If your child seems stuck, try cutting out a set of paper or cardboard squares to move around or let your child draw on graph paper. You might also try a smaller number of chairs, or work to find several instead of all the possible arrangements.

Teachers can keep such notes in a file for use each year with the same activity.

How to Help at Home

Parents often ask what they can do to help their child with math. Sometimes this is a general request: How do I get my child more interested in and comfortable with math? Other times, the question is more specific: How do I help my child with math homework that looks different and feels unfamiliar to me?

How Do I Help My Child Learn and Enjoy Math?

There's a lot families can do to create a math-friendly atmosphere at home. For starters, they can be encouraged to display a positive attitude toward mathematics—even if they find it difficult or unpleasant, or think they were never any good at it. There are several good books for parents who need help overcoming "math anxiety"; see the "Resources and Readings" for chapter 1 (p. 27). Since some children think excelling in math is "uncool" or that only certain groups (boys, for example) are mathematically inclined, families can work at communicating the message that math is not only a practical necessity, it is something *everyone* can do and enjoy for its own sake.

A math educator, lecturer, and workshop leader says, "One of the most significant things parents can do is to help their children understand the normalcy and the value of struggle in mathematics … Learning math ultimately comes down to one thing: the ability, and choice, to put one's brain around a problem—to stare past the confusion, and struggle forward rather than flee" (Sutton, 1998, p. 9). She sees our society as one that accepts, even admires, struggle in other arenas—parents are proud of children who work hard to master a particular piece of music or an athletic skill. But too often in mathematics, people see struggle as the sign of a lack of ability. This belief in innate mathematical ability is damaging to all children. Those who struggle assume they just don't get it and never will. Those who do not struggle believe their success is the result of ability, but then may lose their confidence the first time they hit a stumbling block. Parents can help their children expect, cope with, and work through the mathematical difficulties and frustrations they encounter.

Another answer for parents looking to help their child with math is to encourage them to find ways to explore math together as a family. Some parents find it helpful to think of reading with their child as a comparable example—what's the mathematical equivalent of reading aloud to your child every day? Mathematics can be fun if families find ways to include everyone in the family and don't focus exclusively on aspects that can cause anxiety, such as speed and memorization. The following two handouts give parents ways to encourage their children to explore and enjoy math for its own sake.

How Can I Help My Child Become Mathematically Powerful?

	Early Years	Middle Years	Older Years

Money	Use money to help your child:
	    recognize coins
	    know the value of coins
	    count coins
		Help your child:
		    make change
		    find coins that make 25 cents
		    save her/his own allowance by
		      opening a passbook savings account
			Help your child:
			    participate in making family budgets
			    participate in grocery shopping
			    begin to manage her/his allowance
			    decide how much allowance can buy

Counting/ Numbers	Involve counting and numbers in everyday activities:
	    Count parts of the body
	    Count things around the house
	    Count past 10
	    Identify numbers on the elevator
	    Identify numbers on street signs
	    Setting the table helps build spatial sense and reinforces 1 to 1 correspondence (I need 4 plates for 4 people, for example)
		Encourage your child to count by 2s, 5s, and 10s
		        Count past 100
		    Look for patterns
			Encourage your child to practice skip counting by 3s and 4s
			
			Count past 1000 (say, count from 650 by 100 "650, 750, 850, 950, 1050... for example)

Math Facts	Help your child start to memorize single digit addition and subtraction problems starting with the doubles:
	    1 + 1, 2 + 2, 3 + 3, etc.
	    5 - 5, 4 - 4, 3 - 3, etc.
		By the end of 2nd grade your child should know addition and subtraction facts to 20 (1 + 19, 2 + 18, 10 + 10, etc.)
		    Your child should also know addition pairs that equal 10 (1 + 9, 2 + 8, 3 + 7, 4 + 6, and 5 + 5)
			By the end of 4th grade your child should know multiplication and division facts to 12 X 12

Time	These are some of the time concepts that you can help your child learn at home:
	    days of the week, months of the year, seasons, minutes in an hour, hours in a day
	    how to read a standard clock (with an hour hand and minute hand)
	    how to schedule time (if you need to do four things, how much time will you need?)		

Measure-ment	Involve your child in activities that encourage measurement like:
	    cooking (fractions, volume, cups, teaspoons, etc., following step-by-step instructions)
	    reading a thermometer (measuring body temperature and measuring temperatures outside)		

Figure 23 These tips for parents span the elementary school grade range. From J. DiBrienza and K. Casey, New York City. Reprinted with permission.

What can parents do?

-Become aware of any mathematics anxiety they have and be careful not to pass along their fears to their children.

-Realize that they don't have to know all of the answers (One of the most helpful answers may be "Let's find out together").

-Talk to their children about the relevance of math to future success.

-Be sure that their children pursue high-quality math courses.

-Find out about enrichment programs.

-Encourage their children's interest in math and let them know they can succeed.

-Have high expectations and check on their progress.

-Ask questions.

Figure 24 More general tips for parents who want to support their children as mathematical thinkers. From J. Thayer, L. Womack, and A. V. Marshall, Milwaukee, Wisconsin. Reprinted with permission.

How Do I Help My Child with *This Kind* of Math?

Many of parents' more specific questions about math homework can be answered early in the school year by following suggestions described earlier for Back-to-School presentations or newsletters, with additional communication throughout the year as needed. Being really clear from the beginning about homework expectations and responsibilities can prevent anxiety. Everyone needs to know that homework is the *child's* responsibility. Children will come home understanding the assignment and what's expected of them, and parents will receive information about the homework and how they can help. At the same time, teachers find it crucial to share with parents the strategies students are likely to be using.

> Parents refer back to what they understand and how they learned math … They think we're dumbing down the curriculum because we're not sending as many problems home and the practice is not there the way they remember it. The emphasis on drill is not there, and they feel we're not making children accountable for facts. One of the answers for us has been sharing examples of how a problem might be solved so that when

parents do see two or three problems come home, they have something by which to gauge children's work. It can help them see what they might expect their child to do, or a solution or strategy children would use. It's not enough to just give them directions, "Solve these and show your work." We need to let the parents know what we want.

—*B. Pierce, special education teacher and teacher leader (Arizona)*

Figures 24 and 25 illustrate handouts for parents from two districts using *Investigations,* designed to encourage parents to listen carefully to their children and ask questions of them, rather than simply telling them what to do, where they went wrong, or what the answer is. By helping in this way, parents mimic what teachers do in the classroom—try to follow children's strategies, to understand their logic, and to allow children to discover and correct their own errors. Parents will discover that as children explain their strategies aloud, they often find and fix their own mistakes.

Helpful Things to Say When Your Child Asks For Help With Math Homework...

In order to help your child become a strong and flexible problem solver, we assign a variety of math activities as homework.

Often your child will receive homework that is directly connected to the TERC math curriculum. You can recognize the TERC pages because they appear torn out of student books. On the back of these "Student Sheets" is a section called "To the Family." This section helps explain the concepts the worksheet is designed to reinforce. It also lists the necessary materials and brief explanation of the activity. By reading this section, you can help your child successfully complete the work.

Games may also be assigned for homework. The TERC units use games as motivating ways to help children learn and master concepts. We play the games in school and expect you to play the games at home, too. Games are to be taken seriously! When your child asks you to play a math game, notice that your child has to remember and explain rules, create a strategy, and use math as well. Games challenge children's minds.

We also assign open-ended problems (multi-step word problems) or performance tasks ('measure this...', 'collect data about that...'). Many teachers call these "Problems of the Week." Often the problem of the week challenges your child to try to use all of her/his math knowledge to solve an unfamiliar problem. Sometimes children complain that "the teacher didn't teach me how to do this kind" and the children are correct, in a way. We cannot ever teach your child how to do every kind of problem. Instead, we teach your child strategies to solve a wide variety of problems. When your child asks you for help, try not to jump in with an answer.

Instead, try helping your child get started by using these prompts:

1. Does this remind you of other problems?

2. What have you come up with so far?

3. Where do you think you should start?

4. What is the problem asking you to do?

5. Would drawing a picture or diagram help?

6. How can I help you (without giving you the solution)?

Figure 25 School-wide guidelines for parents on how to help with homework, used as a handout. From J. DiBrienza, K. Casey, and S. Nye, New York City. Reprinted with permission.

What about Flashcards? workbooks?

Some parents will ask about using flashcards and workbook pages or about teaching the "standard" algorithms at home. Teachers handle these questions differently, thinking hard about what works best with their own beliefs, their classroom style, and the particular community in which they teach.

> I think communication with parents is really key. I don't believe that doing something different [like rote math homework] to make the parents happy is going to do it. I think it will just confuse the child because this is not what's happening at school. I think that what's happening in school should be reinforced at home.
>
> —R. Christiansen, grades 1–2 teacher (Massachusetts)

> Children are not getting rote memory homework every night, and parents don't understand why. I try to explain to them what we are doing by sending the parent letter from each unit and inviting them in to visit our classroom. But some still challenge me on those issues, and some are pushing those multiplication tables at home with their second grader. So I try to explain to parents the difference between rote memorization and understanding. I ask, "Could he build it for me in cubes? Does he understand what 3 × 4 really means?" If they say, "Well, no," I say, "What we're trying to do is develop a really strong understanding of what mathematics is." The thing that is really helpful is for them to actually come in and see it because even when I explain a lesson to them it's just not the same as seeing their child in action.
>
> —T. Caccavale, grade 2 teacher (New York)

Some teachers try to point out the practice with basic facts and the four operations that is provided in the curriculum and describe the kinds of activities that will be sent home to achieve the same goals. Parents who are worried about facts and operations are often unaware that there are other approaches; but they are often open to suggestion, so some teachers keep on hand copies of *Investigations* games and activities for "extra work." The more specific the suggestions, the more empowered the parent will be to carry them out. For example, a teacher might send home some games with notes like these:

> I hear that you are worried about how Max is doing with his addition combinations. I agree that's something he needs to be working on—I'd like the children to know their combinations to ten by the end of October. Here are two activities—Turn Over Ten and Tens Go Fish—he can work on at home. These games specifically work on combinations to 10. (Later in the year we will focus on other special combinations like doubles, doubles plus and minus 1, and combinations that make 20.) It would be very helpful if you could play these games with him. He can explain the rules to you since we have played them in class.

You asked about helping Allison with her multiplication facts, and I think it's great that you want to tackle this together at home. We've been doing some activities in class that focus on multiplication pairs and would be perfect for Allison to be working on at home: Arranging Chairs Puzzles, Multiplication Pairs, and Count and Compare. Two of these activities use array cards, which remind me of the flashcards you were asking about, except these cards are more visual. On the array card for 4 times 5, the kids can see the total number of squares (20), the dimensions (4 rows of 5 or 5 rows of 4), and how it looks compared to other facts that equal 20 (it's half as long as 2 by 10, for example). As Allison uses these cards, she will be learning to visualize the facts and their relationships, with the goal of learning to use them fluently.

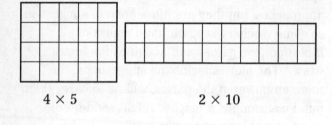

4 × 5   2 × 10

When parents seem convinced of the need to use flashcards or worksheets, teachers can offer ideas about how to use them in ways that meaningfully complement the curriculum and what it is trying to accomplish in math. For example, parents can be told the following:

- If you use workbook sheets, suggest that children only solve "the problems which have even answers, or the ones where you have to borrow when you subtract, [or] … the two problems which have the greatest and least answer on the page, [or] the problems where there are exactly two digits in the answer" (Raphel, 2000b, p. 7). This helps children search for patterns among problems, think about every problem on the page, practice estimating, and build number sense. Ask children how they figured out which problems they needed to solve, and how they solved the ones they did.
- If you use flashcards, encourage children to tell you how they knew, how they figured it out, or how they remember (or might learn to remember) each fact. You might ask, "Did you use something you knew?" or "How would knowing 3 × 3 help you with 3 × 4?"
- You might sort through the flashcards to think about which facts your child already knows and which facts he or she still needs to work on. You can both see mastery develop as you weed out more and more cards. A homework

assignment that supports this work with facts is described in Annette Raphel's book: How many *different answers* are there in the times tables from 1 × 1 to 9 × 9? As she notes, children are often relieved to find that there are only 36; it makes the task feel within reach (Raphel, 2000b, p. 24).

- Children might do activities with flashcards, such as drawing 10 cards randomly and putting them in order from least to most. Or, they might pick a fact that they don't yet know and think of one or more different ways to figure it out.

With some parents, teachers may want to discuss the methods students are using in class in more depth, sending home a note or having a conversation along these lines:

I understand you're worried about Marisol learning how to add two-digit numbers. We spend a lot of time looking at many different ways of adding and subtracting. We think about which make sense for particular numbers and which ways are efficient and accurate. What lots of people are surprised to find out is that there isn't just one way to solve an addition problem. There are many good methods, or algorithms, that work. The standard algorithm often comes up in our classroom, and we talk about it like any other algorithm— how does it work? *Why* does it work? How is it like other methods?

What I've found with teaching children math this way, based on their understandings about numbers and operations, is that they often move from left to right, dealing with the largest part of the number first. So for 46 + 37, they often start by thinking 40 and 30 is 70, or even 46 and 30 is 76. When I used to teach *just* the traditional algorithm, my students used to worry about when and what to carry; they couldn't always tell if a story problem called for addition or subtraction. They would start from the right, like I taught them to, and they would talk about bits and pieces of numbers. For example, they might say "6 and 7 is 13 so I put down the 3 and carry the 1. Or, do I put down the 1 and carry the 3?" Or, they would write the whole 13 underneath the line and get an answer of 713. If they forgot the steps, they would end with an answer that didn't make sense, but they wouldn't realize it. Now, they often know if they've made a mistake because they've thought about the largest part of the problem first. Plus, their own strategies use ideas about place value that are critically important in the traditional algorithm, but aren't as evident in that algorithm: Working from the left, they *know* that the 4 in 46 is 40.

If you share the standard algorithm with Marisol at home, I hope she can make sense of it and compare it to other ways of solving the problem. She is developing a good sense of tens and ones, and I'd like her to keep working on those ideas.

It is important to start where parents are—in their beliefs about mathematics, math education, and what their child needs. Some parents will feel that drill and practice with flashcards and worksheets, or learning the long division algorithm, are essential for their child's educational success. Teachers shouldn't expend effort telling parents what *not* to do, or dictating what they *must* do. Energy focused on helping parents understand homework, how they can help their child with it, and why it is important can establish and widen the common ground for schools and families.

Never say to parents, "No, you can't." You just don't say that. They're the parents. They're more committed to that child than you ever will be. There isn't one right way to do anything.

—*D. Shein-Gerson, grades K–5 math coordinator (Massachusetts)*

Conclusion

Because homework assumes a partnership with families, there are things for teachers to consider *beyond* its usefulness in the curriculum. For example:

- What materials are required? Do all families have access to those materials?
- How much participation from families is required? What feedback am I getting from parents about the amount of homework? about the content? about their relationship with their child around homework? Am I asking too much of families who are already stretched too thin?
- What about children whose families cannot participate? What about children and families who do not speak or read English? What about those who cannot read?

Implementing a well-balanced homework policy that takes into account the various needs and expectations of those involved can be difficult. It requires teachers to be thoughtful and purposeful in their assignments, to be respectful of children and their families, and to know well their mathematical goals for children. It is work that may seem easier if teachers remember "the power of homework to create shared mathematical experiences and meaningful mathematical conversations between parents and children" (Raphel, 2000a).

Resources and Readings

A number of publications from the U.S. Department of Education offer ideas on homework, especially Nancy Paulu's (1995) *Helping Your Child with Homework* (available in both English and Spanish). In addition, the Department of Education has used material from Paulu to create a flier called "Learning Partners: Let's Do Homework!" (also available online), which can be reprinted in school newsletters or used as a handout at parent conferences.

A book by one *Investigations* author, *Beyond Facts and Flashcards: Exploring Math with Your Kids* (Mokros, 1996), is written specifically to help parents do more *Investigations*-like math with their children at home. This can be a useful resource to suggest to parents. Another educator describes ways to help with math at home, using the *Investigations* curriculum, in *Helping at Home* (Kline, 1999; article available online). Parents who ask about a reference book to help them become more familiar with school mathematics might be referred to *A Mathematics Handbook: Math on Call* (Great Source Education Group, 1998).

In her book *Math Homework That Counts: Grades 4–6*, Annette Raphel (2000b) addresses questions teachers often ask, such as "Why give homework?" and "What makes a *good* homework assignment?" She provides math homework activities in four categories: as practice, as preparation, as extension, and to emphasize creativity. This book also includes a section for parents, "What You Can Do to Help Your Child with Math Homework This Year." Also informative is the section titled "General Research Findings About Homework." This book is a useful resource for teachers who want to establish a standard homework policy or are considering a revision to theirs.

For a report on a 1998 survey of how parents and teachers view parental involvement in homework, see *Playing Their Parts: What Parents and Teachers Really Mean by Parental Involvement* (Public Agenda, 1999). Excerpts are available online at the Public Agenda website. In particular, see "Finding 7: Homework Complete with Yelling and Crying."

The "Ask an Author" feature of the CESAME Support Site for *Investigations* Users offers one response on creating additional homework assignments and includes lists of books and websites that offer interesting math problems suitable for homework.

Chapter 7
Helping Parents See the Math

Investigations offers a new image of what an elementary mathematics classroom can be—children making sense of serious and complicated mathematical ideas, talking with and listening to one another defend such ideas, using manipulatives to model situations and build geometric constructions, and explaining and recording their thinking in a variety of ways.

The unfamiliarity of a new math program like this can be disconcerting to some parents, who may "see teaching practices that diverge from their own school experiences as an abandonment of academic rigor" (Shepard & Bliem, 1995, p. 25). They may say, "This looks interesting and engaging, but where's the *real* math? How can I gauge how my child's doing if I don't understand what's happening?" Many will want information to help them assess their child's math experiences, particularly in comparison to their own. Others will wonder how to evaluate their child's math performance, as an individual and as a member of a class.

Parents need to be able to see and respect the mathematics in the work their children do, understand the ideas children are working to make sense of, and see evidence of progress in that work. Educators must help them do that. Schools and teachers who have been successful in achieving this goal say that it is crucial to work on many different levels, using a variety of approaches to reach both *as many* families as possible and each family *as many times* as possible. The more information and experience parents have with mathematical ideas, with doing mathematics themselves, and with understanding their child's mathematical thinking, the better.

There are primarily two places to reach parents: at the school and in the home. This chapter offers ideas for communicating about mathematics during the brief, informal time parents are at school, during planned occasions such as parent conferences, and through papers and projects that can be sent home.

When Parents Come to School

Parents come to school at different times and for different reasons. They drop their children off and pick them up, come to school functions and performances, stop by the office and classroom for information, and attend Back-to-School Nights and conferences. This time is often brief and harried, offering little chance for true interaction with a teacher. However, there are a number of casual but informative ways to catch parents' attention, spark their interest and excitement in the math program, and provide positive images of what learning math is all about.

There are so many ways to get parents in. Involve some parents in the classroom, the ones that will eagerly learn about this curriculum along with you. And if you can find somebody like that? The word of mouth from one or two parents who really see and understand what's going on is worth its weight in gold. The parent workshops we did brought parents in and were very valuable. Some schools do math activities with kids and parents together, the way we did at our "breakfast share." One of the first grade teachers has a Problem of the Day on the board every morning and encourages parents to come in and work on the problem with their child.

—*N. Buell, grade 4 teacher (Massachusetts)*

Bulletin Boards, Displays, and Exhibits

Most rooms in an elementary school dedicate certain areas to exhibiting student work, and it is easy to make sure that one always displays mathematical work. Even simple displays can give parents a sense of the role that mathematics plays in the classroom, help them interpret the math in their child's written work, and help them see progress in their child's learning.

In one school, two teachers set up a display several times a year that shows a range of students' responses to the same problem. They record and label each child's strategy on chart paper and post this display in the hall outside the room. Occasionally, they show every student's work; this way parents can see their own child's strategy and compare it with those being used by the entire class. Giving the bulletin board a title and some explanation can help parents see the math and learn about what the teacher notices in student work (see figures 26 and 27).

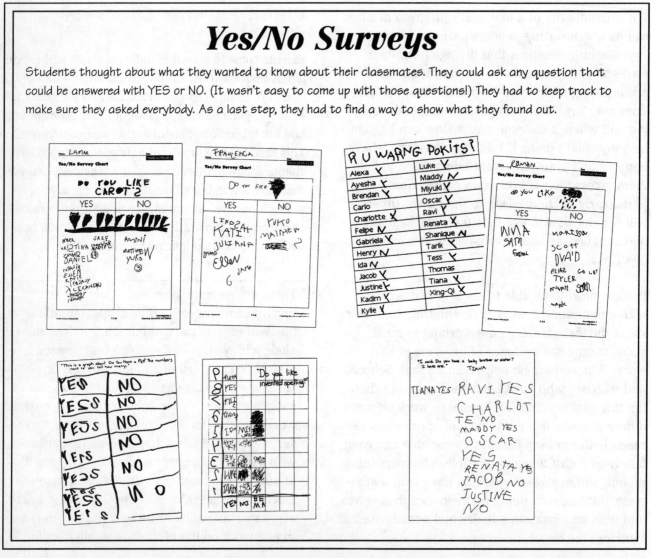

Figure 26 A display like this would help parents understand a kindergarten data activity.

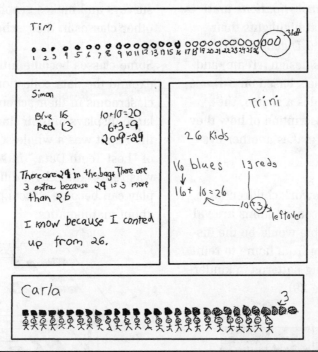

Enough for the Class?

We have been solving "Enough for the Class?" problems: If there are 16 blue cubes and 13 red cubes, are there enough cubes for everyone in our class to have one? How many would be left over? Or, how many more would we need so that everyone could have one?

Here are 4 ways students in our class solved this type of problem. Notice that children use pictures, numbers, and words to show their thinking. How would you figure out if we had enough, too many, or too few cubes for everyone to have one?

Tim

o o o ○ o o o o o o o o o o o o o o ○ o o o o o o o o ○○○ 3 left
1 2 3 4 5 6 7 8 9 10 11 12 13 14 15 16 17 18 19 20 21 22 23 24 25 26

Simon

Blue 16   10+10=20
Red 13   6+3=9
             20+9=29

There are 29 in the bag. There are
3 extra because 29 is 3 more
than 26.

I know because I conted
up from 26.

Trini

26 Kids

16 blues   13 reds
  ↓
16 + 10 = 26
           10 (+3) leftover

Carla

3

Figure 27 This second grade teacher displays several different strategies for solving the same problem.

We have a lot of things hung up in the hallway, which is one way to let people know what's going on—for other teachers as well as for parents. Often, conversations happen because somebody saw something out in the hall.

—*N. Buell, grade 4 teacher (Massachusetts)*

Some schools have a bulletin board for math work in a major hallway or foyer where many school visitors will see it. This might display a strand of math over the grades (for example, geometry from K through 5) or be a rotating bulletin board that passes from class to class or from grade level to grade level over the course of the year. One school devotes an entire hallway to math; another posts a range of student work for each Problem of the

Week; still another occasionally displays photographs of students doing math in classrooms and teachers doing mathematics together as part of their own professional development.

Displays can also showcase work that is not of the paper-and-pencil variety, such as pattern block designs, geoblock constructions, or even photographs of block constructions that had to be dismantled. The quilt designs of "favorite fourths" that children make on geoboards and matching dot paper (in a fourth grade *Investigations* unit) make an attractive display that highlights their work with both fractions and 2-D geometry (see figure 28). When fifth graders design, create, and find the volume of paper models based on 3-D solids, their final report includes a sketch, the model itself, and a written description of how they found the volume. This work makes another eye-catching display.

Exhibits can also reflect homework children have done, showing how families' contributions are valued and built upon. An example would be the display of patterns children bring from home to reinforce their work with repeating patterns in kindergarten and grade 1 (see figure 29).

Class and School Projects

Larger class projects that involve people throughout the school and the wider community also convey a sense of the math program to parents. For example, in a second grade *Investigations* unit, students investigate the number of teeth children in their class have lost. They decide how they will count missing teeth and how they will keep track of and organize their data in order to represent them. (The unit also provides comparative data from classes around the country.) The class then surveys and makes graphs that show the data for other classes in their school.

Some classes become intrigued with this project, expand the data collection to include even more classrooms in their school or district, and make large displays of their findings. In one school, the result was a whole-school representation of "Lost Teeth Data," in which each grade level was represented by a different color. Such a display can become a focal point for conversations about mathematics.

Figure 28 A "favorite fourths" display demonstrates to school visitors one way children come to understand fractional amounts and ideas about area.

Figure 29 A table display (top) shows second graders' work with dividing rectangles into fractional parts, while another one reflects support from home for a unit on pattern for kindergarten and grade 1.

There could be a box or posted sheets of chart paper to collect people's comments on the graph. For example, viewers might respond to prompts like these:

- When I look at this graph, I wonder …
- From your data, I can tell that …
- Your data make me think …

The class can then gather feedback about what people were able to learn from its graph.

One school has an all-school meeting every Friday afternoon for student performances and presentations. Parents are always welcome. One meeting each month focuses on math or science. One presentation featured students in two classrooms who, for a project in a grade 5 *Investigations* unit, investigated injuries on their school's playground. They decided what groups to survey and what counted as an injury. They developed some recommendations for improving their playground's safety based on the data they collected, and they presented it to the wider school community during this all-school time.*

Special projects like this have the power to pique the interest of not just parents, but other students, teachers, and administrators as well. They convey a rich picture of the mathematics that's happening in a particular classroom.

* Annette Raphel (2000b) shares problems used in her school-wide assemblies and describes one such assembly in depth in *Math Homework that Counts: Grades 4–6*, pp. 49–52.

Bridging School and Home: Math Problem of the Week

When I became involved in my children's school as a parent volunteer, I noticed that there were numerous opportunities for children to pursue extracurricular art, reading, music, and even writing. But there were no readily accessible ways for them to pursue math outside of what was offered in their classroom. To fill that need, I designed a Math Problem of the Week program. My goals were:

- to give elementary schoolchildren an opportunity each week to choose to do math that was strictly optional
- to spare teachers from extra work by accepting full responsibility, as a parent, for the distribution, collection, grading, or management of the process
- to provide problems that would be varied, interesting, and challenging to students ranging from kindergarten through grade 5
- to acknowledge the efforts of all students choosing to work the problems, whether they made that choice once all year or each and every week
- to raise the visibility of mathematics in our community, both in the school and at home

Getting the program started was fairly easy because the school has a widely read, parent-produced weekly newsletter that is sent home each Monday with all students. I announced and explained the new program to children and their families in an article that included the first two problems, one for students in K–2, the other for children in grades 3–5.

The first week, 24 students turned in solutions. A first grader and a third grader each won prizes at lunchtime drawings. Children did not need the correct answer in order to win a prize; they did need to submit work that showed their thinking.

continued

continued

The winners were allowed to pick a prize from assembled items purchased for $1.50 or less: pencil holders, hairclips, candy, small toys, and other odds and ends. In the second year, prizes were ice cream cone certificates, eliminating the need to stock and store a prize box. (Finding a local business that is willing to donate prizes is an idea worth pursuing. Other options might include snacks from the lunchroom or credit at the school store.)

The only request I made of teachers was that they help hand back the problems. Every Tuesday evening, I reviewed the problems, wrote responses to the children, and prepared envelopes with the children's names for the Wednesday drawings. On most papers, my comments were about the mathematical thinking the children applied to the task. My goal was to keep every comment encouraging, since the children had freely chosen to do this work.

By the end of the school year, nearly 200 different students (out of 550 in the school) had submitted a solution to a problem at least once, and three students had worked the problems every week for 19 weeks. Each week, at least one student who had never before turned in a solution did so.

Parents commented that the Math Problem of the Week became part of their households' Monday dinner-table routine, and teachers in the lunchroom overheard conversations among children about the poster-sized problems hung on the wall of the cafeteria. Families would talk over approaches and solutions and even debate what the problem for that week was really asking. As one child said, "The Problem of the Week is a kind of family math problem. My mom or dad usually helps me with it. I think grown-ups all learn from it."

A third grade parent shared the following: "Susan makes the problems engaging and accessible by using humor and featuring school staff as characters in the story problems. Because she takes the time to put comments on every paper, students who participate also get to have an exchange about math with an adult who is not the teacher or parent."

Some parents reported that their children saved the problems until the weekend when they had more free time to think. By allowing a full week before solutions were to be turned in, all children had the chance to consider the problems at their leisure.

In the program's second year, some teachers began using the Problem of the Week as a weekly problem-solving activity. Children in those classrooms were given extra points for completing the problem.

Principal Bob McAllister noticed the impact this program was having on the community: "The Problem of the Week has been enthusiastically received by families. Student interest is overwhelming in the cafeteria each Wednesday when the winners of the drawings are announced. I would like to see the program replicated in other buildings because it has been successful here. It very much reinforces the idea that practicing math problem solving can happen for fun, outside of the classroom."

—*S. Pfohman, parent volunteer (Portland, Oregon)*

Parent Volunteers and Visitors

A relatively simple way to give parents a real taste of what math is all about, without much extra effort, is to welcome them into the classroom as visitors and volunteers. Some schools have standard open hours for parents to visit classrooms; some specify that such time is to be spent on reading or math. Teachers sometimes do this individually, scheduling open hours for parents to visit. Some schools offer math classes for parents, which can create a group of parents willing to volunteer in classrooms during math. These offerings do not reach only the parents who attend; many schools cite the beneficial effects of a few parents on the family community in general.

I have parents coming and volunteering … They marvel at how the kids are thinking. "How do they do this?" And they learn to think the same way as the kids. They are very instrumental in talking to other parents. They're really the ones who spread the word that this mathematics makes a lot of sense. Because they *do* talk when they are at Little League, or the supermarkets, or wherever—they talk about the kids and what they are doing in school.

—*R. Christiansen, grades 1–2 teacher (Massachusetts)*

I have parent helpers in math. They come in during math time and walk around the room helping children. They may take a small group of children who are having a difficult time in one area and play a game that builds on that concept. It's great to have this parent support. They see what's going on inside the classroom firsthand and are quick to share the excitement with others. The community enjoys hearing about good things happening at the school from these involved parents. It's been very beneficial to have parents in the classroom, for me and the children.

—*L. Altherr, grade 1 teacher (Arizona)*

Inviting Parents In: A Principal's Perspective

In New York City, there's an Open School Week, the week we give out report cards, and many parents come into school. There's one week in the fall and one week in the spring, throughout our city. And from that it struck me, when parents started seeing the progress of a lesson, and what came out of it, and the discussion from the children that comes out of an *Investigations* lesson, it really made a difference. You know, suddenly they understood it. I had a pool of parents who would come in and say, "Now I understand why these things are happening at home because I saw that lesson in the classroom." All of a sudden a lightbulb went on in the parent's mind that, "Although I didn't learn this way, I understand the rationale for it and have a deeper respect for this kind of a curriculum."

It really hit home that they understood because when we would have a Math Night, those parents would say, "Oh, yes, I saw that in my child's class, during Open School Week, and now I really understand why it's presented in that way." To make this an opportunity for everyone, this year I made the third Friday of the month a math morning—parents as math buddies.

The parents are, for the most part, very much engaged with our school. There is a segment that needs to be pulled into the school, and we're constantly trying to find ways to bring them in. … Math and literacy nights are huge, but those events bring in the parents that don't necessarily need to come; it's the *others* that we want to see. For those parents, who may not be as articulate or as educated as some of the others, it may feel uncomfortable or embarrassing to be in those large groups. But in a small situation, such as their child's classroom, it's a lot friendlier for them.

—*A. Carillo, principal (New York)*

Inviting Parents In: A Teacher's Perspective

We have what's called Family/School Partnership, where parents come in the first and third Friday of each month. The first Friday is literacy, and the third Friday is devoted to math. One father asked me early on where the math textbook was. I said, "There is no textbook, there's a work activity book. It will be going home every now and then, but not every night. Watch for a baggie and an explanation of whatever activity we're going to be doing." He wasn't too thrilled with this, so I said, "You know what? Why don't you come in on the third Friday this month?"

So he came in, and we did the riddle activity "Guess My Number." This was a fairly easy activity, not too complicated. I modeled for him first, of course, and then we broke up into groups, and some of the kids had their chance to try to stump him. And he did pretty well, working with his own small group of children. Then we all came together and talked about "What did you notice?" and "What clues were given?" and "As a strategy, what clues would you use first?" And lo and behold, he loved the whole thing. I mean, he said, "I will come back." It's hard for him to take off from work, but he said, "I will come back."

I feel it's a matter of exposing them—so when their child comes home with a work activity book, or a sheet, or a baggie of number cards, the parents don't wonder "What are you supposed to do with this?" Instead, after visiting the classroom, the parents start to see, "Hey, this is how it's being done, and this is the language, and this is what I should be saying to my daughter. This is why she comes home and is doing math with splitting numbers instead of carrying over." It gives them a sense that they understand what the program is about. So bring the parents in! Once you hook them, then I think it will be a lot easier.

—*I. M. Marcial, grade 3 teacher (New York)*

Back-to-School Night or Open House

I start off at Back-to-School Night saying, "Here's a problem we did two weeks into the school year, and here are six different ways that six different kids did it." They seem to find that pretty powerful. I usually try to show parents their own child's work, and they usually end feeling the way I used to, saying, "Wow, I had no idea that kids could do this, that they would know that much."
—*N. Serafin, grades 3–4 teacher (Arizona)*

Back-to-School Night is a prime opportunity to share information about the math program. Many teachers ask parents to mentally solve a math problem that their children have solved in the first few weeks of school. When parents share their methods for solving it, they are often surprised to hear several different ways shared. Teachers then share a variety of the children's strategies for the same problem and talk through the mathematical ideas children are making sense of. For example, suppose the problem is 25 + 38:

"Jerome first added the 20 and the 30. He started with the tens and then moved to the ones and dealt with what was left. So Jerome understands that the 2 and the 3 are actually 20 and 30 and that adding those first will actually get him pretty close."

"Nicola saw that 38 was close to 40, and she knew that would be an easier number for her to think about. So she added 25 and 40 and then took away the two extra she had added onto the 38 to make it 40. She understands that she can change numbers to make them easier, and she is able to keep track of and compensate for the changes that she makes."

Comparing the children's strategies to those the parents used is often a fruitful conversation:

"How is Nicola's strategy similar to the one suggested by Mrs. Torres, who added 25 and 35, and then 3 more?"

Also valuable is a discussion that compares the children's strategies to the traditional algorithms and introduces the idea of computational *fluency*, which is one of the goals of *Investigations*. Fluency can be explained as including three ideas: *efficiency*—is the child's strategy easy for him or her to carry out and keep track of?; *accuracy*—does the child get the right answer?; and *flexibility*—can the child choose a strategy based on the numbers or situation in the problem? (Russell, 2000a and 2000b). Looking at the children's strategies in this light, how do they stack up against the traditional algorithm? What do their strategies convey about what the children understand about addition? about place value?

> On the second day of school, I present an addition problem to my class and we look at all the different ways we can solve it. Usually there are four or five different strategies that I record on chart paper and post on the bulletin board. Then on Back-to-School Night, I share the different strategies the students have come up with for solving this one problem. I tell parents, "You may see this strategy, or you may see this strategy, or you may see this strategy."
>
> Before Back-to-School Night, some of my students say about a particular strategy, "My mom didn't want me to do it that way," and I tell them, "She will—after Back-to-School Night next week." I talk the parents through the mathematics and really try to get them to understand the process of learning.
>
> —D. Gordon, teacher leader (Arizona)

Parent-Teacher Conferences

Another more formal opportunity teachers have to "talk math" with parents is conference time. Some teachers build in a shorter conference in the beginning of the year, and most schedule official conferences twice a year. Many teachers see this as a critical opportunity to sit with parents and really look at their child's mathematical thinking and math work. What are the child's strengths? Where is he or she struggling? What kinds of strategies is the child using to solve number and computation problems? geometry and spatial problems? How comfortable is she working with data? How is he doing with the basic facts? How are you as a teacher pushing the child to the next level in each of these areas? How are you working to challenge (or support) children at each end of the range?

It is important to keep in mind the research that shows how important and powerful such conversations can be. In one study:

> Overwhelmingly, parents indicated that they learn the most about their child's progress by talking with the teacher. … Parents offered comments that emphasized the value of receiving specific information about their child's strengths and weaknesses … In this study, third-grade parents considered report cards, hearing from the teacher, and seeing graded samples of student work to be much more useful in learning about their child's progress than standardized tests. Though in interview data parents often mentioned the need for comparative information to know how to interpret their own child's progress, they trust the teacher to tell them how their child is doing in relation to grade-level expectations or to other children in the class. (Shepard & Bliem, 1995, pp. 26, 31)

> At the beginning of the year, I have 15-minute conferences with parents so that I can hear from them about their goals and expectations for their child for the year. It's nice to be able to meet with parents right away and begin to feel connected with them. During these conferences this year, a lot of concerns came up about math. Parents were concerned about how their children were doing in math, whether they needed extra help or extra challenges. I would note that and then, a few weeks later, either through a phone call or a letter, I would let them know how things were going.
>
> —R. Musser, grade 4 teacher (Massachusetts)

I had a parent in a conference say, "I'd like you to give some math that's a bit more challenging, this is way too easy for my child." I said, "Let me show you something in his math journal." We looked, and it was evident in his work where the child was able to understand and do the problem, and even more evident, on the next page, where he was *not* able to do the problem. I said, "Look, at this point your child is very comfortable and can answer these questions, but here (looking at the next page), he doesn't have the understanding for solving these problems. So, for me to raise the numbers or to put him in a more difficult situation when he hasn't even grasped this concept would be unfair." And the parent said, "Oh, OK." I am trying to help parents move from what they perceive their child knows and understands to actual conceptual understandings. A child's own math work is the best indicator of these understandings, and as the teacher, I try to act as a guide to show and interpret this information for the parents.

—*D. Gordon, teacher leader (Arizona)*

This time, I really took time during my parent/teacher conferences to show parents the math. I talked to them about how their child solved problems and showed them how I planned to move their child on from really inefficient strategies to more efficient ones.

—*D. Ong, grade 3 teacher (Arizona)*

Reaching Parents at Home

Written communication is another way to reach parents with mathematical information and images of their child's mathematical work. Research suggests that parents particularly appreciate seeing graded samples of their child's work. In one study, third grade parents said that such "informal sources help them learn about the quality of education by giving them firsthand information about the school curriculum, what expectations were being set, and how caring the teacher is with students. In particular, parents said that seeing the actual work that students brought home let them judge whether what was being taught was worthwhile" (Shepard & Bliem, 1995, pp. 26–27). Many teachers supplement student work with additional information, either from the *Investigations* curriculum or from their own hand.

Investigations Family Letters

Each *Investigations* unit includes a Family Letter that explains the mathematics, gives examples of problems and student strategies, and suggests related activities that can be done at home. Some teachers send home the Family Letter for each unit while others use the ideas in them to write their own.

I usually rewrite the letters to parents myself. We don't regularly give homework in kindergarten, but what the Family Letters suggest feels like a really manageable request—games to play and concepts to explore at home. And the parents seem to appreciate the suggestions in the letters. Most parents want to do math with their children but don't always know what to do. The Family Letters help the parents work with their children at home in a way that is in sync with their classroom experiences.

—*K. Sillman, kindergarten teacher (New York)*

Teacher Notes and Math Emphases

Teacher Notes from the units can help parents understand the mathematics children are tackling, the ways children struggle with and make sense of mathematical ideas, and the strategies teachers are using to help, challenge, support, and push children further. Some teachers copy Teacher Notes straight from the unit and send them home as is, or attached to a newsletter. Teachers find certain notes to be particularly helpful; for example, a third grade teacher sends home "Two Powerful Addition Strategies" early each year. A second grade teacher likes to send home "Students' Addition and Subtraction Strategies" and "Developing Numerical Strategies," and a fifth grade teacher shares "Two Important Ways of Building Numbers" and "About Cluster Problems." Others may borrow ideas from a Teacher Note as they craft their own letter to families about particular math topics.

> There's a Teacher Note in the combining and separating unit that explains why we teach children the way we do. I rewrite this note for parents. Because a lot of times, the children will be doing *Investigations* in school, but when they're with their parents, their parents tell them to use the algorithm. So I send home this letter and also explain at parent conferences what I want them to do, and how and why; then they'll do it at home as well. And parents have been very open to it. I haven't met any parents who say no.
>
> —*S. Bernow, grades 1–2 teacher (Massachusetts)*

Still others use features such as "About the Mathematics in This Unit" or the Mathematical Emphases listed throughout each unit to craft helpful notes to parents.

> I find that reading the objectives for the unit, and then reading the sessions for one investigation, gives me a global sense of what I'm striving for. Then, if I take a look at each particular session, I get specific goals. In my weekly newsletters, where I update the parents on what we're doing in math and science, I can specifically say, "In math over the next two weeks, children will be working on combining fractions," or whatever the goals are. So when parents see the games and activities coming home, they can say, "Oh, here's how this is coming into play."
>
> —*S. Huard, grade 3 teacher (Massachusetts)*

Teacher-Created Newsletters

School or classroom newsletters are a good way to share examples of student work and, in doing so, offer some images of the math (see figure 30). Some teachers also offer activities to do at home that build on the mathematics on display in the newsletter.

> I send out newsletters with work samples to show what students have been doing and I tell what we'll be doing next. "This month we're working on multiplication. Your child might be doing it with arrays or he might look at friendly numbers. In other words, he might say, "29 times 6 is almost like 30 times 6." When they see the children's actual work with different types of solutions, the parents take some time to look at it, and they think "Oh, that's what they're doing in there."
>
> —*N. Serafin, grades 3–4 teacher (Arizona)*

Portfolios

For a more complete picture, some teachers assemble a packet of each child's work to be sent home (and then returned) at the end of a unit. One teacher has the children write a cover letter about what they have learned; parents read the letter, look through the work, and then sign and return the portfolio. Other teachers gather samples of children's work into a class booklet to share with families (sometimes using the copy machine to shrink more than one paper onto one page).

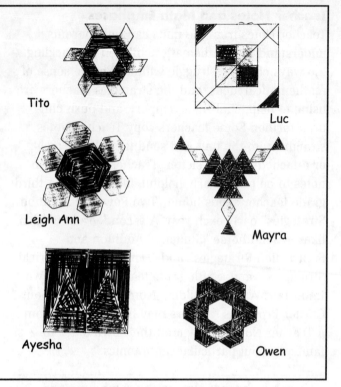

ROOM 12 MATH NEWS
Mirror and Rotational Symmetry

We have been investigating two kinds of symmetry in math class—mirror and rotational. Kyle says that mirror symmetry means "It's the same on both sides of the line." Heather says it's "when you use the same shapes on both sides of the design," and Lauren says, "If you fold it, it will end up the same on both sides." Shane says your design has rotational symmetry if you can "turn the page and see the same thing," and Conor says "it's the same on every side when you rotate it." Can you tell which designs have mirror symmetry? which have rotational symmetry? which have both? (It was challenging to make a design with ONLY rotational symmetry.)

Tito

Luc

Leigh Ann

Mayra

Ayesha

Owen

Figure 30 A fourth grade teacher's newsletter informs families about their class work with symmetry.

Math Journals

An even more comprehensive way to share children's work with families is to introduce a math journal. Students do all their math class work, as well as homework assignments, in this journal. Keeping all the material together in one place provides children with a system of organization and gives families critical information about what's being taught in math class. These journals also provide a reference that children and their parents can use to find the meaning of a certain term or a way to solve a given type of problem.

I had a student who was struggling with factors and multiples, and the parent said, "She told me what she was doing, but she didn't have anything written down. She said she couldn't remember." All the things had been on the board, and we went over strategies in class, but she couldn't remember because she did not write anything down. So now I have them copy strategies from the board into their math journal and write what we've

talked about. If she writes, "these are what multiples are, these are what factors are," and takes her journal home, then the parent has a clue. The child reinforces it by telling her parent what has happened in class, and that is a learning experience, also. I really feel it's a great leap in communication and a help for the child who is struggling.

—*M. Wolfson, grades 3–4 gifted and talented teacher (Arizona)*

Conclusion

Adopting any one of the ideas in this chapter is a step toward good communication between school and home, but the general wisdom from school districts that have successful programs is that a wide variety of approaches, including both one time events and ongoing efforts, is the best way to help parents see, understand, and get excited about the mathematics in *Investigations*.

Chapter 8
Seminars, Workshops, and Classes for Parents

As valuable as a math night can be for communicating with parents, only so much can be done in a couple of hours. Consequently, more and more schools and districts across the country are undertaking work with parents in deeper, longer-term ways, through a variety of multi-session classes or seminars. These schools are trying to do more than tell parents about new standards or explain a new curriculum. They are intent on forging stronger links between families and the school mathematics program.

> The presenter at one evening event "sought to convey the ideas behind the mathematics reform movement to the parents by engaging them in problems requiring mathematical reasoning, sharing examples of students' work, and describing some of her own experiences as a classroom teacher and mathematics learner. ... While the parents seemed to appreciate the lecturer's examples of students successfully solving mathematical problems (many of which involved demonstrations of computational ingenuity), one evening's worth of interesting anecdotes doesn't necessarily provide enough information to reassure parents that this new approach to mathematics is educationally sound, or that it will benefit their own children." (Goldsmith, Mark, & Kantrov, 2000, p. 101)

Districts that are considering in-depth work with families will have in mind their own goals: Do they want a proactive way to address parents' questions and concerns? Is the idea to give parents ideas and methods for helping children with math at home? Do they want to create a pool of parents who understand and support the school's mathematical agenda, who can articulate it to others, and who can serve as classroom volunteers? At the same time, districts will need to find out what parents are interested in. A brief survey or questionnaire, sent out early in the year, can ask parents what they would most like to learn about and what schedules would work best for them. There are logistical concerns as well: Who will teach the classes? Where will they be held? What course materials will be used? Who will attend, and how will they be recruited?

This chapter briefly describes five projects that model in-depth work with parents in widely ranging communities. Evening, morning, and afternoon classes have been offered. Some serve a group that remained steady from week to week, while others are open to any participants who can make it for that particular session. Some serve a fairly homogenous group, while others are characterized by a variety of languages, cultures, and educational levels. Each has been successful in its own community. Following these models is a summary of what facilitators are learning about designing and offering such programs for parents. Considering this section along with the five models can help a school or district create a suitable approach to meet the needs of nearly any community.

MODEL 1: A Parent Academy

Nature of the seminar: A Parent Academy involved four evening classes, each $1\frac{1}{2}$ hours long, held over two months (one class every other week). Two academies were offered, one for parents of children in grades 3–5, the other for grades 6–8. While parents attended the Parent Academy, children could attend a Student Academy run by another faculty member, where they played familiar board games involving strategic planning such as Connect Four, Checkers, Mancala, Tic Tac Toe, and Battleship.

The organizers: The Academies were developed by district teacher leaders Sandy James and Troy Regis and were funded by the Phoenix Urban Systemic Initiative.

General goals: This district hoped to help parents understand how children learn mathematics, particularly through *Investigations* (the district's elementary grades curriculum) and *Connected Math* (the district's middle school curriculum), and to offer support in helping children with math homework.

Source of ideas: To develop the elementary Academy, Sandy James used the *Investigations* curriculum for grades 3–5, as well as *Bridges to Classroom Mathematics* (COMAP, n.d.), a collection of professional development sessions that explore topics and content particular to the *Investigations* curriculum. Troy Regis used the *Connected Math* materials and the district curriculum to design the middle school Academy.

Recruitment: Flyers in both English and Spanish were sent home with students in grades 3–8. It was announced that a Spanish translator would be available at each meeting. As an incentive, participants who completed the Academy received the book *Math on Call* (Great Source Education Group, 1998), as well as a Texas Instruments-34 calculator.

Class content: The *Investigations*-related Academy focused on computation and alternative strategies for solving computation problems. Instructors shared examples of student work to show children's understanding of math and the strategies they use to solve problems. Parents worked on computational and problem-solving activities and talked about how they could help children with math homework. To send the message that mathematics is more than just arithmetic, this academy also explored activities from each of the other strands, giving parents a glimpse of all of the areas their children would explore in this curriculum.

The parents: Each Academy drew a group of 12–15 parents. The teacher leader for grades 3–5 noted that "these parents are even more supportive of what we're doing in class because they see it from a different perspective. Their only criticism was that I didn't give them enough homework!"

> Our "parent math academy" is a place for parents to learn what their children are learning in math, and how, and why. Our academies present challenging math problems to parents, then parents share the methods they use for solving such problems and discuss the math involved. Through these academies, we want parents to see how their children are making sense of math in a deeper manner. As they grow in their appreciation of the field of math, parents are better able to support the math their children are grappling with in the classroom.
>
> —*L. Califano, principal (Arizona)*

MODEL 2: Parent Breakfasts

Nature of the seminar: A series of five parent breakfasts (7:30–9:00 A.M.) was held at the school over a period of several months; parents could attend one or more sessions.

The organizer: Lucy Wittenberg, a veteran teacher with professional development experience in mathematics, developed this workshop series for a small private school in Massachusetts.

General goals: The school wanted something more than a Math Night to involve parents with mathematics and with the newly adopted *Investigations* curriculum. The intention was to inform and educate parents about the program, address specific questions, and give parents a forum to talk with one another as they observed their children working in the new curriculum.

Source of ideas: The video series *Relearning to Teach Arithmetic* (Russell et al., 1999a, 1999b) and units from *Investigations* were used to create this series of meetings.

Recruitment: The principal at this school sent out a questionnaire early in the year, asking what parents would like to learn more about in regard to their child's education. Overwhelmingly, they replied "Math." The workshop series was advertised to all parents, and the school specifically invited those parents who seemed particularly concerned or excited about the new curriculum. Given a history of poorly attended evening events, the school chose breakfast meetings to increase the possibility that parents could attend after dropping their child off at school. The topic of each meeting was announced in the school newsletter a week in advance.

Class content: In order to specifically address real parent concerns, the content was developed partly in conjunction with those who attended. The agendas for each of the five sessions follow.

- *Session 1* To gain a better understanding of what their children were doing in class, parents first solved some mental computation problems. The discussion centered on what it means to have a deep understanding of the four operations; how that supports children in developing strategies that make sense to them; and the mathematical knowledge children need in order to develop strategies that are flexible, efficient, and accurate. Parents were then asked what issues they would like to discuss, and subsequent sessions were organized around their responses.

- *Session 2* This session addressed the question, How does the curriculum meet the needs of different ability levels? Parents examined the range of strategies used to solve multiplication problems in one set of student work. They saw how one problem can address the needs of many different children, because the children are able to enter a problem in different ways that make sense to them. For example, third graders finding the number of legs on a group of elephants might draw a picture and count the legs, repeatedly add fours, or use multiplication facts. The role of the teacher then becomes encouraging children to use strategies that push their thinking.

- *Session 3* This session was characterized mainly by parent-to-parent discussion of how to support children in doing math at home. Issues included children who get frustrated and children who finish an assignment too quickly. The facilitator helped groups think about questions like these: What does it mean when my child says, "I don't understand"? How can I best respond in this situation? How do I know if a problem is too difficult or too easy? How could I change a problem to make it the right level for my child?

- *Session 4* In a session devoted to the role of games, participants looked closely at some multiplication and division games from *Investigations,* ranging from those appropriate for kindergarten to some from the fifth grade units. Parents played each game with a partner and discussed what skills children would be practicing. The facilitator provided a few commercially-available games as resources. (*Math Packs*, TERC, 2000)

- *Session 5* To address questions about assessment, parents solved sample assessment problems, watched students solve the same problems on videotape, and analyzed student work for those problems. The facilitator asked participants to consider, "What do these children know?," "What else would you like to know?," and "What might further their understanding?" The final conversation focused on the school's report-writing system and the criteria teachers use to assess students. Parents had the chance to express to the principal what was useful and frustrating about that system.

The parents: A group of predominantly the same 15–20 parents attended the workshops. According to the facilitator, they ranged from "curious, to supportive, to those with ongoing issues." The principal of the school attended all sessions.

MODEL 3: Mathematics Workshops for Mothers ("Talleres Matemáticos")

Nature of the seminar: This group met at a district middle school every two weeks from September through May, from 10:30 A.M. to 12 noon.

The organizers: Talleres Matemáticos was an outgrowth of the research project "Project BRIDGE: Linking home and school: A bridge to the many faces of mathematics," funded by the U.S. Department of Education/OERI (see Civil, 1998). Led by Marta Civil, a mathematics educator, and Rosi Andrade, a researcher, both at the University of Arizona, the project was a collaboration between university-based researchers and ten teacher-researchers who work primarily with minority and economically disadvantaged students.

General goals: The facilitators hoped to enhance participants' mathematical understandings while also learning what parents thought about math itself and about math in the schools. One goal was to help parents assist their children with (school) mathematics at home; another was to tap into the mathematics these women already knew and used in their daily lives, in order to highlight the connection between school mathematics and the mathematical tasks relevant to typical occupations in the community (e.g., construction worker, carpenter, seamstress).

Source of ideas: A variety of reform-based mathematics curriculum materials informed the creation of these workshops.

Recruitment: These workshops, conducted entirely in Spanish, were started with a group of mothers who were already meeting for literature discussions led by a university researcher. As the mathematics workshops became more regular, additional mothers were recruited through fliers and personal contacts. The group was kept small (6–8 mothers, maximum of 10), so the workshops could be run like a study group in which everybody comes to learn and share knowledge.

Class content: The main focus of these workshops was doing mathematics together as adults, in much the same way that children are asked to tackle mathematics in their classrooms. Facilitators selected open-ended activities with many possible solution strategies, and participants worked in groups to solve the problems. Workshops explored such topics as geometry (occasionally using Logo), strategy and topological games, fractions, probability, patterns, and algebraic thinking.

The parents: The participants in these workshops were mothers, most of whom were working-class, Spanish-speaking, and immigrant. Many were motivated by the desire to assist their children with mathematics at home. Their educational backgrounds were quite diverse, from several years of elementary school to high school. Participants shared their experience with everyday activities involving mathematics. Many of the women sewed and would exchange hints and ideas and demonstrate their methods. Facilitators tried to make the mathematics embedded in such activities more explicit. One participant drew a quarter circle "by holding her measuring tape fixed at one corner of her rectangle (the center) and marking points 25 cm from that point, then joining them to get her quarter circle" (Civil, 1998), allowing an exploration of geometric ideas and relationships.

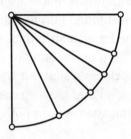

MODEL 4: Morning Math for Parents

Nature of the seminar: This series consisted of four morning workshops, each $1\frac{1}{2}$ hours long (8:00–9:30); participants could attend one or more.

The organizers: This series was developed by Rose Christiansen and Nancy Buell, classroom teachers and teacher leaders in a public school district in Massachusetts. They also lead math workshops for teachers nationally.

General goals: This school hoped to address parent concerns, to provide experience with the math their children were learning and the way they were

learning it, to give parents ways to work with their children at home, and to develop confident classroom volunteers.

Source of ideas: Activities from *Investigations* and *Bridges to Classroom Mathematics*, (COMAP, n.d.), as well as the Marilyn Burns (1994) video *What Are You Teaching My Child?* were used to create these workshops.

Recruitment: The school first sponsored an evening math meeting for parents to talk about mathematics education reform and the *Investigations* curriculum and to explore some specific number activities—including Capture 5, a game from a grade 2 unit, and How Do I Solve It?, computation problems from a grade 5 unit. After a short question-and-answer session, parents who had children in grades 2–4 were invited to the morning workshop series.

Class content: For their focus on the number strand (computation, estimation, place value, mental math, number sense), facilitators presented activities modeled on those children do in the classroom, such as solving mental math problems, Counting Around the Class, and Guess My Number, as well as various *Investigations* games. Parents discussed

- the mathematics in the activities
- how children think about the activities, by looking at sample written work and videos of children (from *Relearning to Teach Arithmetic,* Russell et al., 1999a, 1999b), and by trying to use the children's strategies to solve additional problems
- how to work with children, including questions to ask them
- ways to adapt the games and activities for children who are having difficulty or need more challenge

Parents also received take-home materials to use with their children, and each subsequent workshop began with parents sharing their experience doing the activity at home.

The parents: In the first year, 35 different parents (from a school of 600 children) attended one or more workshop sessions; some attended all of them. That group of 35 had a ripple effect on the rest of the school. There was demand for more sessions the following year and requests that they deal with fractions. In the second year, the sessions explored data, geometry, and fractions. The plan was to set up a two-year cycle of morning workshops for parents, cycling between number and other content as long as interest continued.

> Parent workshops that provide hands-on activities are extremely valuable in helping parents to understand the depth and breadth of the *Investigations* program. These workshops quickly dispel parents' impressions that the *Investigations* program is not rigorous enough, too repetitive, or lacking in opportunities for extension. Through their own participation, parents can appreciate the challenging nature of the mathematical activities and the critical thinking and problem solving that children are engaged in. Our experience has been that parents who participate in the workshops are impressed with the *Investigations* program and communicate this to other parents.
>
> —B. Shea, principal (Massachusetts)

MODEL 5: Developing Mathematical Ideas: Seminars for Parents and Caregivers

Nature of the seminar: This series of meetings was held for 2–3 hours weekly, in the afternoons or evenings, over a 4- to 8-week period.

The organizers: These seminars were first offered by Amy Morse and Polly Wagner and were continued by Morse and Liz Sweeney. All three are veteran teachers in the Boston area who are also experienced math coaches and professional development leaders.

General goals: The facilitators hoped to immerse parents in the language, content, and environments of school mathematics, in order to help them appreciate its complexity and enable them to support their children's learning at home.

Source of ideas: *Developing Mathematical Ideas* (Schifter, Bastable, & Russell, 1999a, 1999b), a professional development curriculum for teachers focused on children's mathematical thinking, and the *Investigations* curriculum, provided much of the course content.

Recruitment: Strategies for recruitment varied according to the target population. One seminar was aimed exclusively at the parents of the 65 third graders in one school. Seminar organizers sent out letters and flyers; the third grade teachers sent home letters of support with children; the school administration wrote a letter of support; and the two grant-funded parent leaders, one Spanish- and one English-speaking, systematically called all of the third grade families in the school. In addition, the principal sent out weekly reminder notices and attended and participated in each session. All communication was in both English and Spanish.

Class content: The DMI Seminars for Parents emphasized four types of activities:

1. *Sharing math histories* In the first meeting, participants shared their experiences and memories of math classes in small groups. These histories included memories of a particular teacher, classroom, or moment; of teaching methods; of specific content areas; or of being perceived as particularly good or bad at math. Then the group looked for common themes among people's stories. This conversation set the tone, established trust, and gave facilitators a window into parents' beliefs. It was typically an emotional discussion that included vivid memories and painful stories, along with more straightforward recollections.

2. *Discussing cases* "Cases" are classroom vignettes that illustrate children's mathematical thinking. In this seminar, written cases (authored by classroom teachers) and videotaped portions of math classes were drawn from the *Developing Mathematical Ideas* (DMI) curriculum. After reading or watching the video, parents talked about what they noticed. The focus was on listening carefully to children, to see what sense they were making of the mathematics. As they puzzled about the logic of a child's idea, parents considered why the idea was difficult or complicated for the child. Through their study of children's work, parents came to understand mathematical ideas for themselves as well.

> Video is a powerful tool for parents to both see children actually articulating their strategies and also to help them appreciate the teacher's craft. It seems to really help parents *believe* that it's possible, that it's happening, and that children are actually discussing mathematical ideas in the same ways the parents are working so hard to do in their own parent seminar.
>
> —*A. Morse, Senior Research Associate (Massachusetts)*

3. *Doing mathematics* At each meeting, parents spent some time doing mathematics themselves. Activities were drawn from the content of elementary school mathematics but framed in a way that challenged adults. For example, at the first meeting, participants mentally solved a computation problem, then described how they did it. This activity quickly demonstrated that the "standard algorithms" are not the only methods suitable for solving math problems. In other activities, parents explored common math games and used manipulatives (cubes, base ten blocks) to solve a mathematical problem.

4. *Assignments: reading, writing, talking, reflecting* Participants completed both in-class and homework assignments. Homework involved reading a case for the next class, solving a problem, or writing further thoughts about a new idea. On occasion, parents were asked to talk with their child (conduct an interview) about a particular idea and then record what happened—or remember it so they could describe it aloud in class. Discussions were a major part of in-class work, and parents were asked at the end of each class to write (or dictate) quick reflections on their work.

The parents: Groups have varied widely. Enrollment ranged from fewer than 10 parents to more than 20. Some groups included teachers and administrators from the schools involved, working alongside the parents as learners. Seminars have served parents in an urban public school where 68 percent of the children are bilingual (Spanish-speaking), a public pilot school, and a small progressive independent school in a middle-class suburb. The formal education of participants ranged from elementary school through Ph.D., often within the same group. Attendees included African American, Latino, Greek, Trinidadian, and Anglo parents, some living below the poverty line, others middle and upper-middle class. Some participants spoke only English; some primarily Spanish, and others only Spanish. One class was conducted simultaneously in English and Spanish with the help of a bilingual teacher as translator.

As facilitators conducted the classes, they made some changes to meet the needs of each particular group. In some instances the length of the seminar was reduced from 8 to 4 weeks, and the length of each class from three hours to two. Seminars were held in the late afternoons or the early evenings, depending on the preferences of participants. Childcare was not offered per se, but a sprinkling of children attended each seminar, either doing their homework or participating in the math.

Things to Consider for Parent Seminars

Existing classes and seminars offer many lessons for those who are contemplating a similar offering. Facilitators are discovering which experiences are particularly powerful for parents and which seem critical. They are learning how to accommodate people from a variety of academic and ethnic backgrounds, people who speak English and those who don't, and people who are and are not comfortable and confident with math, reading, or school in general. Facilitators are learning how to successfully design, offer, and evaluate an in-depth parent course. Finally, they are learning a lot about the effect of such courses on parents' beliefs and attitudes about math and math teaching.

Planning the Content

Paying attention to parents' memories "Facing your mathematical history can be a perilous thing," or so says the leader of a math seminar for parents (Morse & Wagner, 1998, p. 362). Sharing one's personal mathematical history is sometimes a planned activity for all participants. In other seminars, memories of school mathematics come up voluntarily as adults solve a math problem, watch a video of a math class, or talk about what they want for their children. Whatever the situation, this conversation invariably occurs and is often filled with emotion. Here, for example, are not uncommon memories:

> "Third grade—copying my best friend's math (fractions) homework, not having a clue as to what they meant—Painful sessions with my father over word problems, usually ending in tears (mine)—All memories of elementary school were miserable (i.e., humiliation and anxiety)—The only positive experience was geometry."

> "Math class consisted of each kid in turn standing up and reciting the addition tables and multiplication tables. For each wrong answer or missed step, the teacher

would step up and smack the palm of your hand with a ruler." (Morse & Wagner, 1998, p. 361)

Even people who recall math being easy for them often speak of friends or family members for whom this was not true. Other parents say they knew they understood more mathematics—knew that math wasn't just those facts and algorithms—but never had the opportunity to share or further explore those thoughts. This "personal history" is critical to understanding the origins of the questions that parents bring to class. These questions often come from an emotional place. Facilitators note that listening carefully to parents' math histories helps them answer the real concerns behind the voiced questions and talk *to* or *with* parents rather than *at* them.

Making adaptations The range of participants in the five models described earlier is incredibly wide, much like typical elementary school classrooms, where teachers must do their best to support and challenge each child individually. Facilitators must assess each new group and make decisions about how to adapt the seminar to that audience. Cases written in English cannot be used with participants who speak and read only Spanish, nor with those who are not fluent readers. It would be meaningless to offer videotapes in English to participants who speak only Russian or Vietnamese without a translator present. Ideally, seminars include some video of children who speak the first language of the participants, possibly from the school or district hosting the seminar. Translators can translate written cases, assignments completed in participants' first language, the class itself, and/or participants' comments and reflections. Written cases can be read or described aloud to the class. Parents might dictate rather than write their end-of-class reflections.

Finding mathematical activities that are at the right level of challenge for a group of adults can be a similarly daunting task. Facilitators need to think carefully about the individuals in front of them and how to structure and present such mathematical tasks. They need to keep in mind that "for some, doing arithmetic in a school setting, sitting in a chair meant for a ten-year-old alongside other parents who are not yet friends or colleagues, feels intimidating. For a number of us, the experience can conjure up old feelings of shame and a painful remembrance of school as life's choice maker—'smart' folks land here, 'stupid' folks land there. And we all knew that mathematics drew the dividing line" (Morse & Wagner, 1998, p. 361).

Don't assume (or convey the assumption) that the mathematics will necessarily be easy or obvious to those working on the problem, or assume that everyone will feel comfortable volunteering ideas in a mathematics discussion. (Goldsmith, Mark, & Kantrov, 2000, p. 104)

Many facilitators report that participants within a group are engaging with the same problem on several levels. Some are, perhaps for the first time, making sense of the mathematics in a meaningful way. Others are challenged by the realization that there are other ways to solve problems and by trying to understand those ways and how they relate to the one "right" way they have always known. Still others are intrigued with the ways children think about and make sense of mathematics, and how children's strategies can actually show a much deeper understanding of, say, the operation of multiplication than if they simply correctly memorized and used the standard U.S. algorithm.

Doing the math is crucial Facilitators resoundingly agree that *doing math* is crucial; it is the core of the work adults in these classes do. When parents do challenging elementary-school mathematics for themselves, they have a keener appreciation of children's mathematical thinking as they read about real students, watch them on video, analyze sample student work, interview children, and do mathematics with them.

One of the best ways to give people a sense of the kind of mathematical thinking promoted by standards-based curricula is to have them work on mathematics problems. Doing mathematics helps make abstract talk about goals and pedagogies seem more concrete. It gives parents a chance to experience firsthand some opportunities for mathematical reasoning, and may actually help build their confidence in their own mathematical thinking. Doing mathematics also gives parents a chance to see how the curriculum develops certain mathematical ideas. (Goldsmith, Mark, & Kantrov, 2000, p. 104)

Engaging parents with the mathematics is critical in changing their perceptions of math. In fact,

Over and over, parents told us that their perception of elementary school mathematics revolved around memorization and recitation. In some cases, it was painful, in others thrilling, for parents to begin to delve conceptually into mathematics for themselves in the seminar. Parents should upend these perceptions to appreciate the complexities in elementary school mathematics. To hold on to a vision of mathematics as a feat of memorization is to underestimate the work that is possible in classrooms and in mathematics learning. (Morse & Wagner, 1998, p. 364)

Considering Program Logistics
Deciding to create and conduct a seminar for parents involves commitment—of time, people, and resources. Here are questions to think about.

Who is the target group and what's the best schedule? Should the class be offered to the parents of children in a particular grade level? in a band of grades, such as K–2? in the whole school or district? When will it be offered? How will school schedules accommodate this work?

These decisions depend on the makeup of the community and how far along the school or district is in implementing a new curriculum. The number of students and families—as well as the level of interest among parents—will affect the number of classes a school or district wants to offer. Is there a particular effort aimed at one grade level or band? Is one grade level or band particularly interested in or concerned about mathematics? Are parents willing to travel farther to attend a district-level class? Or are they more likely to come to a class in their own child's school, or at a community center? A survey can indicate what times and places work best for most parents. Several classes at different times can accommodate parents with different scheduling needs.

Who will lead the course? The number of seminars to be offered also depends on the number of teachers and others who are willing and able to design and facilitate such a class. Are there people in the school or district who have enough experience with *Investigations* and who are also interested in creating or leading such a course for parents? Are there parent leaders who might do this work, tackle it with a teacher as a partner, or apprentice with a teacher leader? Are there outside collaborators who might be interested in such a project? How will teachers (and others) be compensated for time spent on such a course? How can funds be corralled to support this work?

In the five models described above, different types of people have done this work. Some classes were funded by a grant from an outside agency; others were done on school time or with school funds. Some facilitators are classroom teachers; others are teacher leaders, lead teachers, math coaches, math specialists, or staff developers—people for whom offering such a class is a part of their job. Other projects involve outside collaborators: a consultant, curriculum developer, university professor, or researcher. All have knowledge of and experience with math reform and standards-based curricula, both in theory and in action with children and teachers. They are skilled facilitators, comfortable

moderating a discussion among a diverse group of adults, but they are also able teachers and knowledgeable about mathematics content. Just like *Investigations* classroom teachers, they must have the mathematical knowledge to

- assess the math understandings and abilities of the group before them
- choose appropriate problems
- make sense of and connections among various strategies and participants' ways of thinking
- ask questions that encourage participants to reflect on, clarify, and further develop their strategies

What materials will be used? The models offer a variety of suggestions. Many developers use the *Investigations* curriculum, at least in part, to find problems and information that can be used in a class specifically for parents. Others use materials already available for working with teachers and adapt them to best serve their parent population.

Who will come? Recruiting parents for a multi-session math seminar can be challenging. There are many things to consider. How can the course be publicized to reach the most parents with information about the course, what it offers, and why it is important? What strategies can be used to welcome, accommodate, and involve participants whose first language is not English? who have childcare or transportation issues? who do not consider school a welcoming place? who have difficulties with reading or writing? with mathematics? Chapter 1, "How to Reach and Involve Parents" (p. 21), discusses such barriers to participation and what schools and staff can do to help overcome them.

How can success be gauged? Schools and districts that have given seminars for parents have a plan for collecting feedback from parents. They track who is attending and how often. It is important to be realistic in setting expectations for attendance. At first, the classes might be quite small. As news of the class spreads by word of mouth, future classes might be requested or future seminars better attended.

It is also important to collect data from the parents in these groups: what they are learning, how their thinking is changing, and what impact this seminar has had on their mathematical relationship with their child. Some facilitators gather this information during conversations; others hand out an end-of-workshop survey; and still others use exit cards that participants fill out (or dictate answers for) at the end of each class or at the conclusion of the seminar. A sample course evaluation, for collecting feedback from parents, is shown in figure 31.

What Parents Take Away

Such survey results, in addition to facilitators' own experiences, serve to illustrate how much parents are learning from these workshops, classes, and seminars.

New attitudes about math Through seminars and workshops like the ones described in this chapter, many parents develop new attitudes about mathematics and their own mathematical abilities. They find themselves excited about mathematical ideas—both their own and their child's. As they work through several sessions, parents begin to see that mathematics is something that can and should make sense and that it is something they can successfully tackle.

Morning Math for Parents

Evaluation

How many sessions did you attend (one evening, 8 morning)? _____

We are interested in your reactions to these parent workshops. Your comments will be carefully considered as we evaluate what we did and what we might do in the future. Thank you for your help.

Describe something you learned about mathematics.

_____
_____
_____
_____

Describe something you learned about how children learn mathematics.

_____
_____
_____
_____

What aspect of the workshop had the greatest impact on your thinking?

_____
_____
_____

What changes would you recommend to improve this workshop?

_____
_____
_____
_____

Would you be interested in helping [name of school]'s mathematics program by:

_____ Volunteering in a classroom

_____ Helping organize a student/parent math night

_____ Helping with a special math event during the day

_____ Other (you tell us your idea)

Would you be interested in more workshops next year, to explore mathematics and children's thinking? _____

If yes, do you prefer mornings or evenings? _____

Additional comments

_____
_____
_____
_____
_____
_____
_____
_____

Signature (optional) _____

We have enjoyed working with you!
Rose and Nancy

Figure 31 An evaluation form used by the facilitators of Model 4, Morning Math for Parents. Developed by R. Christiansen and N. Buell, Brookline Public Schools, Massachusetts. Reprinted with permission.

> I find that I now allow more time for really listening to what my son has to say ... I ask him more to explain what his thinking was behind his statements... I am amazed sometimes at his solutions—more elegant, thoughtful, and insightful than what I might have suggested. (Morse & Wagner, 1998, p. 363)

Math content Parents in these courses—which focus mainly on elementary school content—find themselves learning mathematics. It's not that they didn't know how to add, subtract, multiply, or divide (although some do have difficulty with the basic operations). But their understanding of mathematics is changing and deepening. Perhaps for the first time, a participant realizes that everyone does not solve a problem the same way, using one "right" algorithm. Perhaps a mother makes sense of "carrying" and "borrowing" in a way she never did before. Perhaps a step-father realizes that the "secret" ways he has always worked with numbers in his head are legitimate—that this is in fact how many people think. Through in-depth work in elementary school mathematics, parents begin to see and respect the complexities of the seemingly simple ideas children are struggling to make sense of, understand, and use.

Ideas about teaching While participating in a series of classes, parents are also exploring new ideas about teaching and learning in general. For example, some parents realize for the first time the power of working as a group—particularly in mathematics, which for many parents has always meant silent, individual work. As they listen to each other, they learn from each other. As they work together to solve a challenging problem, they share ideas and feel more confident than they would working on their own. Many parents, after being immersed in this work, are struck by the complexities, the challenges, and the sheer amount of work facing teachers of mathematics, even of the very young.

Helping at home Most parents leave these classes feeling better equipped to help their child with mathematics at home. For some, it is the first time they feel capable of this. They talk about listening to their child in a new way and being excited about what they hear, learn, and now understand about their child's thinking. They find that this new way of listening to their child crosses subject areas and deepens their relationship in general.

Conclusion

The facilitators of Model 5, Developing Mathematical Ideas Seminars for Parents, ask themselves the following questions to think about their ongoing work with parents:

- What can happen when parents begin to connect their own past schooling histories with the ways they respond to current math reforms?
- What can happen when parents are considered "learners" and are offered opportunities to rediscover their own mathematical ideas?
- What can we learn from parents, and what can they learn from each other, when parents are openly engaged in the learning process?
- Can the interaction between teachers and parents deepen when parents are involved in their own mathematics learning?
- How might the shift from "informing" parents to "parents as learners" impact the ways we interact with communities and the ways we understand parent involvement in schools?

Teachers are learning as much from parents as parents are from them. They are developing a deeper understanding of the barriers to true partnerships, particularly with regard to mathematics. They are discovering the power of a group of parents who have a deep experience with mathematics, who are often willing and able to talk articulately with other parents, answer their questions, and work in classrooms to support the teaching of *Investigations*. While there is still much to learn and many parents to reach, it seems that one avenue for successfully working *with* parents is creating a respectful mathematics learning community that works together over time.

After the sessions on number and two sessions each on data and geometry, parents went to the school advisory council and said that this needs to be part of our school improvement plan. I had to laugh because what they actually said was, "Every parent needs to participate in these workshops." We can't get every parent to do anything, but I thought it was a real endorsement. And they took over the leadership and the cheerleading for the *Investigations* program. It wasn't a huge number, but they are the parents that are in the building, they're the parents that are the opinion leaders and that talk about what's going on. And they became very vocal in a very positive way about the program. Other parents stopped asking teachers, "Why are you doing this?" The message got out that this is really good instruction, and it's really making children stop and think.

—*N. Buell, grade 4 teacher (Massachusetts)*

Resources and Readings

For another description of a mathematics seminar for parents, see "Learning to Listen: Lessons from a Mathematics Seminar for Parents" (Morse & Wagner, 1998).

Educators interested in a series of math nights may want to consider the Family Math series of workshops, described in "Resources and Readings" in chapter 4 (p. 63).

For more on a variety of workshops for parents, see James Vopat's two books, *The Parent Project: A Workshop Approach to Parent Involvement* (1994) and *More Than Bake Sales: The Resource Guide for Family Involvement in Education* (1998). Both books also offer models for developing parent leadership. In fact, *More Than Bake Sales* devotes a whole chapter to the topic "Parent Leadership: It Doesn't Happen Just Because You Say So."

Section Two

Perspectives on the Math Partnership

Chapter 9

A Teacher's Perspective
Engaging Parents as Partners

Margie Riddle

*This chapter is the first of three that offer differ-
ent perspectives on building a math partnership
between schools and families. Margie Riddle is a
veteran elementary teacher of third, fourth, and
fifth grades. She has long been an advocate for
the volunteer participation of community members
and parents in schools. In this chapter, she
demonstrates how one classroom teacher uses
multiple strategies to communicate with parents
and involve them in school mathematics. While
her article echoes other chapters of this book, it
offers a clear picture of how all the pieces fit
together in a particular setting.*

My principal prepared a banner that hung outside
our school office for an entire year, greeting all who
entered. The banner proclaimed, "Every interaction
with a child teaches something." Those words
haunted me as I began each school day that year,
as I'm sure they were meant to do. They were a
constant reminder that there is never *nothing* going
on in students' minds; they are always learning
something. They helped me remember how important each interaction with each child is; they made
me aware that I wanted those lessons to be productive, intellectual, ethical, supportive, and human.

That same year, my principal also had some words
of wisdom about creating successful schools: "It's
all about relationships." That statement helped me
understand that successful schools aren't just the
result of productive interactions between teachers
and students. Rather, they are the result of productive relationships among a large network of adults
who have a stake in what happens in our public
schools. Of course, the adults who have the largest
stake are the parents of our students.

As I thought back on my own role as the parent of
schoolchildren, I was startled to remember both
the intensity of the relationship I felt I had with
their school and the lack of actual contact with my
children's teachers. In fact, that contact was limited to two extremely short (10-minute) conferences
each year, for which my husband and I both had
to make special arrangements to leave work and
cover a lengthy commute. Beyond those two conferences, I received a few notes describing problems my children were having that teachers wanted me to correct, and a few frenzied phone calls of
the same nature. During my two children's entire
school careers, I contacted teachers only about
four times with concerns that we couldn't resolve
with our children at home. Those concerns all
involved something at school that was upsetting
our child or making learning difficult.

As an elementary teacher, I realize the difficulty of
doing much more—of finding and creating opportunities for more teacher-parent communication.
However, this communication is of utmost importance as we work toward changing the way we
teach mathematics. Parents must be key players in
this work. In fact, they are. They are vocal advocates for their children, and they play important
roles on local school boards and committees. But it
is difficult for parents to stay abreast of the latest
wisdom on how best to provide for the health,
education, and welfare of their children. One newspaper headline can easily raise parents' fears.

In order for parents to be effective advocates, they
must be well-informed about the differences
between how their own children are learning
mathematics and how they learned it themselves.

They need to understand that children are exploring concepts within a problem-solving situation, and that they are working cooperatively with other students, sharing ideas and explaining their thinking. They need to know that the mathematics classroom of today has much more in common with the workplace—with collaborative problem solving in real-life situations—than did the classrooms they remember from their own childhoods. They also need to feel confident that their children will acquire the basic skills of mathematics in this setting. To this end, they need to receive information about the program throughout the year, and they need to see the program in action for themselves.

As teachers we all feel extremely close to our students, especially as the year goes on. We care tremendously about their education. However, sometimes we lose sight of the fact that no matter how much we care about our students' learning, their parents care more. They care for the long term, and they care out of love.

In the days when my own children began kindergarten, we parents received a very clear message: We were not welcome beyond the office except for fund-raisers and to serve as requested chaperones. As teachers, we must now put those days in the past. If we are to be successful in changing mathematics education, we need to engage parents as our allies. They need to help us effect change, and to do that, they need to understand what we are trying to accomplish. Many teachers would say, "That's not my job," and suggest that someone else—the superintendent, the curriculum coordinator, the math specialist, the principal—take care of it. I would argue, rather, that it is exactly our job. Being successful with our students requires positive relationships with their parents. No one else can make that happen as successfully as we can.

Building a Relationship with Parents

Making parents our partners requires that we create productive relationships with many adults whom we only rarely meet face to face. Successful relationships of any kind require time, listening, and the development of trust and understanding. Teachers and parents have very little chance to cultivate any of these. It is worth the effort, though, to build a positive relationship with the 40 or so adults with whom we will interact for only one school year. We must remember that every interaction with a parent teaches something too.

From the first moment we meet, even if by phone, we need to do more listening than talking. We need to listen for parents' points of view and truly hear their concerns. Parents want very much for their children to be successful in the world, and they know that success involves mathematics. They know it is useful to have committed many math facts to memory and are therefore reasonably concerned about a math program that doesn't emphasize the memorization of facts in a recognizable or familiar way. They are receptive when we acknowledge their concerns and help them understand that their children will learn the facts they need in a more meaningful way—for example, through the third and fourth grade games that use array cards to practice the multiplication facts. Many parents, after playing array games with their children, remark, "I wish I could have learned my facts this way. This really works because now I can picture them in my mind."

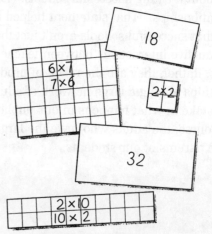

There is no doubt that in mathematics, teachers and parents want success for students. We need to put ourselves on the same side in the struggle to achieve that. If we begin each of our contacts by listening, we will learn a lot and go a long way toward building a trusting relationship.

Good relationships are built on trust, and teacher-parent relationships are no exception. Trust begins with respectful listening and an honest sharing of hopes and beliefs so that you can find common ground. Parents' trust in a teacher grows out of their perception of the teacher's relationship with their child. Looking for honestly positive things to share with parents about their children helps build that trust. Parents trust teachers when they think to themselves, "She knows and appreciates my child."

We teachers must try to understand parents as we seek to build these positive relationships. When we think parents are being critical and are attacking our program, or us, we must remember that parents often do not speak from a position of strength. Especially on the subject of mathematics education, many parents have memories of failure and humiliation. When they express apprehension about a new math program, it's often because they themselves felt unsuccessful in school. Parents want a better experience in school for their children than they had themselves—they just don't know what that would look like. If we can be patient, listen, and try to understand, they will be more likely to listen to us and to realize that we are offering just the change they are hoping for.

If we are to further the changes we are working for in mathematics education, these positive relationships with parents—based on respectful listening, trust, understanding, and appreciation of their children—must be rebuilt each year with a new group of parents. And they must be created when neither side has much time to meet and exchange ideas, even by phone. I believe that teachers need to accept the responsibility to create opportunities where it appears they do not exist.

Expanding Opportunities for Communication

I propose that teachers consider the following as specific opportunities to develop a relationship with parents: phone calls, Open House, using class volunteers, letters home, homework, parent information night, conferences, and report cards. Many of these are things that teachers do all the time. The challenge is to make strategic use of these opportunities, to expand these seemingly small occasions into meaningful experiences that will enable parents to understand our new approach to math education, and to become active supporters of it.

Phone Calls Home

We can make a point of calling the parent of each child in our class within the first week or two of school and again midyear. The first call is simply an introductory call; it is enough to say hello and to share a bit of positive news about the start of the year. This can be a perfect time to mention something mathematical, such as, "I wanted to let you know that Tanisha worked really hard to solve a complicated problem in math this morning. It was such a pleasure to notice that she wouldn't give up until she had satisfied herself that she understood." The midyear call can be a chance to check in with parents about any issues or concerns they may have raised so far. Parents are so appreciative when teachers take note of and respond to their concerns, especially after several months have passed. Calling to say, "You raised concerns in October that Jeremy was having difficulty explaining his thinking in math. I wanted to let you know that he is making good progress. Just yesterday, for instance ..." These phone calls help parents understand that we see them as our partners. They help build positive relationships from the first week of school.

Open House

In most schools, Open House is a casual evening where children bring their parents to meet their teachers and see their classrooms. It can feel like a mob scene, but it's also a great place to inform parents about math and engage them as our allies. For one thing, we can arrange the classroom in such a way that parents are likely to notice math activities and understand their purpose. Letting students decide which math activities they would most like to show their parents will make them more likely to actually do that when they arrive. We can prepare a few brief posters explaining a recent math activity and its purpose or inviting parents to try it out with their child. When children introduce their parents, we can ask, "Did you have a chance to play 'Close to 100' with your dad yet?"

A brief written description of the academic program, handed out at Open House, is a great help to parents. Preparing for Open House is time consuming, but everyone benefits when parents become knowledgeable about the math program early in the year. Finally, many parents feel very shy about coming to school. It's our job to make sure children and their parents know that we value their attendance. Having children spend some time writing a letter or making a card to invite their parents to Open House can ensure that more parents come. The extra encouragement and welcome always increase participation.

Parent Participation in Class

Participating in a math class is perhaps the most effective way for parents to come to understand and appreciate new ideas about school mathematics. It's wise to specifically plan several lessons like this early in the year, advertising them well in advance so parents can adjust their schedules in order to attend. I always choose lessons for which parent help is genuinely needed, and I make sure that the instructions are accessible. Seeing the math firsthand can be a powerful experience for parents. Possible lessons include estimating the weight of apples and then using balance scales to weigh them in grams; conducting a survey that involves pairs or groups of students collecting data from other classrooms; or planning for and then making sandwiches for a soup kitchen. One mother who helped during sandwich making remarked, "I wish my husband could see this. He's a quality control expert, and that's exactly what these kids are working on!"

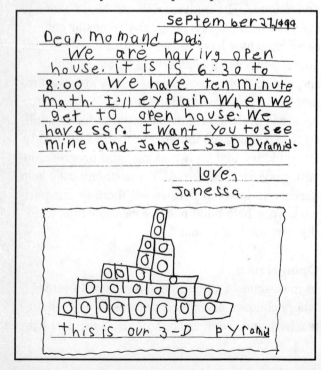

September 27, 1999

Dear Mom and Dad,
    We are having open house. It is is 6:30 to 8:00 We have ten minute math. I'll explain when we get to open house. We have SSR. I want you to see mine and James 3-D Pyramid.

Love,
Janessa

this is our 3-D pyramid

I came to better understand my son's math program from the sheets sent home explaining what the children were doing, the activities we could work on at home, and the assignments themselves—games that all family members played. Also, [we learned more by] completing math assignments at home with him or watching him do them.

—*parent of a child in Margie's class*

April News from Mrs. Riddle's Class

Fractions

As we move into spring at school we are wrapping up several topics of study and moving into some new ones. In math we have finished Landmarks in the Thousands, which focuses on the number system, factors, estimation, and addition and subtraction to thousands. Our next unit will be Different Shapes, Equal Pieces (see the letter on the reverse of this page). It combines the study of fractions with geometry, offering students a spatial model with which to begin to build an understanding of fractions. Perhaps you have noticed the PBS series Thursdays at 2 p.m. (Channel 57) which highlights the importance and changing role of mathematics in today's world. It supports the value of the way we are teaching math at school.

This year's wacky weather has provided us with opportunities to study weather throughout the year. After vacation we will begin another major

Figure 32 This excerpt from the teacher's April newsletter was sent home on the back of the *Investigations* family letter (see below) for the unit the class would be doing next.

Letters Home

Taking the time to write a brief newsletter each month, outlining upcoming curriculum for parents, is time well spent. A letter should go home the first week of school, highlighting units that will be studied, parent help that may be needed, expectations for homework, and supplies that families might be able to contribute. One paragraph should be a short explanation of the math curriculum. As the months progress, ongoing letters—whether from the curriculum itself or written by the teacher—will help parents gradually come to understand the math program. This is an easy way for us to reach out to parents when we don't have the time to see or talk personally with them.

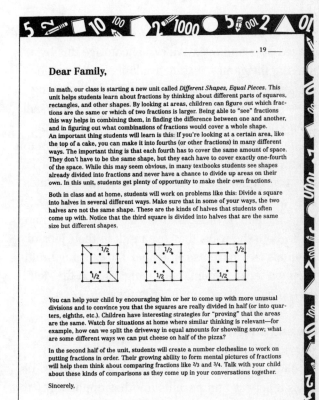

_____ , 19 ___

Dear Family,

In math, our class is starting a new unit called *Different Shapes, Equal Pieces*. This unit helps students learn about fractions by thinking about different parts of squares, rectangles, and other shapes. By looking at areas, children can figure out which fractions are the same or which of two fractions is larger. Being able to "see" fractions this way helps in combining them, in finding the difference between one and another, and in figuring out what combinations of fractions would cover a whole shape.
An important thing students will learn is this: If you're looking at a certain area, like the top of a cake, you can make it into fourths (or other fractions) in many different ways. The important thing is that each fourth has to cover the same amount of space. They don't have to be the same shape, but they each have to cover exactly one-fourth of the space. While this may seem obvious, in many textbooks students see shapes already divided into fractions and never have a chance to divide up areas on their own. In this unit, students get plenty of opportunity to make their own fractions.

Both in class and at home, students will work on problems like this: Divide a square into halves in several different ways. Make sure that in some of your ways, the two halves are not the same shape. These are the kinds of halves that students often come up with. Notice that the third square is divided into halves that are the same size but different shapes.

You can help your child by encouraging him or her to come up with more unusual divisions and to convince you that the squares are really divided in half (or into quarters, eighths, etc.). Children have interesting strategies for "proving" that the areas are the same. Watch for situations at home where similar thinking is relevant—for example, how can we split the driveway in equal amounts for shoveling snow; what are some different ways we can put cheese on half of the pizza?

In the second half of the unit, students will create a number clothesline to work on putting fractions in order. Their growing ability to form mental pictures of fractions will help them think about comparing fractions like 2/3 and 3/4. Talk with your child about these kinds of comparisons as they come up in your conversations together.

Sincerely,

Homework

Math homework can be a chance for parents to learn along with their children and to become more informed about the math program. We can be explicit in our directions about ways parents can help their children, while still encouraging them to figure things out for themselves. For example, "For homework tonight your child will teach you to play the Fraction Cookie Game. Notice how much practice your child is getting with comparing, adding, and reasoning about fractions as you play. Encourage your child to explain his or her strategies to you: "How did you know that the red trapezoid is half?" or "How many green triangles would it take to fill the same space?" Then share your strategies in return: "I knew 6 of the triangles make the whole thing, so 1 of the triangles would be 1 out of 6 or $\frac{1}{6}$."

Many of the *Investigations* games are designed to be played over and over. We can encourage this by making the games readily available—either by having students make their own copies, or by having class sets to borrow. It's a good idea to be sure children know the games well before they take them home, to avoid any confusion. Classroom discussion of strategies used at home by children and their families brings new ideas into the school and validates their work at home. Other interactive homework ideas include having children talk with family members about the ways they use math in their jobs or methods that parents remember for learning multiplication facts. Some families might teach their children number words in other languages.

Parent Information Night

Offering an informational evening program for families to learn about our mathematics program gives teachers and parents another opportunity to understand how much we have in common with regard to educational goals for their children. There are many different ways to structure such a program (see chapters 2–4 of this book for more detail). Our school has met with success by having games from *Investigations* units set up at grade-level stations, with teachers from each grade level explaining rules and helping parents to understand the mathematics their children learn while playing the games. Parents can move from grade to grade and spend as much time as they like with any game. Here, parents and teachers can interact in a more relaxed setting than a conference provides.

At one such math night, I chose to do some geometry Quick Images from a third-grade unit. The parents found the activities intriguing and challenging. They were impressed by the level of mathematics their children were being exposed to, and reassured to learn that children can approach the activity in a variety of ways and with different levels of sophistication. One thoughtful parent of a student with a visual-motor learning disability reflected, "I imagine this is very hard for my child." Her comment gave me the chance to assure her that I had anticipated that her daughter might have difficulty with the activity. She was pleased to know that I had adjusted my expectations for her child, supported the girl's efforts to do her best, and noticed her improvement, which had been significant over time. Such interactions can contribute significantly to the positive relationships between teachers and families.

Conferences and Report Cards

Conferences are one of the few chances teachers have to build productive relationships with parents, face to face. Unfortunately, they generally come late, are too short, are packed with essentials, and are often overlaid with anxiety on both sides. It's helpful if we can find ways to expand upon them. For instance, children can prepare self-evaluations to take home and discuss with their families. We can use these to highlight the math program and to spark a parent-child dialogue about academic issues even before we meet the parents. This puts the child more in charge of the reporting process and also helps the parent prepare for our conference.

> I learned more about Sam's math learning this year through conferences and discussion with the teacher and by seeing Sam apply math skills to everyday tasks (money, figuring out how many days to events, ages, time measurement). Reading over math assignments he'd done in school and brought home that we could talk about with him [also helped].
>
> —*another parent in Margie's class*

To make it clear that we value the input that parents provide, we need to send home reminders about conferences, perhaps the day before each one, and schedule according to parents' preference whenever possible. To make the most of this opportunity—one of the few when parents come individually to school—we can set out children's work and invite parents to come 10 minutes early to look over that work. Parents will of course be looking for information about all subjects, but we can be sure that some of the work (and our conversation during the conference) involves mathematics. I always prepare for conferences by taking some notes, and I begin each one with a positive anecdote or example of the child's success, kindness, or fine schoolwork.

Some issues tend to come up over and over in conferences—the needs of gifted children or battles over homework, for example. I try to save copies of interesting articles on those topics and share them with parents when those issues arise, since I find that parents respect the professional advice of teachers. Finally, of course, conferences are a time for listening on both sides. If the positive relationship is to continue to grow, it must be fostered during the conference.

> Having learned math in a very different way, and having had "math-trauma" when it was time to memorize the times tables (but finally managing to overcome the trauma and learn them!), I wondered how my daughter would learn to be math-proficient by such a different method, wondered if it would actually work … My concerns have been addressed by talking with the teachers and finding that they think Emily really "gets" the concepts … I trust the fact that they believe in this math program, have seen it work, and know how to teach it and evaluate their students.
>
> —*another parent in Margie's class*

Citing the Experts

To help parents become true partners in transforming math education, we must be prepared to document the philosophy behind our math program. For instance, teachers should have copies of and be knowledgeable about the National Council of Teachers of Mathematics (NCTM) *Standards*, their state framework, and their district curriculum. Samples of journal articles, books, and videos can also be useful resources. Parents appreciate being invited to look over or borrow these to become more knowledgeable. When we have these materials available, parents respect our professionalism. I find that they are also more likely to support a program that is clearly based on solid educational research and national and state norms.

Conclusion

As the end of each school year approaches, teachers and parents alike realize that they will be moving on to new school relationships. However, the effort that has gone into creating partnerships during the year can continue to benefit everyone. In the final conference or near the year's end, we can reiterate the benefits of our math program for their children. Many parents appreciate a year-end note that provides—for them and for next year's teacher—specific information about their child's strengths and challenges in math. With such a note, parents have the information they need to become advocates for an appropriate math curriculum for their child.

Parents are more likely to take on the role of advocate when they have lots of information to back them up. When a mother can articulate clearly what her child needs to succeed in math, she will become an advocate. If she says, "My daughter does well in math when she is encouraged to draw pictures to help explain her thinking," she becomes the teacher's ally.

As teachers, we need to understand and welcome the importance of the relationships we build with parents. We need to accept that, in some measure, our success in improving our mathematics program will depend on informing and supporting parents as they seek the best education for their children. In many ways, our success with parents mirrors our success with their children, and it is "all about relationships." We are challenged in working productively with parents by having so little face-to-face contact and so little time. For that reason, we need to start from the first week of school, building positive partnerships that will grow and thrive during the year. If that is our agenda, we will be partners, and we will work together to achieve what we both want.

Resources and Readings

For another teacher's perspective, see Nancy Litton's *Getting Your Math Message Out to Parents* (1998). She discusses strategies she uses to engage parents with her math program (including newsletters, Back-to-School Night, parent conferences, homework, classroom volunteers, and family math nights) and shares examples of newsletters, student work and portfolios, and math night agendas.

Chapter 10

One Parent's View

Becoming a Parent Leader

Susan Pfohman

In the spring of 1999, Portland (Oregon) Public School District's Board selected Investigations in Number, Data, and Space *as its new math curriculum for the elementary grades and* Connected Math *for the middle school. The decision came after a year of study by a selection committee of teachers and administrators. During a public hearing, Susan Pfohman, parent of eight children, offered her support for the adoption in testimony to the school board. What follows is the story of how that one parent became a valuable force in the work of changing mathematics teaching and learning—first, as a parent volunteer in one school, and then as a Parent Leader involved with many schools in her district. She speaks of the inspiration she drew from training sessions in mathematics and of seeing the power of parents to influence the choices schools make. From her perspective, she offers recommendations to other districts for identifying and supporting parents who might take on the role of Parent Leader.*

My Mathematical Background

I grew up in a household where mathematics was revered. When my siblings and I attended public school in the 1960s, our math education involved following memorized steps and procedures. We carried to add and borrowed to subtract, never thinking about the value of any of the numbers being manipulated. I multiplied and did long division with the best of them, without any feel for the magnitude of the numbers I was using and without estimates of the answers I might get. I saw geometry, strictly in the form of theorems and proofs, for one year in high school. I worked my way through all of the procedures of algebra, trigonometry, and pre-calculus (then called Senior Math) without it having any real meaning for me. Even though my

math education didn't encourage mathematical sense-making, I had a very positive attitude toward mathematics, cultivated at home, that ultimately carried me through. I earned a degree in civil engineering and worked as a structural engineer for seven years.

Classroom Mathematics: A Parent Volunteer

In 1995, I had preschool children at home and no plans to return to the workforce in the near future. That's when I began volunteering in my children's school. I let my children's teachers know I was available and that I hoped to tutor children in math. My focus was on mathematics because I had experience, interest, and a level of comfort with the subject. Looking back, there was much I didn't know about elementary mathematics, working with schoolchildren, or even tutoring. But I had a positive attitude about the value of math and a willingness to be open to what I saw children wrestling with.

The teachers directed me to resources that they wanted taught and students who needed the attention. Interestingly, the students most frequently referred were those functioning above grade level, those whom teachers felt weren't being challenged sufficiently by their day-to-day math lessons. In the second year, my daughter's second grade teacher encouraged me to practice open-ended problem solving and to strategize with a dozen 6- and 7-year-olds as they began to approach more complicated math problems. In my older daughters' third-fourth-fifth grade blended classroom, I taught hands-on algebra and geometry from *Investigations* to groups of six students at a time. This was also the year I instituted a Problem of the Week project (described further on pp. 109–111). By the end of my second volunteer year, I was spending one entire day per week in the school.

The Wider Context of Mathematics Reform

During my second year of working in classrooms, several different things affected my thinking about mathematics, furthered my knowledge of the wider context of mathematics reform, and connected me to other people who were interested in improving mathematics teaching and learning for children.

As an active classroom volunteer and a parent of two elementary-aged children, I had questions about math at school. I wondered about the disjointedness of the curriculum that I was observing as my children moved from grade to grade. I wanted them to be progressing, and I wanted to *help* make that happen. I was also curious about the materials I was being asked to use with students, as a tutor.

That same year, I ran for and was elected to Site Council, a group of teachers, parents, and administrators who are responsible for writing, updating, and implementing the district-mandated School Improvement Plan. I now had a place to ask further-reaching questions and learn more about the math curriculum, both schoolwide and districtwide. Had I not been elected to Site Council, gathering that kind of information would likely have been more difficult. At monthly Site Council meetings, I heard teachers' concerns about curriculum and could ask my own questions about curriculum in general and math in particular.

At the same time, I discovered that our school (and six other local schools) had an opportunity to be part of a mathematics restructuring project. The Mathematics Education Collaborative (MEC), a nonprofit organization, was founded to help schools learn to work with their parents and the public. MEC was launching a grant-funded mathematics professional development effort in Portland. MEC's work would bring parents, teachers, administrators, and the public at large to the table in an attempt to develop knowledgeable advocacy for quality mathematics in local schools. The effort

would involve evening sessions for the public, support for administrators, intensive work with a Mathematics Support Team at each school, and a series of nine-day mathematics content courses. When I heard about the project, I asked our principal if there was any way for me to become involved. He inquired, and as a result I was invited to participate, with teachers from five schools, in quarterly, two-day teacher-training sessions conducted by MEC staff.

I was excited to have an opportunity and a forum to explore the questions I'd had about math education. I was now going to be meeting regularly with people who shared my interest in the teaching of math at the elementary and middle school levels.

Training in Classroom Mathematics

During the first quarterly session of MEC staff development, I joined all of the other participants in working on a fraction "menu." A menu is a learning environment designed to immerse students in the study of a mathematical idea or concept, while allowing them to pursue their own thinking on their own time line. Activities are set up around the classroom, and students move from station to station, exploring an idea with different tools and through different problems. For one and a half days, we used pattern blocks, Cuisenaire rods, tiles, fingers, and graph paper to explore and make sense of fractions.

My experience with this fraction menu was literally life altering. It was so very different from any previous math learning I had done, the contrast was striking. I had more fun over the course of those two days than I'd had in a very long time. I was completely engaged and lost in thought. I was seeing things and understanding relationships, particularly with regard to multiplication and division, which I had never experienced before. No one had ever expected me to see these things. I was excited. It suddenly became utterly important to me to understand how children (and adults) learn. I couldn't stop thinking about what the implications might be for my children, for other students in our school, and for me. Doing the math at MEC training and classes has been the fuel that drives me to work for change; it's what keeps me going. I feel strongly that this is a key to what might keep other parents going too.

After that first training session, participants were asked to go back to their classrooms (all participants except me were classroom teachers) and begin doing "Number Talks," which are primarily mental math activities: "naked number" computation problems, estimating, and sharing strategies for solving such problems (such as rounding, or breaking numbers apart).* I took Number Talks into my daughter's first-second grade combination class once a week. This helped me develop some insight into what young children are capable of learning about number and computation that doesn't rely on first teaching them algorithms. I have watched and listened to primary grade children making sense of addition, subtraction, and even doubling and tripling of numbers. These positive and enlightening experiences continue to intrigue me.

District Mathematics: The Adoption Process

By the following spring, I understood the importance of the decision our district math curriculum selection committee faced. Our district had not been able to afford a new math adoption, complete with texts and staff development, for nearly 11 years. The reason I could never find a thread of continuity in the math curriculum as my daughters moved from grade to grade was that there wasn't one. Individual classroom teachers were either relying on outdated textbooks or on materials and training they had gathered and selected on their own, based on their own ideas about what elementary math should look like and their years of

* The term *Number Talks* describes a process—originally called "Thinking with Numbers Time"—developed by Ruth Parker to help children learn to reason with numbers. After further exploring and developing this idea with Kathy Richardson, she changed the name of the process to "Number Talks."

experience with what they believed worked. We were now on the brink of unifying the efforts of every teacher in every elementary and middle school throughout our district. My new view of the situation was that we had an opportunity to put meaningful mathematics materials in the hands of teachers and students, and I didn't want to see that opportunity slip away.

The elementary selection committee arrived at the consensus recommendation that the board fund the purchase of *Investigations* and *Connected Math*. It then became a matter of making sure the board understood the correctness of that choice. My testimony for the first hearing was written to provide a counter view to what the local daily newspaper had reported about criticism of the proposed curriculum. I wanted the board and the local press to hear that there were parents, like me, who endorsed the proposed adoption. I tried to impress upon board members that *Investigations* was the best choice educationally and socially because it could provide access to mathematics in a way that no other curriculum could. Every child would have a chance to develop powerful mathematical understandings, even those who don't excel at the memorization and rapid recall of procedures and routines.

Anxious about a handful of negative letters received from "back to basics" advocates, the board postponed its decision to adopt the proposed curriculum until public forums were held to air all sides of the issue. At the forum I attended, dozens of interested parents from all walks of life spoke out in support of *Investigations*. The supporters came from all socioeconomic backgrounds, but had one primary message in common: We weren't given the chance to learn mathematics in a way that has worked very well for us, and we wanted something better for our children. Two speakers were vehemently opposed to the proposed selection. Ultimately, *Investigations* and *Connected Math* were officially approved.

During this period of interacting with teachers and district curriculum administrators, I gained a sense of the power that parents have to influence the choices schools make. We have the power to make important changes come about more quickly and decisively when we let our opinions be known. I do feel, though, that it is important for parents to have a sincere interest in the areas of change being considered, to have experience to draw upon, and to have a working knowledge of the issues. If we choose to involve ourselves in the change process, we must prepare ourselves with more than information taken from the Internet or the party line of a particular faction. Rather, we need to find ways to become knowledgeable about current thinking in the field. In this case, I needed to bring myself up to date through articles, books, lectures, and workshops about math education. We should also act out of interest for all students, not exclusively our own children. Lastly, we need to ask ourselves whether our own education has truly served us and can give the children of our community what they need to move forward to productive futures.

Helping to Implement *Investigations*

The following summer, MEC offered a nine-day class on patterns, functions, and algebraic thinking. I enrolled as a member of my school's Math Support Team. I did math from 8:30 A.M. to 3:30 P.M. and brought home problems and manipulatives to do more math at night. I went to class each day feeling that this was the most fun I could have on my summer vacation. I continued to feel that what I was learning about math and about education were changing my views of almost everything around me. I wanted to find ways to support teachers in making the transition to teaching *Investigations*. I also dedicated myself to finding ways to help children make the transition from the pencil-and-paper algorithmic approaches to arithmetic I had learned as a child, to really understanding what numbers are about.

Before the start of the next school year, I met with my daughters' teachers (the two were in a blended third-fourth-fifth grade classroom with two teachers) and spoke with them about how they would be incorporating *Investigations* into their integrated curriculum. They asked me, and I agreed, to teach math to the fifth graders, one hour a day, and to do two "mental math" sessions each week with half the class at a time, all on a volunteer basis.

These teachers trusted my understanding of mathematics and appreciated my eagerness to teach it, even though at the outset my actual classroom experience was limited. They were always available to help me with classroom management and discipline issues. We met regularly to plan, talk over issues, discuss how children's understandings were developing (or not), and brainstorm ways to support students' progress. We worked very hard to stand back and let the children's ideas take center stage. The experience of collaborating has been very powerful; I believe it has made each of us better equipped to teach mathematics. The more classroom experience I get, the more respect and appreciation I have for my children's school and its teachers.

Mathematics for Other Parents

At the request of the math team of Portland Public Schools, I have begun conducting a series of three parent education sessions, focused primarily on answering questions about *Investigations* and mathematics in the city's elementary schools. These sessions have been offered at school sites that request them, with parents coming from schools in the surrounding area. The focus is on introducing the reasoning behind the math adoption, giving parents experiences with several *Investigations* units, discussing how to help children with math at home, and preparing parents to assist as math volunteers in their children's classrooms.

As I conduct these sessions, I find that questions from the parents tend to be more general than specific. Their main concern is whether their children are OK and whether they are learning what they need to know to be successful. Parents' questions generally fall into one of several major categories. They want to know how this curriculum relates to "new math" and whether their children are guinea pigs for just another educational fad. They want to know that their children's progress will be measured in such a way that someone knows what they are really learning. They want to know how to help their children with homework they don't understand. And they want to know that the needs of their particular children are being met and that their children will be well equipped to succeed in middle school, high school, college, and in life.

Overall, the most vocal concern (not to be confused with the most *prevalent* concern) has been, "My child's math abilities are way above grade level. He (or she) is bored and frustrated in math. I'm afraid my child is going to be turned off to math altogether even before hitting second grade."

At every school, and in every session, someone tried to steer the conversation to the needs of his or her particular, extraordinary child. It was usually only one parent per school, and the issue often turned out to be that the child wasn't experiencing the "rigor" the parent had experienced when he or she learned arithmetic. I try to reinforce the idea that of all the programs out there, *Investigations* has the greatest potential to meet the needs of a wide range of children and has built-in extensions. I also mention that the teachers' ability to extend the lessons is likely still developing since the curriculum is so new to them. In each session, I try to help parents understand how lessons allow for a range of depth in thinking and how, over time, teachers and parents will become better at eliciting deeper thinking and at recognizing it on paper.

Often in my conversations with parents, we discuss how to approach teachers with our own new-found understanding of how math can look. I suggest that parents inquire if they would be useful

"as an extra pair of eyes and hands" during math time. If the teacher agrees, they might briefly discuss the extensions for the day's lesson, and the teacher could direct parents to children who are ready for these extensions. (The complicating factors here are teachers who aren't yet sufficiently comfortable or familiar with the curriculum to want help in the room, and parents who might need to do a bit of reading or prep themselves to be truly useful.) This points to the need for a set of extra curriculum units stored somewhere in the school, so parents or other volunteers can read and explore the material they might be helping to teach. Teachers can't lend copies of the units they need to teach from, and other teachers at the same grade level are usually teaching the same unit at approximately the same time of year.

The most prevalent concern among parents has been, "What are the short- and long-term effects on my kids from the standardized and open-ended math assessments mandated by the state?" Without a doubt, people came in with a lot more concerns about the goals of education and the emphasis on testing than anything specific about *Investigations*. If a concern was expressed at all, it was that teachers weren't yet confident enough to trust that the new curriculum would be sufficient preparation for any state test. Instead, teachers are, at some schools, putting third, fourth, and especially fifth graders through pretty rigorous practice tests and test preparation. We spend quite a lot of time in parent sessions talking about where the state assessment came from, what its purpose was supposed to be, and its political ramifications. We also discuss where parents might direct their concerns if they would like to see change.

Perhaps the most encouraging question I hear is, "How can we, as parents, be trained as effective volunteers in the classroom during math time?" At every school where I conducted parent education sessions, one or two parents asked about training and ongoing support so they could provide the best volunteer help possible. These parents wanted to understand the math, but they also wanted to know what is most helpful for teachers. They recognize the challenges teachers face: a wide range of abilities within a single classroom, time constraints, and accountability to the public, parents, and administration. These parents simply want to be of service. Few expressed the need to work in their own child's classroom. They want to be prepared to effectively work wherever they are needed most.

Identifying and Supporting Parent Leaders

At every training session I have conducted, at least one parent per school stood out as a potential parent leader. Such parents share these traits:

- They come to the classes with an interest in better understanding how *Investigations* benefits children. Most have already attended MEC's larger community-wide meeting that describes the changes taking place in the mathematics education community, and they see the value of that perspective.
- They are already involved with their own children's learning and have time and energy to volunteer at school with other students.
- Many have positive math histories and can describe the fun they had thinking creatively about mathematics and numbers as children. They value mathematics for themselves and for their children. It is noteworthy that at least half of these self-selecting, potential parent leaders who expressed positive feelings about their own math education were raised outside of the United States, in either Europe or Asia.
- They recognize and sympathize with the challenges teachers face in classrooms. They are interested in supporting teachers and recognize them as professionals.
- They want to work as effectively as possible at school, and if that means more training, they are willing to acquire it.

- They uniformly express an altruism toward their child's school or classroom and a willingness to work with whatever students the teacher feels could benefit most from the extra attention, time, and support.

The experience of educating parents about mathematics has triggered many thoughts and questions. I believe there are parents like myself in every district who would be willing to invest the time in training and volunteering to support math in their neighborhood schools. Teachers seem to be more inclined to ask for parent help with reading, but there are parents willing to provide volunteer support with math learning as well.

While some ethnic diversity was present among those who stood out as potential leaders, these parents did *not* represent a wide range of socio-economic groups. Parent leaders need to represent more than the middle class, and schools must find ways to involve parents from all walks of life. How do we eliminate or ameliorate barriers that might keep interested parents from taking part? How do we recruit, train, and compensate parents who are or might be interested? What types of training do we offer, when, and for how long? How do we find a variety of roles for parents that capitalize on their strengths, abilities, and availability?

There are people in our community who believe in and support public education to such a degree that they will voluntarily lend support to teachers. Obviously, the responsibility for training these parents cannot fall on the shoulders of teachers alone. How do we provide training to these parents and persuade teachers that these volunteers can be capable of providing meaningful classroom support? The potential to support teachers and help children by developing this largely untapped resource seems enormous. It would not be without its costs in training and supervision, but it may be a resource we can't afford not to develop.

Chapter 11

The Administrator's Role
Involving Parents Right Away

Unlike the previous two chapters, which each featured a single voice (one a teacher, one a parent), this chapter blends the voices of a variety of school administrators, including principals, lead teachers, math coaches, math specialists, curriculum coordinators, and assistant superintendents. Their perspectives and advice come from direct experience with fostering a school-home partnership while implementing Investigations *as their math curriculum.*

As the process of implementing a new curriculum gets underway, administrators have many day-to-day needs to manage—making sure teachers have the materials they need, that the schedule allows more time for mathematics, that there is time built into the day for teachers to meet, that substitutes are available for covering classes, that they make it to the meeting about math with Rory's mom or Juan's dad. Parent and community outreach can get put off as the minutiae of the daily grind eat up administrators' time and energy. However, as one educator points out,

> We have learned that working with parents to bring them into the process is crucial. Until all stakeholders are at the table, it's really difficult to have a productive conversation about what math is and what it should look like for children. Parental and community understanding and support are requirements for successful mathematics restructuring efforts.

> —*P. Lofgren, Mathematics Education Collaborative (Oregon)*

There are very real pressures working against early outreach to parents. Learning how to teach *Investigations* can be a challenge, particularly in the early stages of implementation. Many teachers are being asked to change their teaching in deep and profound ways. Administrators want to respect the risks teachers are taking and the accompanying feelings of vulnerability. They wonder how to ask teachers—who are themselves unsure about these new ways of teaching and learning mathematics—to communicate with parents. As one assistant superintendent for curriculum and instruction said, "I will tell you truthfully, I was very hesitant to bring parents into the game at that point because I knew we were going someplace very different and I didn't want to put teachers on the line" *(K. Coleman, assistant superintendent for curriculum and instruction, Arizona).*

Teachers often feel this tension themselves. "I think one difficulty with being ready to talk effectively about an inquiry approach to mathematics, when it is new to both the school community and the teacher, is that the teacher is still developing an understanding of the philosophy of *Investigations* and how all of this integrates with the curriculum. She sees the deeper learning that is going on but may not feel comfortable defending this philosophy to a group of parents who seem critical of the changes" *(P. O'Brien Broome, grade 3 teacher, Massachusetts).*

Despite all these pressures, when asked what advice they would give schools or districts just starting out with *Investigations*, teachers from districts four and five years into the process respond similarly:

> The one thing I would say is *involve parents right away.* And I think that's really hard for teachers. I mean, "I don't know this program. What is it I'm going to say to a parent?" But invite someone to come in, or have a curriculum coordinator do it. I think the fact that we had PTO meetings was real-

ly important. If you try to shut parents out initially, they're going to make decisions about what's going on, they're going to have their own ideas about what's going on, which may or may not be accurate.

—N. Buell, grade 4 teacher (Massachusetts)

My advice would be to get parents involved from the very start. I think that, just as with teachers, we don't just say, "Okay, here's a new curriculum, we want you to use it." Teachers and administrators need to inform the parents and explain the philosophy behind this way of teaching mathematics: what's going to be different and what to expect. This way parents will know ahead of time that their child is not going to be coming home with lots of drills but will be learning mathematics, including the "facts," in a different way, with more understanding. If parents can see that this curriculum is, in fact, going to help their child to learn mathematics better than the way they learned it, they will become supportive.

—R. Christiansen, grades 1–2 teacher (Massachusetts)

Including Parents in the Plan

While there is a tendency to delay outreach to parents until the curriculum is more established, experience suggests that schools or districts are better advised to develop a plan for parent communication with the following features:

- It is respectful of all the parties involved—their needs, concerns, and issues.
- It builds on the school's and community's strengths.
- It does not rely on *all* teachers, nor does it rely solely on individual classroom teachers.
- It is realistic and practical given the time,

energy, and resources available.
- It takes advantage of those who are most interested, motivated, and supportive.

Much like a gradual implementation plan, which involves phasing in more units each year, a school or district can begin small, with focused and intentional communication designed to open a dialogue and form relationships. A thoughtful process builds on what is learned as more and more people are brought into the conversation. It also acknowledges that this will be an ongoing process as the curriculum is further implemented and as new families and teachers enter the school or district.

Growing Circles of Influence

Including parents in the plan can be a new and challenging idea for administrators who wonder, "But how do we *do* that?" What follows is a model for including parents that one district used to build consensus for the adoption of standards-based materials for the secondary level. They termed this incremental model "Growing Circles of Influence."* Through a succession of meetings, each step involving more people and incorporating support materials that were developed as the need arose, the district gradually learned more about what parents and the community needed in order to understand and appreciate the mathematics curricula the district was adopting. Examining this model can help administrators think about the concerns of various groups of shareholders in their community.

*Sandy Rummel, a principal in the communications firm of Rummel, Dubs & Hill, as well as a parent and school board member in White Bear Lake, Minnesota, developed this model. SciMathMN, a public and private partnership that supports improved student learning in grades K–12 science and mathematics via standards-based, systemic reforms for policy and practice supported the development.

The Inside Circle: Knowledgeable Supporters

This district started by forming an advisory committee with a school board member, a district administrator, a math teacher, two parents, and a community member with a math-related career. This group provided insight into the community and its attitudes toward education. They provided ideas about how to reach various segments of the community, gave feedback on what was planned for future meetings with the various groups, and suggested community members in math-related fields who might participate in an early focus group.

The Second Circle: The Toughest Audience

Next, the group was expanded to include people from the community who were considered knowledgeable and influential—engineers, pharmacists, a CFO, a technical writer from the city paper. The team felt that concerns, if they were to arise, were likely to be voiced by this group. Because of their credibility, support from members of this group could prove to be valuable. Thirty-two people received written invitations from the superintendent and follow-up calls from people whom they knew. The 24 who accepted worked together on a mathematics activity, watched a video, had an open discussion, and received a document that answered frequently asked questions. This group suggested providing more time for discussion and examples of available data. The advisory group used this feedback to refine the parent meetings to come.

The Third Circle: Parents of Students in the Pilots

The process was then opened up to many parents. Seven meetings were held on different dates, at different schools, and at different times in order to give parents as many options as possible. Invitations were sent and cookies served. The sessions began with an ice breaker activity. They included an extended math activity and ample time for conversation. Parents wrote comments on stick-on notes and then sorted and discussed those comments. Parents received the handout of frequently asked questions plus a new handout called

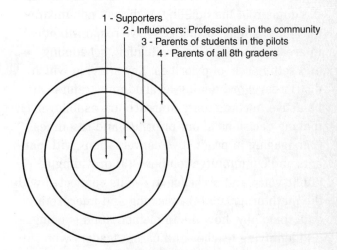

1 - Supporters
2 - Influencers: Professionals in the community
3 - Parents of students in the pilots
4 - Parents of all 8th graders

"Research at a Glance." Twenty percent of the parents of the students in the pilot classes attended. Parents who did *not* attend responded overwhelmingly, on a questionnaire given at school conferences, that this was "because we trust the decisions of our math teachers."

The Final Circle: Parents at Large

The final step took place at student registration for incoming freshmen. As they arrived at the orientation, parents received a large brochure, "Math That Makes Sense," explaining the key elements and benefits of the math curriculum. The curriculum leader explained the program and answered questions. There were relatively few questions, apparently because parents who had been to the previous meetings had already talked at some length with those who had not. Parents had a choice, and 95 percent of the parents of all incoming students chose the standards-based program over a traditional one.

The Role of an Administrator

Once the adoption process is complete, administrators turn to their roles in supporting the implementation of the curriculum. Many activities that involve parents and the community can be the joint work of administrators, teacher leaders, and parent leaders, but there are key tasks specific to the domain of the building or district administrator. For example, principals have responsibilities in areas such as hiring, evaluation, scheduling, and setting school priorities. Key areas in which district-level or building-level administrators can be active in community outreach are as follows: (1) making decisions about priorities and resources; (2) engaging in productive conversations with parents and community members; (3) providing a public voice and presence at events connected with the math program; (4) collecting and interpreting data that show how the implementation is going; (5) identifying teacher and parent leaders who can further this work; and (6) developing school- or districtwide resources for ongoing communication with parents and families. This section discusses each of these key areas.

Decisions About Priorities and Resources

As administrators make decisions about priorities and resources, they need to make working with parents a priority—in both name and action. Hiring staff and allocating resources to support such involvement is one way to do this.

> When I hire teachers … I want people who can be articulate about what they're teaching and who have a rationale, who are able to explain why they do what they do. I know they have to be able to do that for parents, and for others in this community as well.
>
> —*M. Sleeper, principal (Massachusetts)*

Resources need to be corralled and used creatively to move the implementation of *Investigations* forward. Such funds help buy the materials necessary to teach the curriculum well and finance professional development for teachers (while hiring substitutes to enable that). In addition, funding designated for school-home connections can be used for the following:

- creating a parent center within a school
- hiring parent leaders
- hiring translators who are fluent in the languages spoken in the community
- buying refreshments or door prizes for meetings
- funding transportation to and from parent math events or childcare during them
- purchasing an extra set of *Investigations* units for the library, parent center, resource room, or office, to be shared with parents, substitutes, student teachers, support staff, and classroom volunteers

Engaging in Productive Conversations

Administrators need to approach this work with patience. Adopting a new math curriculum like *Investigations* results in many changes that take place gradually, over time. Listening to both teachers and parents is crucial. Regular, ongoing communication must be two-way. Administrators have much to learn from teachers about what's challenging about teaching this curriculum and what would be helpful to them in changing their practice. At the same time, administrators have much to learn from families—about their thoughts and feelings about mathematics, their children, and their children's education and future.

Many administrators accept the role, particularly early in the implementation process, of meeting with parents who have questions or concerns. As the implementation proceeds, they may encourage parents to take questions to the child's teacher or the building principal, as well. Whoever is designated in this role must be able to talk articulately about the program, why it's good for children, and what is being done to support teachers in the early phases of implementation.

> I know that, if parents come to me with a question about this new math program, I can go to my principal and say, "This parent is having an issue, can you help me with this?" I feel comfortable going to him.

He'll help in any way he can, and not just blindly say, "Oh, my teacher is right." That's not the kind of principal he is. He's a good listener for both parents and teachers and can bring the two together.

—*N. Springer, grade 4 teacher (Massachusetts)*

It's very hard to defend a program that you haven't used at least for a full year. There's a certain leap of faith that this is going to be OK for my students, but you don't have a clear picture of how it's going to work out. To defend that program to parents, who have their own concerns about how it's going to work out, is really hard. There needs to be support outside of the classroom. We had tremendous support from our principal, our system curriculum coordinator, and the superintendent. The district's elementary math coordinators did a presentation for parents at every school. Letters went out from the assistant superintendent's office about the curriculum. The message was clear that the use of *Investigations* was a system decision, not the decision of each individual teacher.

—*N. Buell, grade 4 teacher (Massachusetts)*

Parents often raise legitimate and reasonable questions about a new curriculum. Their feedback can give administrators valuable information about how the implementation of a new program is going, where strengths and weaknesses lie, and what might need attention. An administrator in a district that uses a standards-based curriculum explains:

Parental concerns and complaints are often well-founded. With appropriate follow-up, they can provide valuable information about faulty implementation of programs.

The most common complaint I hear about our elementary program is that students aren't learning their basic facts. When I ask parents if they have seen games coming home or if their children mention playing games in school, and they say "no," the problem is clear. Games are the primary vehicle for basic fact practice in that program. By eliminating games, the teacher has eliminated the basic fact practice from the program! The problem is implementation, not the program and not the parents (Briars, 1999, p. 34).

The principal of a low-income school has learned to listen carefully when parents voice concerns:

You know, the world perceives my school's parent population as being kind of nonparticipatory … But, for the most part, when a parent calls with concerns about a curriculum, they're usually correct. I listen, and sometimes I'm amazed.

—*W. Roselinsky, principal (Nevada)*

Administrators stress that it is important to sit down with parents who are concerned about the math program and really discuss their questions and issues. Responding respectfully to parents' concerns with useful information helps them learn more about what is possible for children mathematically.

I've had lunch meetings with parents, and really just listen because that usually works for me. I listen to what they have to say and say, "I agree with that. Now, let me show you where this is in the curriculum."

—*K. Coleman, assistant superintendent for curriculum and instruction (Arizona)*

These administrators say that first and foremost, they listen. They also look together with parents at the mathematics and what the research has to say about math teaching and learning. Being clear about goals and expectations in conversations with parents is particularly important. As one administrator advises:

> I think the thing is to help parents understand, "If you're going to do only operations, you can't teach number sense." We're trying to move toward what youngsters are going to need to know in the future, and they're going to need number sense. We try to be very clear about our expectations. So when parents ask about the multiplication tables I say, "Of course we want those tables. We want every single table from 1 to 12, and we want them by the end of fourth grade."
>
> —*A. Switzer, principal (New York)*

Although parents may be looking for answers that require fairly extensive knowledge of the curriculum, that knowledge is present *somewhere* in most districts. Administrators may need to tap the expertise of other district personnel to find the information and resources that will be most useful to parents. Also, some professional development experiences aimed at teachers new to the curriculum can be equally valuable for principals and other administrators, giving them just the information they need.

> I think that administrators should, as much as possible, involve themselves in the initial teacher training that goes on, because just as this type of curriculum is brand new to teachers, it's also brand new to a lot of the administrators. They need to clearly understand what this type of curriculum looks like and what it means to implement it.
>
> —*M. Scott, grades 1–2 teacher (Massachusetts)*

As instructional leaders within their schools and districts, administrators must strive to achieve a balance in their work with parents. While on the one hand they need to listen intently to parents' concerns and be responsive to those concerns, they also need to communicate to them what is known about best practices in teaching mathematics. Doing this often challenges long-held beliefs about mathematics as a set of speedy arithmetic procedures memorized by rote. Administrators must help both teachers and parents consider new ideas about the possibilities for mathematics in the elementary classroom. Herein lies one of the major challenges for an administrator.

Providing a Public Voice and Presence

Principals and other district administrators are often instrumental in organizing and publicizing math events for parents. They also have important roles to play at such functions. Their presence is a show of support, symbolic of a school community that stands united in the work of improving math instruction for all students. They must also play a knowledgeable role. For example, principals might open a parent night with a presentation to the whole group, providing some background on how the school came to adopt *Investigations*, why math is changing, or aspects of the school's implementation plan. This is a chance to establish common ground in terms of mathematics goals for students and to invite parents to share ideas and lend support in whatever ways possible. Principals and administrators can also offer to meet with parents who would like to know more or who have specific issues or concerns.

One administrator recommends four key components for communicating successfully with parents at events such as these:

- Make basic skills visible.
- Provide specific information about how parents can help their children.
- Provide information on assessment as well as curriculum and instruction.
- Listen to parents. (Briars, 1999, p. 34)

An Example of a Math Night Opening

When I do an introduction (at family math nights), I talk about NCTM and what their vision is. I explain that we need a new vision of mathematics for our children. I say, "What we had in the past wasn't good enough. Look at all the people who can't figure out a tip at a restaurant, who don't have an understanding when they pick up the headlines. This is a different generation, and the skills they need are different." You have to tell parents why change is needed and then explain, "This is the plan. This is how we will do it." You have to tell them what we're keeping from the "old way," because that's what people get nervous about, along with what's new. I say, "You still need to know math facts. Children need to learn them. And this is how we teach them." The biggest difference in the new vision is teaching for *understanding*. Children have to understand. I usually put up a problem—say, a two-digit by two-digit multiplication problem—and I say to parents, "That second line—why do you move it over?" Most people don't know. Sometimes they do, but most times they don't, and I talk about that.

I use myself as an example. I say, "I dropped math as a senior because it meant I wasn't going to get all A's, and I wanted all A's, and I didn't think I needed math. Getting A's was more important to me then than math, and that's not acceptable." I also talk a lot about my own kids, how the three had different learning needs, and how my one son needed more help than the others. I say, "You know your own children. If your child needs more support, please help us and here is how …"

—D. Shein-Gerson, K–5 math coordinator (Massachusetts)

Taking on a public role at a parent night has additional meaning; it is supportive of teachers, who often have enough on their plates in organizing a portion of the evening for the families who attend. Some teachers also feel that the overarching message, and the unity of purpose it delivers, is more powerful coming from an administrator than from a single classroom teacher.

At these events and others like them—a school staff meeting, a PTA gathering, a school board hearing—administrators need to think carefully about who might speak on behalf of the math program or present a suitable math activity. Whether an administrator, teacher, or parent, the chosen speaker should be well respected in both the school and home community. Some districts call in collaborators from a local college or from the high school mathematics department. If there will be a question-and-answer period, the speakers need to feel confident with the material, have articulate ways of expressing it, and think quickly on their feet. Inviting students to share some mathematical work or talk about their experiences in math class can also be particularly powerful. Finally, parents or community members who use mathematics in their career can be invited to talk about what children need to be able to do in today's world and how that differs from the education most adults received.

Collecting and Interpreting Data

One key job for an administrator is to keep track of data that may influence decisions about the implementation. Parents are one source of such data. For instance, one group of educational researchers suggests the following:

- Keep logs of visits, letters, and phone calls to principals, department chairs, and central office administrators. When parents have questions or concerns, keep track of the kinds of issues they are raising and note any changes over time. Also note parents' expressions of interest and support for the program.

- Check with teachers about their conversations with parents: What are parents' concerns, how pressing do these concerns feel, and what kinds of support for the program are parents expressing?
- Send short questionnaires to parents to ask about their children's mathematical education. (Goldsmith, Mark, & Kantrov, 2000, p. 124)

By listening to parents, one school found:

> We've had family math nights where parents come with their children to experience the activities. They want more of that. They want to come in and do more activities so they know what [their children are doing in school], and actually do the activities that the children are doing in class. ... We are trying to do it every year, and now they've expressed needs for different levels. "I understand what's going on now, but I want to know more about the actual activities."
>
> —*L. Alloway, grade 1 teacher and teacher leader (Arizona).*

Another school was hearing a lot from parents about homework:

> The issue of homework was coming up and coming up and coming up, so I had a PTA meeting, and I just put on the board all the different requests. "These parents want more. These parents want less. These parents want it on the weekend. These parents never want it on the weekend. These parents want all skills. These people want all open-ended. These parents want Monday through Friday. These want it handed out Monday, collected on Friday." And so the obvious thing is, "See, someone else has to decide these things. It probably should be your child's teacher, right?" Making things public is a very good way of making people more reasonable, if there's some leadership. That's been a credo for me.

> You make things public. And you also get a lot of accountability that way.
>
> —*A. Switzer, principal (New York)*

Still another school used the mathematics section of children's report cards to draft a mathematics report card for parents, designed to take a survey of parents' attitudes about the school's math program. Parents were to rate their feelings about 18 topics. The report card used the following scale:

E Exceeds expectations
S Satisfactory
N Needs improvement
U Unsatisfactory
DK Do not yet have enough information to make a judgment

This administrator was able to get an overall sense of parents' impressions of their math program as well as pinpoint particular areas that parents thought needed work, that required more communication to parents, or that parents supported.

In communicating with the community and collecting data, both formally and informally, administrators need to think carefully about whose voices are and are not heard, and to consider ways to widen the range of those who *are* heard. Who has the administration's ear? What points of view do the most vocal parents typically represent? How large a percentage of the community do they and their views seem to represent? Why do the opinions of a large group of parents remain unknown or unclear? Are there ways to find out more about their thoughts? Only if a district hears from the entire range of parents in a community can it address the most prevalent concerns rather than just the most vocal ones (although addressing the particularly vocal ones is also critical).

> Our conflict has come very specifically from the part of the parent community that is wealthy and has a good education. That's split down the middle, too, because a good portion of that community is happy with

the math curriculum. Parents have left messages on my voicemail or written me letters that say, "Whatever you heard at that parent meeting the other night, I hope that we don't change the math curriculum." I have one mom who said, "I have taken all kinds of high level and graduate level math courses at the university. My child is so flexible in the way she thinks about numbers and the way she solves problems. She has abilities far beyond anything I developed as a young person, and I feel so fortunate to be in this district because of that.

—K. Coleman, assistant superintendent for curriculum and instruction (Arizona)

Some administrators conduct focus groups, interviews, meetings, forums, discussion or study groups, or roundtable discussions with parents to get the data they need. For more on reaching a wide range of parents and families, see chapter 1, "How to Reach and Involve Parents," page 21.

Identifying, Developing, and Supporting Leaders

Communicating and collaborating with parents require much of administrators, but many aspects of this work can be shared. Therefore, one of the first things administrators can do is get some help. The key is developing a cadre of people—teachers and parents—to work with administrators, help teachers work with parents, and work with parents themselves. This group can then decide among themselves how their interests, abilities, time, and energy can best be used.

Teacher leaders Early in the process of implementing a new curriculum, a school or district needs to identify potential teacher leaders, plan professional development to equip them in that role, and set up a plan for ongoing support. Teacher leaders who are knowledgeable about the curriculum can communicate with the parent community in an articulate and confident way. They can shoulder the responsibility for most of the parent work early on, taking

the lead at Parent Nights, meeting individually with parents who want to know more, and opening their classrooms to colleagues and parents who are interested in seeing *Investigations* in action. Even when principals and other administrators understand and are able to articulate the philosophy of *Investigations*, they still need to find people who "get it" on a whole different level—the level that comes from working on math every day with students and teachers. Math specialists, math directors or coaches, curriculum coordinators, staff developers, and assistant superintendents for curriculum and instruction can all be significant leaders as well.

Parent leaders Similarly, schools need to be on the lookout for parents who might be willing to take on a leadership role or participate on school or district committees. In chapter 10, "One Parent's View: Becoming a Parent Leader" (page 14), Susan Pfohman shares some characteristics she notices that can help administrators identify and tap likely candidates. A parent leader can fill many shoes, particularly with training, whether as a volunteer or a paid staff member. Parent leaders can work in classrooms under teacher direction. They can design and distribute flyers to publicize upcoming math events or call parents to encourage attendance. Some parent leaders are open to speaking at district or schoolwide meetings about math. Most are happy to discuss questions and concerns with other parents and might even run regular discussion groups, parent forums, or study groups. Some may bring their energies to a completely new idea.

Administrators should talk with both teacher and parent leaders about the overall plan for communicating with families. What special talents, interests, and abilities do these leaders bring to the task? Would someone be able to host a series of Math Nights? Does anyone have the expertise to create an introductory video for parents or a website with information about the school/district's mathematics program? Are any of these leaders particularly connected to or adept at reaching some particular segment of the community?

Obviously the credit for parental support goes to the teachers who are doing an effective job in the classroom. But we've also spent quite a bit of time in evening meetings, Back-to-School Nights, parent academies, math breakfasts, and family math nights, showing parents what it is the children are doing, explaining why we want the children to understand math, and giving them examples. We encourage parents to participate in hosting math nights. We strive to draw from parents their own special talents and interests related to math. We also ask, "Did math make sense to you? Did you enjoy math?" Most of them didn't. We explain, "We want your child to have a better understanding of math. We don't want your child's education to be stopped because they can't get through algebra, which we know happens all too frequently." We welcome them in the classroom at all times. We tell them: "You can go in your child's room at any time, we're not hiding anything. In fact, we encourage you to join in the mathematical learning in the rooms."

—*L. Califano, principal (Arizona)*

Developing Resources for Ongoing Communication

Administrators can take an active role in outreach activities aimed at informing parents about mathematics. Some write letters laying out the implementation plan or addressing common questions and issues; others regularly send out a school or district newsletter. Still others invest in materials designed to make the curriculum more visible to parents, such as *Student Activity Books* and Investigations *at Home Booklets*. Others create or share resources such as books, websites, handbooks, and videos. Still others tap connections to the local media to disseminate information about the changing nature of elementary school mathematics. Examples of these and other ideas appear in the following pages.

As administrators, we worked very hard to make sure that parents were well informed. We sent out letters describing the implementation plan. We conducted many parent meetings. We worked with teachers so that they would be able to communicate effectively with parents and feel comfortable answering parents' questions. We encouraged teachers to start "Breakfast with Mathematicians" (an extension of "Authors' Breakfasts," at which students had been sharing their writing with parents). I have been very responsive to comments from the community because I didn't want misunderstanding about our math program to evolve. I have written a "computation letter" that explains how we teach computation and how parents can help their children learn math facts. We now have a website on which we list our learning expectations for math and resources for parents to use.

—*D. Shein-Gerson, K–5 math coordinator (Massachusetts)*

Newsletters and letters In one school district, the principal's monthly newsletter always includes a section on math. This section might share a math problem, news of an upcoming Math Night, student work, a response to a particular concern that's been voiced by parents, or descriptions of some of the districtwide mathematics staff development that's been happening. In another district, the math coordinator wrote a letter each year that laid out the implementation plan, where in that process the district was, and what was new that year. She also wrote letters specifically addressing computation and other common questions.

Another district math coordinator sends out a biweekly newsletter, mainly for teachers but also accessible to parents (see figure 33). In a section called "In My Travels …," she shares what she has seen in her visits to math classes across the

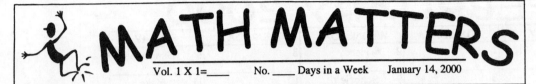

MATH MATTERS

Vol. 1 X 1=____   No. ____ Days in a Week   January 14, 2000

Hello Everyone,

My thoughts are with you as you prepare your report cards. If anyone has any questions regarding the math section, feel free to contact me. In addition to the content and process of mathematics it is often helpful to comment on a child's mathematical disposition. Comments may include things like curiosity, enjoyment, reflection, perseverance, and consideration of other's ideas.

The 100th day of school is February 7th (without snow-days!) The most recent issue of Teaching Children Mathematics includes activities for the 100th day of school. I have seen the magazine in several teachers' rooms. If you can't find a copy, I have one.

If yesterday (January 14, 2000) was the first day of snow in 303 days, what was the last date we had snow? See if your kids can figure it out!

☺ Blake

"QUOTABLE QUOTES"

"The mathematical sciences particularly exhibit order, symmetry, and limitation; and these are the greatest forms of the beautiful."

Charles Babbage (1792-1871)

In My Travels I...

- Worked with third & fourth graders to help them understand what it means to explain how you solved a problem.
- Talked to a second grade teacher about determining to what extent the kids understand subtraction!
- Met with a principal to plan for a PTO meeting.
- Shared end-of-the-unit assessments with grade 2 teachers.
- Previewed Shapes, Halves and Symmetry with second grade teachers piloting Investigations.
- Met with a second grade class to talk to them about my visit to Japan. We will learn to count to ten in Japanese!
- Attended a SPED job-alike meeting. We planned a meeting to talk about strategies for kids who need support around number sense and computation strategies.
- Met with Yolanda Rodriguez to continue planning the 4-7 grade level meeting on mathematics.
- Previewed a unit with new, or new to the grade, third grade teachers.
- Worked with three third grade teachers to correlate the Learning Goals, Investigations and supplementary materials to determine where we need to "fill in the gaps" to ensure the Learning Goals are being fully implemented in our classrooms.
- Didn't travel very far! Sorry to those I missed as a result of the flu!
- Attended a meeting at the DOE to revise the state mathematics frameworks. A very interesting process!

"Add"itional Information

- I am thinking about scheduling an Exemplars workshop for August 2000. In order to do the planning it would be helpful to know who is interested in attending. If you would like to participate in a 2-day workshop please let me know via email ASAP. Thanks!
- If you are looking for a literature connection for multiplication stories check out, Amanda Bean's Amazing Dream by Cindy Neuschwander.

Figure 33 Pages from different editions of a newsletter from district math coordinator B. Munro, Wellesley, Massachusetts. Reprinted with permission.

FEBRUARY 2000

	MONDAY		TUESDAY		WEDNESDAY		THURSDAY		FRIDAY
31	Upham	1		2	Hardy	3		4	Hunnewell
7	Bates 100th Day!	8		9	Schofield	10		11	Fiske
14	Hardy	15		16	Upham	17		18	Hunnewell
21			VACATION !!!						
28	Bates	29		1		2	Schofield	3	Fiske

DOMINO SOLITAIRE

This is a game for all ages. My 85-year-old grandmother just learned how to play and then she taught me! Put out a set of 28 dominoes in one long row. Count from zero to twelve and touch the dominoes in sequence as you count. When you get to twelve, start at zero again. If the number you say matches the sum of the pips on the domino, take that one out of the row. The object is to take all the dominoes out of the row. It is great for kids who need to practice their addition pairs to twelve!

How is your Number Sense?

Give your "number sense" a test as you try to solve these riddles! There will be five in each Math Matters. Look for the answers in the next issue!

Example: 16 O in a P
Answer: 16 ounces in a pound

1. 7 D of the W

2. 12 S of the Z

3. 52 C in a D

4. 200 D for P G in M

5. 32 D at which W F

MATHEMATICAL W.O.W.

- Word of the Week:

PIPS
Did you know that the dots on a domino are called pips?

- Websites of the week:
www.lab.brown.edu/investigations
This is the CESAME support site for Investigations. It has some great resources!
Thanks to Kelly Harper for suggesting it as a featured site!

Blake Munro
Elementary Mathematics Coordinator
Wellesley Public Schools   446-6200 Ext. 1020

Figure 33 (continued)

district. Other sections include a mathematical word and website of the week, math activities or problems, and mathematical quotes. This newsletter also lets people know her schedule and announces meetings and workshops for specific groups (e.g., "Attention Third Grade Teachers").

Teacher and parent leaders can help with such newsletters. In one school, a parent leader takes on the publication aspects of getting out a newsletter while another collects samples of student work from classes around the school to use as illustrations. In another school, children themselves wrote a newsletter (see figure 34). They shared their thoughts about mathematics and *Investigations*, explained strategies for solving particular problems, and told about their favorite math activities. The administrator who organized and published this piece of work wrote an introduction and added a math report card that parents could use to grade the school's math program.

Sharing resources Administrators can take the lead in establishing a check-out system of useful math resources for parents. These might be located in the front office or library and could include books, manipulatives, activities and games, curriculum units, articles, and journals. A list of relevant websites could be made available, and in the library a computer could be set up with those sites bookmarked for parents to explore.

Sharing a particular book An administrator in one community that was adopting *Investigations* discovered one particularly useful resource for parents, *Beyond Facts and Flashcards: Exploring Math with Your Kids* (Mokros, 1996). Written by an *Investigations* author, this book offers many ideas to help parents work with their children on mathematics that goes far beyond drill and practice, just as the *Investigations* curriculum aims to do in the classroom. The administrator let families

know about the book and the opportunity to purchase it. Parents who were interested could drop off a check at the front office by a particular date. The school then placed one large order and distributed copies to parents when the books arrived. To build on this idea, a discussion group could be established for people reading the book.

Problem of the day In another district, an administrator has instituted a "Problem of the Day" program, posting problems on two computers in the school cafeteria. The problem is changed for different lunch periods, depending on the grade levels of the children present. Students talk about the problem in line or as they eat. At the end of lunch period, the answer is announced, and a few strategies are shared. Each problem is either taken from past versions of the state mathematics test or designed to be similar. In addition to imbuing the schools' culture with more mathematics, this program offers a response to parents who are concerned about children's performance on the high-stakes test.

Tools provided by the curriculum The *Student Activity Booklets* and Investigations *at Home Booklets*, available for purchase with the curriculum, are another way districts have responded to parental concerns about the lack of a traditional student text.

The Investigations *at Home Booklets* were developed specifically to address parents' desire to know more about their child's math class. Available for every unit in grades 1 through 5 and under development for kindergarten, these booklets provide a summary of what's happening in math class for each curriculum unit, alert families to potential homework assignments, suggest activities for exploring mathematics together at home, and encourage practice by providing activities and games (along with materials and instructions).

What Does Math Class Look Like?
What Are Students Doing and
What Is the Teacher Doing?
by Hannah Harris

Investigations Math really helps you to not just do a math problem, move on to the next one, then move on to the next one. In fifth grade we do a lot of writing down and explaining our strategies. If you were a parent and you looked on your child's paper, you would see many words and explanations. Sometimes there may be more words on the paper than numbers. There is a simple reason why this method may be a better way to learn math; students could do one thousand three hundred and forty six multiplied by eleven and never understand how they got the answer. If you are doing another problem that is harder, you will have an easier time if you know how you solved the first one.

In *Investigations Math*, there are no textbooks or workbooks. Instead, the students have sheets with one or two problems, and half a page each. We get these kinds of papers a lot. This helps people because there is not as many problems and you'll just focus on those two problems and you can't move on to more. Sometimes the problems are "cluster" problems. In a cluster problem, there are three or four easy problems that you have to use to get to the main, harder problem. Another thing we do is "quick images", which we sometimes do during "Ten Minute Math". Quick Images are when the teacher shows a design or a pattern of dots on the overhead projector. The teacher will show it for three seconds and then cover it up. The children have to draw the image and do the best they can. Then, the teacher will show it again for three seconds and then kids will revise their drawings if they need to. Then, the teacher will ask everyone what they saw, noticed, and wondered about what they saw. Sometimes the patterns look like lightning bolts or stairs. This helps to build up memory, visual thinking, and it helps you look carefully and think quickly.

In class, sometimes kids will be working separately, but a lot of times they will be working with a partner or in a group. When we are working on something in *Investigations Math*, the teacher will come around and see what and how we are doing. If we need help, she will help us. Sometimes we just need a little nudge, a push forward on what we are doing. She does not just say, "Well, do this and this and let us start working." She will give us examples or questions in the middle and ask us if we understand. *Investigations Math* is a well liked program in fifth grade and it is very helpful.

Investigations:
The Nature of Homework
by Haley Deutsch

The nature of homework in the new *Investigations Math* program is much different than what is usually used (textbooks, workbooks, etc.). Mostly there are worksheets, but they are different than traditional worksheets. Instead of 30 easy problems, there are two or three harder problems that require a lot of strategizing.

Usually multiplication problem worksheets have a lot of memorizable problems. On an *Investigations* worksheet, it is not like that. There are four problems that help you figure out a bigger problem that cannot be done from memory, such as 36 X 42.

Another Investigations homework assignment is to play number games with a friend. This raises more awareness of math and numbers than a bunch of problems on a textbook page. Other math homework can be boring, but *Investigations* homework is surely not!

Figure 34 An administrator at the Newtown Friends School in Newtown, Pennsylvania, edited a special edition of the Parents Association Newsletter, "Rainbow Connection." This newsletter shared the experiences of third, fourth, and fifth graders with *Investigations*, in their own words. It featured many samples of student work along with essays, like these by two fifth grade students. From D. Forman. Reprinted with permission.

Some schools and districts have found the *Student Activity Booklets* similarly useful. Developed as an alternative to copying the blackline masters in the back of the unit, each booklet contains everything needed for an individual student to complete all the class and homework for one unit.

> Investigations *at Home* does far more to explain to parents the mathematical emphasis for the current unit than any textbook I have ever seen. If parents want to know what their children are doing and how to help them, these slim booklets are invaluable. I have seen plenty of parents confused by the lessons in traditional textbooks. I do not believe that textbooks are a panacea for effective parent communication and education. Textbooks are not written to or for parents and offer no direct support to parents who probably were educated differently as children. The Investigations *Student Activity Booklets* also clearly show parents what their kids are doing on a daily basis. The parents of my students seem perfectly happy with them.
>
> —*M. Taft, grade 5 teacher (Massachusetts)*

Introductory video for parents One large urban school district decided to create a video specifically for parents, just as they had done for teachers who were new to *Investigations*. The video introduces the curriculum to parents, gives them a sense of what *Investigations* classrooms will look like and the mathematics they will focus on. All the footage came from classrooms in the district. The video also talks to parents about what they can do at home to support their child in math, and includes interviews of district parents talking about the *Investigations* curriculum and what it offers their child. Other schools or classrooms have become intrigued with the idea of a video that could be sent home with each child in consecutive weeks, something like a class pet. The video would include some general information that was the same each

time, but also some specific footage of the "child of the week" at work in mathematics. Such a video might be part of a kit that also includes game instructions, readings, and manipulatives. At some point, then, parents might be told, "Pause the tape now and play [name of a game] with your child."

Creating a website Developing a school website, or expanding the current one to include information on mathematics, is another way administrators might share information with parents and the community. At its most basic, such a site might provide information of a general nature about the curriculum and its philosophy, as well as publicize upcoming events where parents can learn more. If particular teachers, students, or parents with technical expertise volunteer, they could post more detailed information for a particular grade level, perhaps sharing images of students' work, notes from teachers, students' thoughts about math, and information about specific mathematical projects. Other grade levels or individual classrooms could then be encouraged or challenged to do the same. Some administrators also recommend interactive bulletin boards on the Web for posting ideas and holding discussions. One existing board is the CESAME Support Site for *Investigations* Users, which has discussion groups on multiple topics for teachers, leaders, administrators, and parents.

Tapping the local media Aware of the power of television, radio, and newspaper reports, some administrators are thinking more widely about the media, any connections people in the school community have to these outlets, and how those connections might be used in support of the implementation process. "Districts can be strategic about using newspapers, radio, and school newsletters to carry stories about mathematics education reform, new curriculum possibilities, and students' classroom activities. The media can also serve as a way to keep community members updated about adoption efforts within the district and can provide a forum for dialogue about district plans" (Goldsmith, Mark, & Kantrov, 2000, p. 105).

Conclusion

> While professional development may result in improved mathematics instruction in individual classrooms, long-lasting, school-wide change calls for substantive, ongoing, schoolwide support. For this to happen, the leadership of the building principal is essential. (Burns, 1999, p. 1)

This is also true for district-level administrators such as math coordinators and superintendents of curriculum and instruction. Leaders who hope to develop and implement a strong program of family involvement, particularly around mathematics, would do well to give careful thought to the following questions:

- How can I best set the tone of this school as a learning community, a community of people that respects all individuals, is curious, and listens to and learns from each other? How can I communicate what I expect to see in classrooms, from children and from teachers? what I expect to see in school-home interactions?

- How do I communicate that the goal is true partnership, working *with* parents? That partnership is about far more than talking *to* or *at* parents, explaining to them, or telling them—much as mathematics is about far more than a teacher dictating from the board?

- How do I communicate that this is the job of the entire school? People have different interests, abilities, and expertise, but everyone needs to find a role to play, a way to be a part of developing this community. How do I best match people to roles?

- How can we, as a school community, work to understand and overcome the barriers that seem to prevent true family involvement in many school settings? How can we encourage parents to join us in working together for the best mathematics education for their child? How can we make our school the kind of place where all parents will feel respected, comfortable, and welcome? How can we as educators become the kind of people parents would want to have as partners in educating their child?

- How can I help families learn about mathematics and about this curriculum? What is my role in initiating, supporting, and conducting activities that reach out to the community? What is my role in finding and helping teachers or parents to do this work? What is my role in hearing parents' and teachers' concerns and responding in respectful and useful ways?

- How will I encourage teachers to reach out to the community and communicate with parents? What do I expect of teachers? How do I respect the risk teachers are taking and their feelings of vulnerability? In particular, what teacher-parent communication do I expect in these early stages? Have I communicated this to teachers? Do teachers know what resources and options are available for responding to parents' questions and concerns?

- How will we give parents a new image of what mathematics is and simultaneously demonstrate where and how traditional math content (i.e., facts and computation) is taught? How will we engage them with the ideas so that they have a broader view of mathematics and of our mathematical goals for children?

Administrators in schools or districts that are successfully implementing *Investigations* say that while their role as school managers has been important, what has been critical is their instructional leadership. These administrators set priorities and guide the school or district toward achieving them. The decisions they make about spending, scheduling, hiring, evaluations, and professional development support teachers in the day-to-day challenges of implementing a new curriculum and in improving their instructional practice. As a result, parents see images of quality mathematics instruction schoolwide.

At the same time, administrators must make special efforts to connect with families, to talk about the recent changes in math teaching and learning. True partnership with parents and families must be an important priority, and administrators must allocate resources for this work. Administrators not only provide a supportive public presence, they take an active role in conversations with families about the math program. In addition, administrators are finding that they need to develop teacher and parent leaders who can both share in this work and offer particular expertise. Both people and resources are critical in helping administrators support parents and families in learning more about a new math program like *Investigations*.

References

Baratta-Lorton, M. (1995). *Mathematics their way: 20th anniversary edition.* Menlo Park, CA: Addison-Wesley.

Battista, M. T. (1999, February). The mathematical miseducation of America's youth: Ignoring research and scientific study in education. *Phi Delta Kappan 80* (6), 425–433. Available online.

Briars, D. (1999, January). A tactic for educating parents. *The School Administrator.* Available online.

Burns, M. (1992). *About teaching mathematics: A K–8 resource.* Sausalito, CA: Math Solutions.

Burns, M. (1994). *Mathematics: What are you teaching my child?* [Videotape]. New York: Scholastic. Also available in Spanish.

Burns, M. (1998). *Math: Facing an American phobia.* Sausalito, CA: Math Solutions.

Burns, M. (Ed.). (1999). *Leading the way: Principals and superintendents look at math instruction.* Sausalito, CA: Math Solutions.

Civil, M. (1998, July). *Parents as resources for mathematical instruction.* Paper presented at the Adults Learning Mathematics (ALM-5) Conference, Utrecht, Netherlands.

Coates, G. D., & Stenmark, J. K. (1997). *Family Math for young children.* Berkeley, CA: Regents, University of California.

COMAP. (n.d.). *Bridges to Classroom Mathematics.* Lexington, MA: Author. Available from The ARC Center, 781-862-7878 x50.

Corwin, R. B., Price, S. L., Storeygard, J., & Smith, D. (1995). *Talking mathematics: Resource package.* [Video package]. Portsmouth, NH: Heinemann.

Crittenden, A. (2001). *The price of motherhood: Why the most important job in the world is still the least valued.* New York: Metropolitan Books.

Curcio, F. R. (1999, February). Dispelling myths about reform in school mathematics. *Mathematics Teaching in the Middle School 4* (5), 282–284. Available online.

Cushner, K., McClelland, A., & Safford, P. (2000). *Human diversity in education: An integrative approach.* Boston: McGraw-Hill.

References

Economopoulos, K., & Russell, S. J. (1998). *Coins, coupons, and combinations: The number system.* A grade 2 unit of *Investigations in Number, Data, and Space.* Glenview, IL: Scott Foresman.

Eisenhower National Clearinghouse. (1998). Family Involvement in Education. ENC: *Focus for Mathematics and Science Education, 5* (3).

Ensign, J. (1998, February). Parents, portfolios, and personal mathematics. *Teaching Children Mathematics 4,* 346–351.

Epstein, J. L. (1995). School/family/community partnerships: Caring for the children we share. *Phi Delta Kappan, 76* (9), 701–712.

Epstein, J. L. (1996). Perspectives and previews on research and policy for school, family, and community partnerships. In A. Booth & J. Dunn (Eds.), *Family-school links: How do they affect educational outcomes?* (pp. 209–246). Hillsdale, NJ: Lawrence Erlbaum.

Epstein, J. L., & Dauber, S. L. (1991). School programs and teacher practices of parent involvement in inner-city elementary and middle schools. *The Elementary School Journal, 91* (3), 289–305.

Fey, J. (1999, May). Standards under fire: Issues and options in the math wars. Keynote session at the Show-Me Project Curriculum Showcase. Available online at http://showmecenter.missouri.edu/showme/perspectives/keynote1.html.

Ford, M. S., Follmer, R., & Litz, K. K. (1998, February). School-family partnerships: Parents, children, and teachers benefit! *Teaching Children Mathematics, 4,* 310–312.

Fuller, M. L., & Olsen, G. (1998). *Home-school relations: Working successfully with parents and families.* Boston: Allyn and Bacon.

Funkhouser, J. E., Gonzales, M. R., &. Moles, O. C. (1997). *Family involvement in children's education: Successful local approaches: An idea book.* Washington, DC: U.S. Department of Education. Available online.

Glenn Commission. (2000). *Before it's too late: A report to the nation from the National Commission on Mathematics and Science Teaching for the 21st Century.* Washington, DC: U.S. Department of Education. Available online.

Goldsmith, L. T., Mark, J., & Kantrov, I. (2000). *Choosing a standards-based mathematics curriculum.* Portsmouth, NH: Heinemann. Excerpts available online.

References

Great Source Education Group. (1998). *Math on call: A mathematics handbook.* Wilmington, MA: Author.

Hart, A., Smyth, M., Vetter, K., & Hart, E. (1996). Children, teach your parents well: Communication in mathematics between home and school. In P. C. Elliott (Ed.), *Communication in mathematics, K–12 and beyond* (1996 yearbook, pp. 180–186). Reston, VA: National Council of Teachers of Mathematics.

Henderson, A. T., & Berla, N. (1994). *A new generation of evidence: The family is critical to student achievement.* Washington, DC: Center for Law and Education (originally, the National Committee for Citizens in Education).

Hewlett, S. A., & West, C. (1998). *The war against parents: What we can do for America's beleaguered moms and dads.* Boston: Houghton Mifflin.

Hidalgo, N. M., Siu, S., Bright, J. A., Swap, S. M., & Epstein, J. L. (1995). Research on families, schools, and communities: A multicultural perspective. In J. A. Banks (Ed.), *Handbook of research on multicultural education,* 498–524. New York: Macmillan.

Hiebert, J. (1999, January). Relationships between research and the NCTM Standards. *Journal for Research in Mathematics Education 30* (1), 12–13. Available online.

Hildebrand, C., Ludeman, C. J., & Mullin, J. (1999, March). Integrating mathematics with problem solving using the Mathematician's Chair. *Teaching Children Mathematics, 5,* 434–441.

Hirigoyen, H. (1997). Dialectal variations in the language of mathematics: A source for multicultural experiences. In J. Trentacosta (Ed.), *Multicultural and gender equity in the mathematics classroom: The gift of diversity* (1997 yearbook, pp. 164–168). Reston, VA: National Council of Teachers of Mathematics.

Kamii, C., & Dominick, A. (1998). The harmful effects of algorithms in grades 1–4. In L. J. Morrow (Ed.), *The teaching and learning of algorithms in school mathematics* (1998 yearbook, pp. 130–140). Reston, VA: National Council of Teachers of Mathematics.

Kenschaft, P. C. (1997). *Math power: How to help your child love math, even if you don't.* Reading, MA: Addison-Wesley.

References

Kliman, M., Russell, S. J., Tierney, C., & Murray, M. (1998). *Building on numbers you know: Computation and estimation strategies.* A grade 5 unit of *Investigations in Number, Data, and Space.* Glenview, IL: Scott Foresman.

Kline, K. (1999). Helping at home. *Teaching Children Mathematics, 5* (8), 456–460. Available online.

Lappan, G., Fey, J. T., Fitzgerald, W. M., Friel, S. N., & Phillips, E. D. (2002). *Connected Math.* Upper Saddle River, NJ: Prentice Hall.

Lewis, D. E. (2000, January 9). Games, brainteasers that can get you a job: Employers obsessed with teamwork, creativity, say old-fashioned interviews alone just don't cut it. *The Boston Globe,* pp. C1, 7.

Litton, N. (1998). *Getting your math message out to parents: A K–6 resource.* Sausalito, CA: Math Solutions.

Mason, D. (1998). Capsule lessons in alternative algorithms in the classroom. In L. J. Morrow (Ed.), *The teaching and learning of algorithms in school mathematics* (1998 yearbook, pp. 91–98). Reston, VA: National Council of Teachers of Mathematics.

McDiarmid, G. W. (1992). *Kathy: A case of innovative mathematics teaching in a multicultural classroom.* Teaching Cases in Cross-Cultural Education. Fairbanks, AL: University of Fairbanks.

Mokros, J. (1996). *Beyond facts and flashcards: Exploring math with your kids.* Portsmouth, NH: Heinemann.

Mokros, J. (2000, January). *The* Investigations *curriculum and children's understanding of whole number operations.* Retrieved from CESAME Investigations Math Support Site at www.lab.brown.edu/investigations/resources/studresults/.

Mokros, J., Russell, S. J., & Economopoulos, K. (1995). *Beyond Arithmetic.* Parsippany, NJ: Dale Seymour.

Moles, O. C. (1996). *Reaching all families: Creating family friendly schools.* Washington, DC: U.S. Department of Education, Office of Educational Research and Improvement. Available online.

Morse, A. B., & Wagner, P. (1998, February). Learning to listen: Lessons from a mathematics seminar for parents. *Teaching Children Mathematics, 4,* 360–375.

References

Murnane, R. J., & Levy, F. (1996). *Teaching the new basic skills: Principles for educating children to thrive in a changing economy.* New York: The Free Press.

National Assessment of Educational Progress. (1983). The third national mathematics assessment: Results, trends, and issues (Report No. 13-MA-01). Denver, CO: Educational Commission of the States.

National Council of Teachers of Mathematics. (1989). *Curriculum and evaluation standards for school mathematics.* Reston, VA: Author.

National Council of Teachers of Mathematics. (1991). *Professional Standards for Teaching Mathematics.* Reston, VA: Author.

National Council of Teachers of Mathematics. (1995). *Assessment Standards for School Mathematics.* Reston, VA: Author.

National Council of Teachers of Mathematics. (1998, February). Beyond the Classroom: Linking Mathematics Learning with Parents, Communities, and Business and Industry. *Teaching Children Mathematics, 5.* Reston, VA.

National Council of Teachers of Mathematics. (1999, December). *NCTM News Bulletin.*

National Council of Teachers of Mathematics. (2000). *Principles and standards for school mathematics.* Reston, VA: Author. Available online.

National Council of Teachers of Mathematics (NCTM). (2000). Setting the Record Straight About Changes in Mathematics Education: Commonsense Facts to Clear the Air; Commonsense Facts About the NCTM Standards; and Commonsense Facts about School Mathematics. Available online at http://www.nctm.org/news/speaksout/commonsense.html.

National Research Council. (1989). *Everybody counts: A report to the nation on the future of mathematics education.* Washington, DC: National Academy Press. Available online.

Paulu, N. (1995, September). *Helping your child with homework.* Jessup, MD: U.S. Department of Education, Office of Educational Research and Improvement. Available online. Also available in Spanish.

Peressini, D. D. (1998, February). What's all the fuss about involving parents in mathematics education? *Teaching Children Mathematics, 4,* 320–325.

References

Poynter, L. (1998). Teacher Advice on Connecting School and Home. Family Involvement in Education. *ENC: Focus for Mathematics and Science Education, 5* (3). Eisenhower National Clearinghouse.

Price, J. (1996, November). President's report. *Journal for Research in Mathematics Education, 27* (5), 603–608.

Public Agenda (1999). Playing their parts: What parents and teachers really mean by parental involvement. New York: Author. Excerpts available at Public Agenda Online at www.publicagenda.org/specials/parent/parent.htm.

Raphel, A. (2000a, March). *Homework: Research and practice*. Presentation at the *Investigations* Implementation Institute 2: Administrators as Leaders, Parents as Partners, Billerica, MA.

Raphel, A. (2000b). *Math homework that counts: Grades 4–6*. Sausalito, CA: Math Solutions.

Richardson, K. (1997a). *Math time: The learning environment*. [Video package]. Norman, OK: Educational Enrichment.

Richardson, K. (1997b). *Math time: Thinking with numbers*. [Video package]. Norman, OK: Educational Enrichment.

Richardson, K. (1998). *Math time: A look at children's thinking*. [Video package]. Norman, OK: Educational Enrichment.

Rubenstein, R. N. (1998). Historical algorithms: Sources for student projects. In L. J. Morrow (Ed.), *The teaching and learning of algorithms in school mathematics* (1998 yearbook, pp. 99–105). Reston, VA: National Council of Teachers of Mathematics.

Russell, S.J. et al. (1998). *The Investigations in Number, Data, and Space Curriculum*. White Plains, NY: Dale Seymour Publications.

Russell, S. J. (2000a, May). Developing computational fluency with whole numbers in the elementary grades. *The New England Mathematics Journal, 32* (2), 40–54. Available online.

Russell, S. J. (2000b, November). Principles and standards for school mathematics: Developing computational fluency with whole numbers. *Teaching Children Mathematics. 7* (3), 154–158. Available online.

Russell, S. J., Smith, D., Storeygard, J., & Murray, M. (1999a). *Relearning to Teach Arithmetic: Addition and Subtraction*. [Video package]. Parsippany, NJ: Dale Seymour.

References

Russell, S. J., Smith, D., Storeygard, J., & Murray, M. (1999b). *Relearning to Teach Arithmetic: Multiplication and Division*. [Video package]. Parsippany, NJ: Dale Seymour.

Russell, S. J., Tierney, C., Mokros, J., Goodrow, A., & Murray, M. (1998). *Implementing the* Investigations in Number, Data, and Space *curriculum*. Grades 3–5. Glenview, IL: Scott Foresman.

Schifter, D., Bastable, V., & Russell, S. J. (1999a). *Number and operations, part 1: Building a system of tens*. Developing Mathematical Ideas. Parsippany, NJ: Dale Seymour.

Schifter, D., Bastable, V., & Russell, S. J. (1999b). *Number and operations, part 2: Making meaning for operations*. Developing Mathematical Ideas. Parsippany, NJ: Dale Seymour.

Schifter, D., Bastable, V., & Russell, S. J. (2001a). *Geometry: Examining features of shape*. Developing Mathematical Ideas. Parsippany, NJ: Dale Seymour.

Schifter, D., Bastable, V., & Russell, S. J. (2001b). *Geometry: Measuring space in one, two, and three dimensions*. Developing Mathematical Ideas. Parsippany, NJ: Dale Seymour.

Schifter, D., Bastable, V., & Russell, S. J. (in press). *Statistics: Working with data*. Developing Mathematical Ideas. Parsippany, NJ: Dale Seymour.

Secada, W. G. (1992). Race, ethnicity, social class, language, and achievement in mathematics. In D. A. Grouws (Ed.), *Handbook of research on mathematics teaching and learning* (pp. 623–660). New York: Macmillan.

Senk, S. L., & Thompson, D. R. (Eds.). (in press). *Standards-oriented school mathematics curricula: What does the research say about student outcomes?* Hillsdale, NJ: Lawrence Erlbaum.

Shepard, L. A., & Bliem, C. L. (1995). Parents' thinking about standardized tests and performance assessments. *Educational Researcher 24* (8), 25–32.

Silverman, H. (2001, April). *Developing parent leaders*. Presentation at a meeting of the National Council of Supervisors of Mathematics, Orlando, FL.

Stenmark, J. K., Thompson, V., & Cossey, R. (1986). *Family Math*. Berkeley, CA: Regents, University of California. Also available in Spanish.

Sutton, S. (1998). Beyond homework help: Guiding our children to lasting math success. *ENC: Focus for Mathematics and Science Education: Family Involvement in Education 5* (3), 8–11. Available online.

References

Swap, S. M. (1993). *Developing home-school partnerships: From concept to practice.* New York: Teachers College Press.

TERC. (1990). *Used Numbers: Real data in the classroom.* Primary (K–3) and Middle grades (4–6). [Videotapes]. Parsippany, NJ: Dale Seymour.

TERC. (2000). *Math packs.* Cambridge, MA: Author. Distributed by Pearson Learning.

Thompson, V., & Mayfield-Ingram, K. (1998). *Family Math: The middle school years,* Berkeley, CA: Regents, University of California.

Tobias, S. (1993). *Overcoming math anxiety.* New York: W. W. Norton.

U.S. Department of Education. (1995). *Learning Problems: Let's Do Homework!* Available online: http://www.ed.gov/pubs/parents/LearnPtnrs/home.html

U.S. Department of Education, Office of Educational Improvement. (1997). *Overcoming barriers to family involvement in Title I schools: A report to Congress.* Washington, DC: Author.

Vopat, J. (1994). *The parent project: A workshop approach to parent involvement.* York, ME: Stenhouse.

Vopat, J. (1998). *More than bake sales: The resource guide for family involvement in education.* Portland, ME: Stenhouse.